ANGELS A TO Z

ANGELS
A TO Z

A WHO'S WHO OF THE HEAVENLY HOST

Matthew Bunson

 THREE RIVERS PRESS · NEW YORK

ACKNOWLEDGMENTS

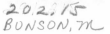

There are a number of individuals to whom a special debt of gratitude is owed for their help in the preparation of this volume. Among them are the staffs of several libraries, especially of Sahara West Library; Dakila Divina, Ariel Foxman, and Elke Villa of Crown Publishers, Inc.; and Ann Patty, editorial director of Crown, for her confidence. Most important, a very special thanks is owed to Jane Cavolina, my editor, for her trust, friendship, patience, and boundless enthusiasm, not to mention her many gifts as an editor.

Copyright © 1996 by Matthew Bunson

All rights reserved. No part of this book may be reproduced or transmitted in any form or by any means, electronic or mechanical, including photocopying, recording, or by any information storage and retrieval system, without permission in writing from the publisher.

Published by Three Rivers Press, New York, New York.
Member of the Crown Publishing Group.

Random House, Inc. New York, Toronto, London, Sydney, Auckland
www.randomhouse.com

THREE RIVERS PRESS is a registered trademark and the Three Rivers Press colophon is a trademark of Random House, Inc.

Printed in the United States of America

Design by June Bennett-Tantillo

Library of Congress Cataloging-in-Publication Data
Bunson, Matthew.
Angels A to Z : a who's who of the heavenly host / by Matthew Bunson
1. Angels—Dictionaries.   I. Title.
BL477.B86   1996
291.2'15—dc20   95-52232

ISBN 0-517-88537-9

10   9   8   7   6

FOREWORD

An angel who might, for whatever reason, find itself in even a
modestly sized bookstore just about anywhere in the world
would perhaps be both pleased and amused at the renaissance of the last years in the appreciation, honor, and even
reverence given to his celestial brethren by mortals. The glorious residents
of the heavenly halls are found today in books, cards, posters, stationery,
paintings, videos, jewelry, and even candles. Angel merchandise decorates
homes throughout the Orient, Africa, Europe, and the Americas, and people of all faiths agree that at no time has the spiritual strength and concern of the angels for all of humankind been more needed than on the
troubled planet of our own era.

The foremost modern expression of mortal concern with the angelic, however, is in the area of books. An angel (or human, for that matter) can find works on the timeless wisdom of angelic love, self-help tips
encouraging the reader to become more like the angels, and philosophical
and spiritual speculation on all aspects of the angelic nature. Many of
these works are today considered classics in the field of angel studies, such
as those by Sophy Burnham, Malcolm Godwin, Gustav Davidson, and
John Ronner, with new angel books appearing every year. The angel
might thus rightly ask why another book has been published about his
kind at a time when it seems that nothing further could possibly be contributed to the subject.

Angels A to Z is, in fact, needed and timely and does, it is hoped,
have something more to contribute to what has proven to be a near endlessly interesting field of study. This reference work is intended to permit
the reader to find in one easy-to-use, handy reference volume a com-

pendium of angel lore, traditions, imaginings, and speculation, from millennia distant to our own age. Such information is spread out in a host of
volumes and studies, many now largely unobtainable or exceedingly difficult to find. This book additionally aspires to provide what its subtitle declares: a *Who's Who* of the heavenly host.

In these pages the reader will find virtually every angel who has
graced the earth with its wisdom or who has been said to have wandered
the corridors of the heavenly mansions surrounding the throne of the
Lord. A census compiled during the Middle Ages by a certain cardinal of
Tusculum (a position of some importance in the medieval Church) estimated that there were some 399,920,004 angels in the cosmos. It is not
the ambition of this book to provide coverage on *all* of these angels—as if
their names were known anyway—but it does seek to offer complete, unusual, and interesting details, stories, legends, and traditions concerning
angels from the beloved to the virtually unknown.

Beyond these angelic biographies, *Angels A to Z* offers, for the first
time, coverage of every other aspect of angelology, including the incarnations of angels in art, literature, poetry, and film. Further, there are easy-
to-consult sections on the main angelic attributes (their creation, gender,
powers, etc.), angel wings, angels in the Bible, and the appearance of angels over the centuries. There are also the views on angels as expressed by
the world's major religions and cultures.

The current popularity of angels can be attributed to a number of
reasons. There are those who derive enormous comfort from a simple
certainty in the existence of angels. In this sense, angels stand as eternally
vigilant guardians, helpers, and guides of humanity in times of darkest and
most terrible need. Further, in a society in which organized religions are
facing strife and challenge from within and without, angels are a powerful
means of connecting with a spiritual existence without the need to adhere to a specific dogma or religious structure. Angel lore is today so
much a part of the human consciousness less through one all-encompassing tradition or school of thought than through a mélange of peoples,
creeds, and even literary and artistic customs. Angels are their own spiritual tradition, one that has undergone transformation and alteration by
each generation "discovering" the heavenly host in all of its glory. Finally,
and perhaps most important, throughout history one thought has proven
powerfully constant and nearly universally accepted by Jewish writers,
Christian saints, Muslim scholars, and followers of the New Age: The
angel is one of the most beautiful expressions of the Concern of God for
all of his creations, an idea beautifully expressed by Tobias Palmer in *An*

Angel in My House: "The very presence of an angel is a communication. Even when an angel crosses our path in silence, God has said to us, 'I am here. I am present in your life.' "

Implicit in the existence of the angel is the inseparable reality of what it does. As St. Augustine wrote: "Angels are spirits, but it is not because they are spirits that they are angels. They become angels when they are sent. For the name *angel* refers to their office, not their nature. You ask the name of this nature, it is *spirit;* you ask its office, it is that of an angel, which is a messenger." Be it as a minister of comfort and solace to the suffering or desperate, as the bringer of joyous tidings of an impending birth, or as a feared and fearsome warrior of destruction, the angel engages in each moment of angelic activity upon the earth as the fulfillment of a vital part of its purpose and an affirmation to the mortal that there is another realm beyond our own. The name *angel* is itself in fact derived from the idea of messenger, first in the Hebrew *malakh* and then in the Greek *angelos,* and its most famous appearances in history have come as part of its delivering of some divine message or declaration.

This does not mean that angels are exclusively messengers. As spirits created by God, they are also servants, caretakers, and worshipers. They serve the purposes and needs of the Lord by fulfilling any and all tasks assigned to them (the duties bestowed being ever equal to their specific natures as expressed by their affiliation with one of the highly varied angelic choirs). According to many sources in angel lore, only the angels, archangels, and principalities ever have anything to do with humanity, so it stands to reason that the other six choirs would have their own jobs and obligations. One of the most significant caretaking tasks is that of maintaining order and beauty in the cosmos. Beyond even these awesome responsibilities is the one of greatest joy to the angels: that of circling the divine throne to sing in endless praise of God. An undertaking that might sound rather dull or pointless to many, this sharing in the celebration of the Lord is said to be the highest honor sought by angels and the one carried out with greatest skill by the seraphim, cherubim, and thrones, the three higher choirs who are the finest reflection of the divine essence. The music of the angels, described as the music of the spheres, is beyond human comprehension.

It is, of course, a matter of debate as to whether angels do actually exist. In the Middle Ages, when miracles and other supernatural happenings were thought to occur with astonishing regularity, angels were an accepted part of life, with the relics and saints. St. Francis was visited by one when he received the stigmata; Pope St. Gregory I beheld one over what came to be called Castel Sant'Angelo; and Thomas Aquinas, considered the most rational thinker of his age, was encouraged by them in his dreams. It was only in the time of the rationalists of the seventeenth and eighteenth centuries that angels were declared absurd or unlikely. Such a blithe dismissal would not last. Today, polls regularly find that a vast majority of the public firmly accepts belief in angels. Such polling confirms that contemporary angel interest is far more than a fleeting moment of spiritual excess in the otherwise irascible and ephemeral realm of pop culture.

Whether one embraces the so-called cult of angels or dismisses it as a mere flight of fancy, one indisputable benefit has been derived from their visits—real or imagined—to the earth. They are the inspiration for a stellar body of artists and literary giants: Giotto, Michelangelo, Titian, Dante, Milton, Blake, Fra Angelico, Dürer, Doré, Singer, Aquinas, Rossetti, and Shakespeare, to name but a few. It is their faith and labors on behalf of the angels, as much as the nine choirs themselves, that this book celebrates.

A **BADDON** The angel of the bottomless pit, as named in the Hebrew; in Greek he is called Appolyon. Abaddon is named specifically in the Book of Revelation as the leader of the terrible locustlike beings sent from the abyss to torment the unbelievers. "As their leader, they had their own emperor, the Angel of the Abyss, whose name in Hebrew is Abaddon and in Greek Appolyon" (9:11). In the same sources (20), Abaddon binds Satan for a thousand years: "Then I saw an angel come down from heaven with the key of the Abyss in his hand and an enormous chain. He overpowered the dragon, that primeval serpent which is the devil and Satan, and chained him up for a thousand years. He hurled him into the Abyss and shut the entrance and sealed it over him, to make sure he would not lead the nations astray again until the thousand years had passed. At the end of that time he must be released, but only for a short while." Other identifications of Abaddon in lore include him as an angel of death

Abaddon, the angel of the bottomless pit; from a woodcut by Albrecht Dürer.

and a dark angel, or even as a demon, serving in the abyss, perhaps to be considered Satan himself. Another use of his name is to denote not an angel, but a place, synonymous with the abyss itself, or hell. The poet Milton, in his *Paradise Regained,* wrote: "In all her gates Abaddon rues, thy bold attempt." In yet another source, *The Greater Key of Solomon* by the great occult scholar S. L. MacGregor Mathers, Abaddon was significantly powerful enough to be used by Moses as a means of invoking the terrible rain that descended upon Egypt. (See also *Abyss, Angel of the,* and *Bottomless Pit, Angel of the.*)

🙊 **ABALIM** The name used in the Hebrew for the corresponding choir of angels in Christian lore called the thrones. Abalim means "great angels." They are also known as the arelim. (For other details see under *Thrones.*)

🙊 **ABATHAR MUZANIA** An angel-like being found among the Mandaeans, a sect of Gnostics that flourished in the first to second centuries A.D. in modern-day Iraq. This angel is responsible in their lore for weighing the souls of the deceased to determine their worthiness. For this task he uses a set of scales. He is also called the angel of the North Star.

🙊 **ABBATON** A traditionally useful name for conjurations and summonings, as noted in *The Greater Key of Solomon* (by S. L. MacGregor Mathers). Abbaton is supposedly a powerful angel of God himself, applied to the conjuring of demons and forcing them to perform various deeds.

🙊 **ABDALS** A group of mysterious beings who figure in Islamic lore. Said to number seventy, the abdals (meaning "substitutes") are known only to God and fulfill the essential task of permitting the world to continue in existence. Similar to the Just in Jewish lore, the abdals are spiritual (or perhaps angelic) caretakers of the earth. They are not immortal, however, and when one of them dies their number is kept constant by God, who secretly appoints a replacement.

🙊 **ABDIEL** An important and valiant angel who plays a leading role in Milton's *Paradise Lost* in standing firm against the call of Satan to the angels to revolt against God. A member of the angelic choir of the seraphim, Abdiel is described by Milton as the "flaming seraph." His great moment comes during the first day of fighting in the war in heaven. He routs the rebellious fallen angels Ramiel, Arioch, and Ariel, and even Satan himself is driven back by the "mighty sword stroke" of the seraph. There has been some question over the years as to whether Abdiel has any roots in Jewish or Christian legend or lore or was merely a creation of Milton. The angel, in fact, was mentioned during the Middle Ages in the mystical Jewish work *The Book of the Angel Raziel,* traditionally attributed to Rabbi Eleazar of Worms. Abdiel's name means "servant of God." He was described by Milton as "unshak'n, unseduced." (See also *War in Heaven.*)

🌀 **ABRACADABRA** One of the most ancient of all charms, used to protect the user (or wearer, when adapted as an amulet) from disease, toothache, and spiritual assault. Meaning "I bless the dead," Abracadabra was said to have originated in one of two ways. It was perhaps formed from the Hebrew declaration *he brachah dabarah* ("speak the blessing") or from the Hebrew words *Ab* (Father), *Ben* (Son), and *Ruch a Cadsch* (Holy Spirit). Its association to angelology stems from its use in summoning an angel to provide assistance. When recited or chanted, it is spoken repeatedly, each repetition dropping the last letter until only the letter *A* remains. As an amulet, it is hung around the neck and tied with a linen thread, the words being written upon fine parchment:

ABRACADABRA
ABRACADABR
ABRACADAB
ABRACADA
ABRACAD
ABRACA
ABRAC
ABRA
ABR
AB
A

🌀 **ABRAHAM** The honored and so-called Father of the Jewish People, one of the greatest patriarchs of the Old Testament, and a figure known in the Muslim faith as the "friend of God." Abraham was also the recipient of several significant visitations by angels. While some have made the suggestion that the three visitors to his camp to announce the impending destruction of Sodom and Gomorrah were angels (named in some accounts as Michael, Gabriel, and Israfel), it is considered more likely that the three impressive men who stood before him were, in fact, the Lord, especially as in the Book of Genesis (18) the three always use the personal pronoun "I." The visitors predict the birth of Abraham's son, Isaac, an event that Abraham's wife, Sarah, greets with total incredulity, even laughing out loud before realizing the grievous offense she had committed. There is a custom, however, that the birth of Isaac was prophesied by the great archangel Michael. The coming of Isaac was so remarkable because both Abraham and especially Sarah were considered far too old to bear children.

Abraham is visited by the three mysterious strangers who announced the destruction of Sodom and Gomorrah; by Gustave Doré.

Abraham was tested in a most extreme fashion soon after the birth of Isaac. Instructed to take his son to Mount Moriah, Abraham was told to sacrifice his beloved son. Obedient to the will of the Lord, the patriarch prepared to put Isaac to death as a burnt offering. His hand was stayed by an angel, who expressed the Lord's pleasure that he was so faithful but also enunciated the important teaching that there should be no taking of life in the name of the Lord.

Abraham is also connected to angel lore in several ways that go beyond Scripture. By custom, for example, he was even accompanied by his own special guardian or guiding angel. The name of this angel is given as Zadkiel, the angel appearing in Jewish lore as the master of mercy and compassion. It is thus Zadkiel who is thought in some sources to have stayed the hand of Abraham on Mount Moriah, although that act has also been attributed to Michael. In an even more interesting tradition, consistent often with the other great patriarchs of the Old Testament, Abraham was taken to heaven and, like Enoch and others, was transformed by the will of God into an angel. (See also *Bible* and *Old Testament*.)

ABRAXAS In the teachings of the Gnostics, the name used for the Supreme Being, the source of the divine emanations through which all things were created. Included in the emanations are 365 spirits, thought to have their own heavens. Interestingly, the sum of number 365 is said to equal or correspond to the numerical value of the seven Greek letters used to spell "Abraxas." These seven numbers also served as a mystery symbol of God; moreover, they were thought to be the basis of the magical incantation Abracadabra.

As Gnostic thinking developed, Abraxas became the creator and leader—or prince—of the aeons, the eternal beings or divine manifestations that emanated from God. Abraxas was ruler of their 365 heavens and helped to perform a kind of intermediary role between the Supreme Being and those who exist on the earth. The name Abraxas was thus not surprisingly used in charms and talismans and was intended to provide divine protection and blessing. (See also *Aeon*.)

ABYSS, ANGEL OF THE The angel with authority over the nearly endlessly deep place, considered another name for hell and also termed the "Bottomless Pit." The abyss is the abode of Satan and his legions of fallen angels; it is additionally the place to which the souls of the condemned are consigned for an eternity of punishment and torment. This angel, keeper of the keys of the abyss, is also called the angel of the bottomless pit, identified most often as Abaddon.

ACCUSING ANGEL, THE The name given to the angel who "accuses" the sinner of the action; it is also applied to Satan, who, in the role of "the accuser," tests all humanity in its faithfulness toward God. The most famous incident involving Satan as the accusing angel is recounted in the Old Testament tale of Job. It is also used as a name for Samael.

ADABIEL According to the 1635 treatise on angels, *The Hierarchy of Blessed Angels,* by Thomas Heywood, Adabiel is one of the seven archangels, with authority over Jupiter or Mars. It is thought that his name might be a version or variation of Abdiel.

🏮 **ADAM AND EVE** The first human family, who resided in Paradise, the Garden of Eden, until their expulsion following the eating of the forbidden fruit from the tree of knowledge. Adam is considered in three senses: a personal name (Adam himself), an individual who bears within himself the attributes of all humanity, and humanity itself. Adam, as the first man, was supposedly created by God out of the dust or dirt of the earth. According to legend, his creation came about when the Lord dispatched the angels Gabriel, Michael, and Israfel to gather earth from different depths. They were unable, however, to complete their task because the earth itself would not give up its dirt, as it predicted that humanity would turn against the Lord, and it preferred to avoid the unpleasant experience altogether. Disappointed in the failure of his trusty lieutenants, God chose a new angel, Azrael, to fulfill the task. More determined, Azrael dragged the dirt out of the earth's grasp and brought it to the Lord. As a reward, Azrael was made the angel of death. The fact that he gathered soil from all over the world and of differing colors is used to explain the variety of colors and peoples who subsequently populated the globe.

Adam would have dealings with the angels—both righteous and fallen—in the time following his first appearance, but the very prospect of his creation also is traditionally thought to have had the most far-reaching consequences in heaven. Many angels, including Satan (also called Iblis in the Islamic custom and incorrectly named Lucifer in later accounts), were adamantly opposed to the rise of humanity. In the case of Satan, he refused to follow the command of the Lord that all angels should bow down before man. As the Qur'an (Koran) noted: "And when We said to the angels, Be submissive to Adam, they submitted, but Iblis [did not]. He refused and was proud, and he was one of the disbelievers" (surah 2:34). There supposedly followed the war in heaven, so beautifully presented in Milton's *Paradise Lost* as the heavenly host was divided over the question of humanity. The angels supporting Satan were ejected from heaven and fell, becoming the inhabitants of a hell of their own creation by their pride and disobedience.

Satan would attain some measure of revenge upon Adam and his wife, Eve, however, for he tempted the first couple to consume the forbidden fruit and so caused the great breach between God and humanity, sin. After many years of bliss, in which Adam and Eve apparently walked with God in the garden and in the company of the angels, Paradise was suddenly denied them. They were expelled by an angry cherubim at the order of the Lord, their expulsion beginning the story of humanity on the earth. A mighty cherubim, his burning sword facing in all directions, stands guard at the entrance of Eden to prevent any from approaching the tree of life. As for Adam and Eve, they would go forth and, as the legends declare, beget humanity, the story of their family and descendants detailed in much of the Old Testament. In some tales Adam was taken to heaven after his death, but others declare that he went to Sheol to await the coming of the Messiah with the other figures of the Old Testament; he was thus taken to heaven by Christ after the savior's descent into hell and the freeing of all who had anticipated his arrival. A rather touching tale has the grave of Adam dug by the angels Gabriel, Michael, Uriel, and Raphael, who lovingly returned him to the earth from which he had come. (See also *Eden, Garden of.*)

ADIMUS An angel who was long venerated by the Christian Church, but in 745 was included in a list of angelic servants declared by Church officials to be henceforth ineligible for honor by the faithful. The cause of this decision was the paucity of scriptural evidence for his existence and works. He was one of a number of angels, including the famed Uriel, who were removed from the angels to be venerated, the decision formally undertaken by a Council of Rome.

ADIRIRION An angel found in Jewish mystical traditions. Adiririon is a powerful servant of the Lord, ranked as a chief among the angelic orders. His name, however, is also connected with the name of God, and it was used on amulets as a preventive for the evil eye.

ADOIL An angel-like being mentioned in the apocryphal Second Book of Enoch. Adoil was actually a kind of explosive emanation or spiritual essence created by God. Out of this unique being God brought into existence all material things in the world: "And I commanded the lowest things:'Let one of the invisible things descend visibly!' And Adoil descended, extremely large. And I looked at him, and behold, in his belly he had a great light. And I said to him, 'Disintegrate yourself, Adoil, and let what is born from you become visible.' And he disintegrated himself, and there came out a very great light. And I was in the midst of the great light. And light out of light is carried thus. And the great age came out, and it revealed all the creation which I had brought up to create. And I saw how good it was."

🐚 **ADONAI** The term or name used since an early time by the Hebrews as a substitute for the sacred name of God, Jehovah (Yahweh),
which was ineffable and incommunicable. Adonai was thus read or
recited silently when it appeared in sacred texts. A Hebrew plural for
the word *adon* or lord, Adonai additionally substituted the tetragram-
maton, the four letters (JHVH, JHWH, YHVH, etc.) routinely used
for the word of God. In most translations of the Bible, Adonai is expressed as Lord. It also denoted a group of angels, especially in the
tradition of Gnosticism, the heretical Christian sect of the first centuries A.D. (See also *Elohim.*)

🐚 **AEON** In the original Greek sense, a great period of time, normally
considered infinite or indefinite; over time, aeon became associated in
the teachings of Gnosticism with an order of spirits or angelic beings
who exist eternally and are emanations of the Godhead. According to
Gnostic thought, there was a first aeon who emanated from God and
from which the next aeon was said to have been emanated. In this
sense each aeon used part of its own divine power or essence to emanate other aeons, each successive generation possessing less power
and divine essence because the aeons from which they were born
also possessed less essence than the one before them. As there was less
of the divine in each successive aeon, there was a greater risk of error
or mistake. This propensity for failing gave the Gnostics their means
of explaining the creation of the flawed and sin-filled material
universe.

Some Gnostics taught that the head of the aeons, their prince or
ruler, was Abraxas (or Abraxis). There were also to be found two important aeons: Pistis Sophia, the female personification or embodiment of wisdom, and Dynamis, the male personification of power.
The exact number of aeons is varying, but the most common number
given is 365. The prevalence of acceptance of the aeons as spiritual
beings to be respected is attested by the fact that many authorities in
the centuries prior to the sixth century A.D. placed them on a par
with the sefira (see *Sefiroth*) and also counted them as one of the ten
(or more) acknowledged orders or choirs of angels. They were subsequently dropped after the standardization of the orders by the sixth-
century theologian Dionysius the Areopagite. (See also *Archons.*)

🐚 **AHIAH** A half angel mentioned in the famed collection by Louis
Ginzberg, *The Legends of the Jews*. Ahiah is the son of fallen angel Se-

myaza, the onetime seraph who descended to the earth and cohabited with a human woman. (See also *Semyaza*.)

AHURA MAZDA The supreme deity of the Zoroastrian religion, which prospered in the Persian empire and the regions of the ancient Near East and was propagated by the prophet Zoroaster in the seventh to sixth centuries B.C. After spreading throughout Persia, the belief in Ahura Mazda was able to reach its zenith under the Persian king Darius I (r. 522–486 B.C.), who commanded that his subjects should worship the great god. In the teachings of early Zoroastrianism, Ahura Mazda was the creator of all things. This theology changed over succeeding generations so that the deity became the prime figure of goodness, compared with the equally eternal figure of evil. The two were forever locked in struggle, their main place of conflict the earth. In still later thinking, Ahura Mazda was known as Ormazd and was the twin brother of Ahriman. The sons of Zurvan (equated with Time), they do battle in epochs until the final triumph of Ahura Mazda at the end of time. In the early Zoroastrian cosmology, Ahura Mazda was the progenitor of two great spirits, Spenta Mainyu and Angra Mainyu—the former a spirit of light and goodness, the latter one of darkness and evil. He was later aided by six attendant spirits, the amesha spentas, who are considered the Zoroastrian equivalent of the archangels. (See also *Amesha Spentas* and *Zoroastrianism*.)

AKATHRIELAH YELOD SABAOTH In Jewish lore, a truly powerful angelic being, so formidable that his name (meaning "Akathrielah, lord of hosts") was used for God. His place in the heavenly order is to stand above the other angels in judgment. He was seen by the famed rabbi Eliosha ben Abuya when the latter was granted the great honor of actually visiting heaven while still alive on earth. Abuya gave a description of Akathrielah as standing at the very entrance of paradise.

AKHAZRIEL An angel mentioned in Louis Ginzberg's *The Legends of the Jews*. Akhazriel is ranked, as his name decrees, as the "herald of God," and he is used by the Lord to give declarations and divine pronouncements. Thus he was dispatched to inform Moses, the great Lawgiver, that Moses' prayer to have a longer time was not to be granted; Moses' death had been declared as arriving, and Akhazriel was charged with telling him that. (See also *Moses*.)

🦚 **AL-ZABAMIYAH** A group of nineteen angels who were mentioned in the Qur'an. Their task is to act as divine guards in the Islamic view of hell. Ambriel, an angel with a varied portfolio, is ranked as a prince in the choir of thrones. Among his other major positions are head of the zodiacal sign of Gemini and the patron angel of the month of May. Ambriel also appears in the Qabalistic tradition of the Jews.

🦚 **AMESHA SPENTAS** Called also the amshaspendas, the amesha spentas were the holy immortals, the six or seven spirits created by the great god Ahura Mazda in the Zoroastrian religion to assist him in the ordering of the universe. The amesha spentas are equated with the archangels of later understanding and are said to serve the Supreme Deity as virtually attendant deities. They were given various qualities and ultimately received exceedingly personalized attributes: truth (Vohu Manah); immortality (Ameretat); salvation (Haurvatat); desirable realm or dominion (Ksathiara); highest righteousness (Asha Vahista); and pious devotion (Spenta Aramiti). It can be said that the amesha spentas emanated (were emanations of) Ahura Mazda and reflected his most magnificent traits. Each amesha spenta, however, also had a diametrically opposite and equivalent archangel or spirit of evil. These seven evil attributes eventually came to represent the famous seven deadly sins, while the amesha spentas served as the foundation of the seven virtues. (See also *Ahura Mazda* and *Zoroastrianism*.)

🦚 **AMITIAL** See *Truth, Angel of the.*

🦚 **ANABONA** An angel listed in the famous occult work *The Greater Key of Solomon,* by S. L. MacGregor Mathers. He is described as the angel by whom (or through whom) God created the world. According to Hebrew legend, the name Anabona was heard by Moses when the Lawgiver was given the Ten Commandments.

🦚 **ANAEL** See under *Haniel.*

🦚 **ANAFIEL** Also called Anaphiel, he is the leader of the eight superior angels of the Merkabah, the mystical Jewish conception of ascending heavens. In this role, Anafiel has the high honorific role of serving as chief bearer of the seal and the keeper of the key to heaven's halls. According to the Third Book of Enoch, it was this angel who carried the great patriarch Enoch to heaven, where the latter was turned into the all-powerful angel Metatron. In a testament to Anafiel's own authority, however, Jewish legend tells of his performing the unpleasant task of punishing Metatron for some transgression; he whipped Metatron sixty times with tongues of fire. He is described in the Book of Enoch as "the honored, glorified, beloved, wonderful, terrible, and dreadful Prince."

ANAHITA A female angel found in Zoroastrian teachings, the ancient religion of Persia, Anahita is ranked high among the angelic beings.

ANAKIM The name given to the children born out of the union of mortal women with the fallen angels who had descended to earth. The Book of Genesis records that the angels (called here "the sons of God") "looking at the women, saw how beautiful they were and married as many of them as they chose" (6:1–2). The result of these marriages were the anakim. Derived from the Hebrew word *anak,* meaning giants, and also called the nephilim, these giants were said to be so tall that they literally touched the sun. Described in Genesis as "men of renown," the giants were actually mortal, existing without the benefits of any divine blood, inheriting none of the angelic attributes of their fathers. Among the angels listed as the sires of the anakim are Semyaza, Azza, and Azael. (See also *Nephilim.*)

ANGEL (Choir) The ninth and final order of angels according to the organization of the celestial hierarchy as created by the sixth-century theologian Dionysius the Areopagite; the angels belong to the third and final triad of choirs, with the archangels and principalities, the primary focus of their existence being the caretakership of humanity and the world. While the lowest ranked of all angelic beings—if one accepts the idea of a regulated angelic organization—angels are nevertheless members of the heavenly host and thus possess the profound and beautiful attributes given to them by their Creator. They are beings of pure spirituality and exist to fulfill the tasks given to them by God. Chief among these are to act as messengers of the Lord to the earth and guardians of the human soul.

The angel is thus the member of the heavenly host closest to humanity in its labors and concerns. The guardian angel, for example, the angelic being supposedly assigned not only to every living soul, but to places, churches, and even nations, is chosen from among the ranks of the ninth choir. Further, the angels are the heavenly residents who are most often mentioned in the Old Testament as making direct interventions upon the earth, be it to rescue Meshach, Shadrach, and Abednego from the fiery furnace; bring manna to Elijah; or speak to Abraham, Moses, and a host of other prophets and patriarchs. They also regularly appeared in the New Testament, proclaiming the birth of Christ, warning Joseph to flee from the wrath and evil of King Herod (and to return to Palestine after Herod died), and rescuing St. Peter from prison. Angels have also been seen throughout much of subsequent history by assorted saints—they used to help St. Zita in her kitchen chores, and a guardian angel was visible to Gemma Galgani—and to ordinary men, women, and children, touching their lives with an impact that is often inexpressible in mundane human terms.

An angel from *Paradise Lost;* by Gustave Doré.

It is precisely with the human, however, that the members of the ninth choir are most often concerned, but their specific mission on the earth is quite varied, depending upon the desire of the Lord. The word *angel* is derived from the Greek *angelos* and the Hebrew *mal'akh* (or *malak*), both meaning "messenger." Thus, one of the central tasks of the angel is to act as a messenger of the Lord. They might deliver joyous news, such as the birth of Christ in Bethlehem, or word of impending destruction and woe, such as the three mysterious visitors to Abraham who foretold the obliteration of Sodom and Gomorrah. Angels also carry out God's justice and fight against evil in the world. They do this through both physical and spiritual means. In the realm of the senses, they act, as St. Thomas Aquinas put it, upon the imagination to encourage the mortal from sin, further giving strength (when possible) to the soul to overcome temptation or to seek penance when some sin has been committed.

Quite spectacular have been the physical or material appearances of the angels, visitations that give some expression to the incomprehensible strength and power granted them by God: one angel destroyed an entire Assyrian army, and another wiped out seventy thousand Israelites to punish David for his pride. Far more subtle are angelic appearances, called angelophanies, touched upon earlier, namely the granting of help and assistance to simple good souls most in need of aid. Such incarnations, like the archangel Raphael in the Book of Tobit, are totally without the recognition of the mortal that the person who has shown up at some moment of crisis or danger is actually a resident of heaven. (See *Angelophany.*) Angels also observe all of human history, perhaps recording every human act to provide a clear statement of the development of each soul at the time of its judgment in the next world and laboring behind the scenes of human affairs to direct the world's evolution and progress toward peace and spiritual enlightenment. In this they oppose the efforts of evil to sow chaos, discord, and war. Finally, they are said to appear to many individuals at the approach of death, offering encouragement and solace as the soul begins its journey into the new life beyond the world.

In heaven angels provide valuable service, in proper fulfillment of their natures as purely spiritual beings and the will of the Creator. As beings who, ages ago, chose and embraced the love of God, angels partake in the blessed and pure light of the Lord. They ask nothing more than the incomparable honor of giving worship to their Maker, a beloved duty for all angels regardless of their place in the celestial hierarchy. They give thanks to God for their creation and the bringing into existence of the world and the cosmos, and they reportedly fill the heavens with joy every time another soul has achieved salvation. While ranked last of the nine choirs and hence the least perfect of all angels, according to Thomas Aquinas, angels nevertheless have a vital role to play in maintaining the heavenly order and the equilibrium of all the universe. They possess a full share in God's love and grace and are completely content with their place in heaven. This was expressed in Dante's *Divine Comedy* when the poet inquires of Piccarda in *Paradiso* (Canto III): "Long ye for a higher place, More to behold, and more in love to dwell?" She and other spirits only smile gently and reply:

> . . . *If we should wish to be exalted more,*
> *Then must our wishes jar with the high will*

Of him, who sets us here . . .
Rather it is inherent in this state
Of blessedness, to keep ourselves within
The divine will, by which our wills with his
Are one. So that as we, from step to step,
Are placed throughout this kingdom, pleases all,
Even as our King, who in us plants his will;
And in his will is our tranquility:
It is the mighty ocean, whither tends
Whate'er creates and nature makes.

Dante proclaims his understanding by observing:

Then I saw clearly how each spot in heaven
Is Paradise, though with like gracious dew
The supreme virtue shower not over all.

The choir of angels is said to be headed by several angels, including Adnachiel and Chayyliel, but the most well-known is Gabriel. (For more information on the nature and existence of angels, see *Choirs* and *Guardian Angel*.)

ANGEL OF THE ABYSS See *Abyss, Angel of the;* see also *Abaddon* and *Bottomless Pit, Angel of the*.

ANGEL OF DEATH See *Azrael* and *Death, Angel of*.

ANGEL OF THE LORD See *Lord, Angel of the*.

ANGEL WRAPPED IN A CLOUD A "mighty angel" described by St. John in the Book of Revelation. This unnamed angel came down from heaven "wrapped in a cloud, with a rainbow over his head, and his face was like the sun, and his legs like pillars of fire. He had a little scroll opened in his hand." The scroll he would later give to John, commanding him to eat it. The writer found it "sweet as honey in my mouth, but when I had eaten it my stomach was made bitter. And I was told, 'You must again prophesy about many peoples and nations and tongues and kings' " (10:1–2, 10–11).

ANGELIC DOCTOR The title given to St. Thomas Aquinas (d. 1274) in honor of his enormous achievements in theology and especially his writings on angels. (See *Thomas Aquinas, St.,* for details.)

ANGELOLATRY The improper veneration or even worship of angels. Angelolatry is a kind of exaggerated belief and reverence of angels and is condemned by the Catholic Church, for such worship is due exclusively to God. In the early Christian Church, there was considerable discussion and, at times, confusion over the proper way of honoring the angelic servants of the Lord. Some felt it was entirely appropriate to honor them, but others felt it smacked of idolatry, a charge to which the Church was exceedingly sensitive in its first centuries, struggling as it was with the forces of paganism. Gradually, however, the revering of angels was permitted, leading to the extensive listings of angels and angelic choirs by such writers and theologians as Dionysius the Areopagite. By the eighth century, however, Church officials felt that the speculation was increasingly excessive, so in 745 a council of leaders was convened in Rome. Here a group of angels was removed from the list of angels to whom it was proper to give veneration (Adimus, Tubuas Raguel, Sabaoth, Simiel, Inias, and Uriel). The modern Church, particularly since Vatican Council II (1962–65), has deemphasized the place of angels, and today angelolatry is not a common problem faced by the Church, although some critics of the New Age movement warn against an understandable obsession with angelic intervention. (See also *Rome, Council of.*)

ANGELOLOGY The broad term given for the study of angels and all things pertaining to the angelic and the celestial hierarchy. It can be said that angelology began at the earliest time when humans first wondered about the nature and attributes of angels, or whatever name they gave to divine messengers or emissaries of heaven. The Bible was subsequently one of the main sources for the study of angels, with its many references to the angelic, although only two angels were actually named in the Jewish Old Testament, Michael and Gabriel, with a third angel, Raphael, named in the Book of Tobit. More angels were mentioned in the New Testament, especially so in the Book of Revelation, where angels play a leading part in the events of the Last Judgment. Beyond the Bible, there is a host of so-called apocryphal and pseudepigraphical writings that were not accepted into the canonical writings of the Bible, either by the Jewish faith or by the Christian. These works, such as the Books of Enoch, the Book of Jubilees, and numerous Gospels, often contain extensive details about angels and their place in the heavens. While they are not accepted as writings of revealed faith, such compendiums of lore remain some of the most interesting sources for the supposed characteristics, attributes, and hierarchy of the angels.

The golden age of angelology was during the Middle Ages, specifically in the twelfth and thirteenth centuries, when Christian scholars, members of the intense intellectual movement called Scholasticism, gave much thought to the place of angels in God's Creation, their functions and attributes, and the organization of the entire heavenly host. Much of their research was based on the work of earlier writers, such as the sixth-century Dionysius the Areopagite (or Pseudo-Dionysius), who is credited with designing the generally accepted organization of the angelic choirs. The foremost angelologist, perhaps of all time, was St. Thomas Aquinas (d. 1274), who devoted a part of his mammoth theological work *Summa Theologica* to angels. (See *Thomas Aquinas, St.*)

In the era of the Renaissance and the subsequent Enlightenment, angels fell out of favor as objects of serious study; nevertheless, they remained potent and favorite subjects of art and literature, reaching their literary zenith in *Paradise Lost* (1667) by John Milton, a work ranked with Dante's *Divine Comedy* as one of the foremost sources for the angelic. In modern times the angel has undergone a truly remarkable rebirth, standing as one of society's great expressions of the divine, the spiritual, and the endless possibilities of the transformation of the soul with the help and encouragement of the entire realm of the sacred. Spearheading the flowering of contemporary angelology have been the works of such eminent writers as Mortimer Adler, Gustav Davidson, Sophy Burnham, and Terry Lynn Taylor.

ANGELOPHANY The technical term used for the visit or visitation by an angel. The name implies the intensely mystical and religious significance of any appearance by angelic beings. Angelophanies have been reported throughout human history, ranging from the famous interventions of the Old Testament to the involvement of angels in the affairs of later mortals, to the sudden arrival of the heavenly messenger into the lives of seemingly ordinary men, women, and children. Among the host of historical examples are St. Joan of Arc (d. 1431) and Pope St. Gregory the Great (r. 590–604). Joan was supposedly guided by the archangel Michael in her brilliant campaigns against the English during the Hundred Years' War (1337–1455), and her hearing the voice of the angelic played a major role in securing her condemnation by the English in 1431 and her being burned at the stake for heresy and witchcraft. Pope Gregory the Great also had dealings with St. Michael, beholding the angel descending upon the mausoleum of Emperor Hadrian during a plague in Rome. He took the vision to mean that the plague would stop—which it did—and so renamed the mausoleum the Castel Sant'Angelo in St. Michael's honor, the Castle of the Holy Angel.

As is clear from these two events, the angelophany rarely leaves the recipient unchanged or unaffected. These examples are also among the better known. Many angelophanies occur to individuals or saints who never report them to anyone or who are not believed. There are hundreds, perhaps thousands, of such angelic visitations throughout the world, with only a few recognized as a celestial foray or actually noted, recorded, and made public. Such are the claimed numbers of angelophanies that entire books have been written on the subject and organizations devoted to their study.

In Christian custom, it has been declared that there are ways of telling whether a possible angelic visit is truly by a heavenly being or by an infernal one. One supposedly surefire method is the sensation one has during and after the incident. Should one be at great ease during the visit and then sick at heart or ill afterward, it is said that the visitor was a denizen of the territory of the fiend; if one is stricken with a mixture of awe, terror, and dread during the event and great peace or even joy afterward, the guest was probably angelic. There is, of course, to be remembered the lesson learned by Abraham in the Book of Genesis, when he was visited by three travelers (angels or perhaps God himself). Often one may be asked for help by a stranger; the supplicant may be a human in distress or it may be an angel in disguise, the angelophany hidden from mortal eyes, but not from the angel or its Master.

🞕🞕 **ANGELUS** A popular prayer recited in honor of the Annunciation of the angel Gabriel to the blessed Virgin Mary that she would bear the child Jesus. In Catholic practice, the Angelus is recited at 6 A.M., noon, and 6 P.M. Its common name is derived from the first word of the opening line, in the original Latin: *Angelus Domini nuntiavit Mariam* ("The Angel of the Lord declared to Mary"). The prayer is as follows:

> *The Angel of the Lord declared unto Mary.*
> *And she conceived by the power of the Holy Spirit (Hail Mary).*

Behold the handmaid of the Lord.
Let it be done to me according to your word (Hail Mary).
And the word was made flesh.
And dwelled among us. (Hail Mary).
Pray for us, O Holy Mother of God.
That we may be made ready of the promises of Christ.
Let us pray.
Pour forth, we beseech you, O Lord, your
grace into our hearts; that we, to whom
the Incarnation of Christ your son was
made known by the message of an angel, may
by His passion and cross,
*   be brought to the*
glory of His Resurrection;
*   through the same*
Christ Our Lord. Amen.

ANNUNCIATION, ANGEL OF THE The traditional title given to the archangel Gabriel in his role as messenger of God to the Virgin Mary to announce the incarnation of Christ. As was recorded in the Gospel of Luke (1:26–31): "In the sixth month the angel Gabriel visited in the city of Galilee named Nazareth, a virgin betrothed to a man whose name was Joseph, of the House of David; and the virgin's name was Mary. And he came to her and said, 'Hail, O favored one, the Lord is with you!' But she was greatly troubled at the saying and considered in her mind what sort of greeting this might be. And the angel said to her, 'Do not be afraid, Mary, for you have found favor with God. And behold,

The archangel Gabriel announces to the Virgin Mary the coming of Christ; from *The Annunciation* by Christus Petrus, Gemaeldegalerie, Staatliche Museen, Berlin (COURTESY ART RESOURCE).

you will conceive in your womb and bear a son, and you shall call his name Jesus.' " Gabriel also prophesied the conception of St. John the Baptist by Mary's kinswoman Elizabeth, declaring, "For with God nothing will be impossible." (See also *Gabriel.*) The Annunciation—and hence Gabriel—has been the subject of artists throughout the ages, including Tintoretto, Fra Angelico, Leonardo da Vinci, and El Greco.

APOCALYPSE See *Revelation, Book of.*

APOCALYPSE, ANGEL OF THE The title given to a number of angels and even several historical figures. The angel of the apocalypse is looked upon as an angel who brings tidings of the impending end of the world and imminent judgment of the human race. Among the angels who are suggested in this role are Michael, Gabriel, Orifiel, Raphael, and Haniel. Two saints, much revered, can also lay claim to the honor. The first is St. Francis of Assisi (d. 1226), one of the very rare figures in Christian history who is considered in legend as having been taken to heaven and transformed into an angel following his death. The other is St. Vincent Ferrer (d. 1419), a renowned Spanish preacher who was said to possess the ability to predict coming events (he once prophesied the arrival of grain ships in a city when they were desperately needed); St. Vincent also regularly called upon his listeners to repent everywhere he journeyed across Christendom.

APOCRYPHA The broad title given to those writings that were initially included in the Greek version of the Old Testament (the Septuagint) but were later excluded by the non-Hellenic Jews from their accepted books of the Old Testament. These writings were largely adopted into the canonical (or accepted) books of the Christian Old Testament but were later removed by Protestant leaders during the Reformation and the organization of their own Bible. Apocryphal literature, however, is also found among the Jews and the Christians with great bodies of works that were, for various reasons, rejected by the leaders of the faiths as unauthentic or holding theological positions that were contrary to those of the established teachings. In Christianity, for example, a large number of texts were unacceptable because they espoused the teachings or were influenced by the heretical movement of Gnosticism, which was quite contrary to existing doctrine. (*Entry continued on page 22.*)

APPEARANCE OF ANGELS

❦

Largely through the brilliant and imaginative creations of artists over the ages, angels are today easily described by young and old alike. Some are said to be beautiful beings (of often nonspecific gender), with wings of pure white feathers; they are dressed in white, perhaps with cords of gold, or gleaming armor; they carry harps, other musical instruments, or fiery swords; and they have lovely halos or auras of the brightest golden hue. Other angels are delightful little cherubs, chubby childlike beings with tiny wings, circling figures of the Madonna and baby Jesus; they are more reminiscent of Cupid than the fell beings who destroyed Sodom and Gomorrah.

While immediately recognizable, such common visions of the angel are only partly supported by Scripture and the personal experiences of those fortunate souls who have actually met members of the heavenly host, and the idea of the cherub is actually entirely the work of artists. Angels appear in the Bible and in apocryphal writings such as the Books of Enoch in shapes and sizes that are radically different from anything the average person could conceive. There are, for example, the powerful images of Ezekiel's cherubim as they

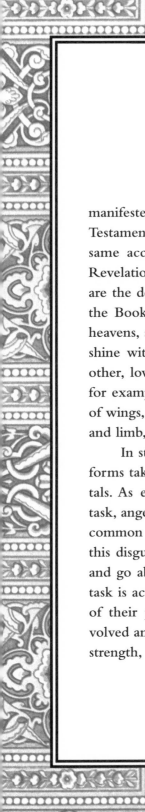

manifested themselves at the river Chebar in the Old Testament (see *Cherubim* for details), the thrones in the same account, and the dread angels of the Book of Revelations in the New Testament. Even more striking are the descriptions of the angelic princes of heaven in the Books of Enoch. These angels stand as tall as the heavens, send out lightning with their every look, and shine with a light that is unapproachable even by the other, lower angelic ranks. The great angel Metatron, for example, is covered with 365,000 eyes and 36 pairs of wings, and every fiber of his being, every hair, organ, and limb, is a living, pure flame.

In stark contrast, but still to be considered, are the forms taken by angels when visiting the world of mortals. As empowered by the Lord to accomplish some task, angels can take any shape or visage. But the most common is that of a simple man, woman, or child. In this disguise, angels are able to move among humanity and go about their work largely unnoticed. Once their task is accomplished they disappear, leaving not a trace of their presence beyond the memories of those involved and the fruits of their charity: hope, joy, renewed strength, and health.

While not included in the sacred texts, many apocryphal writings (and so-called pseudepigraphical works—texts written in a style of canonical books and supposedly authored or named after some biblical figure) make for fascinating reading and very often include extensive details about angels. Among the most famous angelologies are the Books of Enoch, the Book of Jubilees, and the Gospel of St. Bartholomew.

APOLLION Another name for the angel Abaddon, the angel of the bottomless pit.

APPEARANCE, ANGELIC See box on pages 20–21.

APUTEL An angel greatly respected by the Hebrews. The priests who entered the "holy of holies" in the tabernacle of the Great Temple of Jerusalem wore a plaque on their breasts that bore his name. By using his name, a trained and powerful sorcerer was reputed to be able to raise the dead.

ARAQIEL Also called Arkiel and Saraquael, an angel mentioned in the First Book of Enoch as being ranked among the infamous two hundred fallen angels who taught humanity certain kinds of knowledge. Although arrayed with the evil angels in this account, Araqiel is also considered a good angel in other sources, such as the Sibylline Oracles. For example, he is credited in some accounts as one of the angels who carry the souls of deceased persons to heaven and before the throne of God for judgment.

ARARIEL An angel of the waters, Arariel was recognized as having authority over the oceans, and as such he was asked for help by fishermen in catching fish large enough to tell a tale. There is also a tradition that Arariel would cure stupidity.

ARCHANGEL (Choir) One of the accepted choirs of angels as established by the sixth-century theologian Dionysius the Areopagite; the archangels are ranked eighth in the nine choirs, above angels and below principalities. In the division of the angelic hierarchy into three triads of three choirs each, the archangels belong to the third and lowest triad (with angels and principalities). The chiefs of the choir are given as Michael, Gabriel, Raphael, Metatron, Barachiel, and Barbiel, although of them Michael is most commonly mentioned as leader. The archangels are perhaps the most confusing of the angelic orders, for aside from being a distinct part of the heavenly host, their name is used frequently for virtually every angelic being superior to the ordinary (if one can call them that) angels—in the sense of members of the ninth choir. This peculiar situation is exacerbated by the long-standing tradition declaring archangel Michael the captain of the host of the Lord, technically meaning that a member of the second-lowest choir in all of heaven is superior in rank even to the mighty seraphim. The roots of this dilemma may be traced to the development of angelology in Jewish lore and during the Middle Ages. In the initial understanding of angels, there were only two ranks, angels and archangels. Over time, however, they were joined by the other orders, such as the cherubim

The seven archangels; from a woodcut by Albrecht Dürer.

and thrones, until an entire hierarchy of blessed spirits had been formulated by scholars and writers. In Christian times the archangels, because of their close association with humanity, were placed on the lower level of the angelic lists. Thus, with such angels as Gabriel, Raphael, and Michael named as archangels, they were simply grouped with their fellow members, regardless of their obvious and attested importance in heaven. It is possible to argue additionally that archangels are given the full task of leading the host of heaven anytime it sets off to do battle with the forces of darkness. They were thus in charge of conducting the so-called War in Heaven, which was precipitated by the Fall of Lucifer and his fellow angels, and they will

THE
SEVEN ARCHANGELS

While the archangels are said to constitute a separate choir or order of angels within the celestial hierarchy, there are also declared in tradition a group of archangels who stand above not only their own choir, but higher than nearly all of the angelic orders regardless of their place in the heavenly host. These most august of angels are members of several choirs at once, being honored as the heads of the angelic bodies while fulfilling the leading offices in heaven; they are also most appropriately termed "princes of the seven heavens," and according to the Third Book of Enoch, each is attended by 496,000 myriads of ministering angels (a myriad in archaic terminology denotes either a vast number or perhaps ten thousand). Islam recognizes only four archangels (Michael, Gabriel, Israfel, and Azrael), and other customs say twelve, but the most common number for these mighty angels is seven. This number is supported by occult lore and appears in many sources, such as Revelation (8:2), the First and Third Books of Enoch, and the Book of Tobit (12:15); in the latter writing, the archangel Raphael declares his membership as "one of the seven holy angels who present the prayers of the saints and enter into the presence of the glory of the Holy One."

Far more uncertain are the actual members of this group of princes, although almost every possible list has two or three names in common: the famous and beloved angels Michael and Gabriel, along with Raphael. The First Book of Enoch states them to be Raphael, Uriel, Michael, Gabriel, Zerachiel, Remiel, and Raguel. The Third Book of Enoch appoints Michael, Gabriel, Satqiel, Sahaqiel, Baradiel, Baraqiel, and Sidriel. The best-known list belongs to Dionysius the Areopagite, who names Michael, Gabriel, Raphael, Uriel, Chamuel, Zadkiel, and Jophiel.

appear once more—if Scripture is to be accepted—at the end of the world.

Archangels are among the few angelic beings mentioned specifically by name in the Old Testament. In the Book of Daniel, Michael is referred to as "one of the chief princes," and he is joined by Gabriel. Even more specific are references in the New Testament, such as in the Letter of Jude (1:9): "But when the archangel Michael, contending with the devil, disputed about the body of Moses, he did not presume to pronounce a reviling judgment upon him, but said, 'The Lord rebuke you.' " As is clear from their appearances in Scripture, the primary duty of the archangels is to carry out the will of God as it relates directly to humanity. They bring to the world the prayerful blessings of the Lord and the special concern of God for each and every human life. It is for that reason that the archangels—like their close counterparts the angels—are said to intervene so regularly in the affairs of men and women, be it on a battlefield, in an impending disaster, or in the private anguish and sorrow of the living. In each case they impart a portion of their incalculable compassion and love, giving comfort, solace, or fortitude at the darkest of moments.

The number of archangels has long been a source of great discussion among angelologists. Traditionally there are seven archangels (for their names, see *Archangels, Seven*), although who they are and what they do has been given variously in different sources. Most of the lists name at least four angels in common: Michael, Gabriel, Raphael, and Uriel; Michael and Gabriel are attested to in the Old Testament, as is Raphael (who appears in the Book of Tobit, which is considered apocryphal by some faiths). Uriel is not named in the Bible, but in assorted noncanonical writings, especially those of Enoch where he is included in the lists of archangels (under the name Suruel). Of all the named archangels, though, the Christian Church has retained only three: Michael, Raphael, and Gabriel. The others, including Uriel, were removed from the lists of those eligible for veneration because of the absence of any scriptural support and their presence in dubious legends. That there are seven archangels is attested to in the Book of Revelation (8:2): "Then I saw the seven angels who stand before God. . . ." There is also the list of seven archangels in the First Book of Enoch and the princes of the seven heavens in the Third Book of Enoch. Against all of these sources is the Islamic teaching that places the number of archangels at four. Two, Michael and Gabriel, are named in the Qur'an; the other two are not named, but Islamic tradition holds them to be Azrael, the angel of death, and Israfel, the angel of the trumpet. (See also *Choirs*.)

ARCHANGELS, SEVEN See box on pages 24–25.

ARCHONS Eminently powerful spiritual beings, said to be equated with the aeons and also with the archangels. The archons were created in the teachings of the Gnostics (the early heretical movement in Christianity) and were said to have been born by the will of the Gnostic deity Demiurge. In the dualistic thinking of the Gnostics—in which the material world is considered evil—the archons were equated with beings of evil, in large part because they had the duty of governing the running of the world, a place of inherent wickedness. In Gnostic thinking, the archons were said to number around twelve (or perhaps seven). In the latter count, they corresponded to each of the known planets; other sources spoke of their coordinate place with the zodiac. Their other terrible purpose was to imprison the souls of humans in the sin-racked material bodies and so leave them trapped in the wicked realm of the world, unable to free themselves and pass upward into the divine light.

In the last sense, the archons (or a variant of them) appeared in the lore of the Merkabah, the mystical Jewish sect. Here they work against the progress of souls along the route of the seven heavens, conspiring with the hosts of evil spirits and challenging angels. Some thinking, on the other hand, declares them to be synonymous with the angels, specifically the great angels who assist God in the running of the world. In this understanding they are not at all evil, and over the years the archons have been said to include such renowned angels as Michael, Uriel, Raphael, and Gabriel. (For details on angels governing nations, see under *Guardian Angels*.)

The leaders of the archons vary depending upon the source that is used to find out who they are. In one Gnostic reference they are counted as Sabaoth, Ialdabaoth, Jao, Ailoaios, Oraios, Astanphaios, and Adonaios. In another source, the *Papyri Graecae Magicae* ("Papyrus of Greek Magic"), there are five archons, their names for the most part far better known than the other Gnostic list: Uriel, Gabriel, Michael, Raphael, and Shamuil.

ARIEL An angel or spirit best known as a character in William Shakespeare's *The Tempest*. According to this play, Ariel is an "ayrie spirit" who is freed from painful confinement in a cloven pine by Prospero after being imprisoned there by the witch Sycorax for being "a spirit too delicate to act her earthy and abhorr'd commands." Ariel performs a number of tasks for Prospero but eventually receives his freedom after ensuring at the end of the work that the royal fleet—bearing Prospero—reaches home safely. There are several uses of the name in the Old Testament, namely in Isaiah (29:1), where it denotes the city of Jerusalem ("Ho Ariel, Ariel, the city where David encamped!"); and in Ezra (8:16), where it is the name of a man. There is also a long-standing tradition that Ariel is an angel, the name meaning "lion of God"; although he is variously described as a member of the angelic hierarchy, he is also at times placed among the evil angels. He is thus, variously, an angel companion of Raphael in his efforts to assist humanity and, in John Milton's *Paradise Lost,* one of the fallen angels who is routed by the stern and obedient seraph Abdiel during the war in heaven.

ARIOCH A onetime angel who fell and joined Satan in his war with heaven. In *Paradise Lost,* Milton described the rather one-sided struggle between Arioch and the angel Abdiel: "Nor stood unmindful Abdiel to annoy, the atheist crew, but with redoubled blow, Ariel and Arioch, and the violence, Of Ramiel scorched and blasted overthrew." In other customs Arioch became a dreadful demon of vengeance. The well-known fantasy author Michael Moorcock used Arioch (Arioc) as one of the powerful deities of chaos in his popular saga featuring Elric of Melnibone.

ARK OF THE COVENANT, ANGELS OF THE The angels who were carved on the Ark of the Covenant (the vessel said to be the repository of the broken Ten Commandments and a truly powerful conductor of God's will). The angels on the Ark have been said to number two or four, depending upon the divine instructions given to Moses and recorded in the Book of Exodus: "And you shall make two cherubim of gold; of hammered work shall you make them, on the two ends of the mercy seat. Make one cherub on one end, and one cherub on the other end; of one piece with the mercy seat shall you make the cherubim on its two ends. The cherubim shall spread out their wings above, overshadowing the mercy seat with their wings, their faces one to another; toward the faces of the mercy seat shall the cherubims be" (25:18–20). According to legend, the names of the two cherubims on the Ark were Jael and Zarall. The Ark—and hence the angels—was carried by the Levites (the priestly assistants) during the wanderings in the wilderness of the Jewish people, but it was eventually placed in the Great Temple of Jerusalem by King Solomon, from which it eventually disappeared. The Israelites did carry it into battle, where its awesome power was unleased upon their enemies. The angel Sandalphon has also been called the cherub of the left hand of the Ark. The Ark has been depicted on a number of occasions in art and even film, perhaps the most notable being in the film *Raiders of the Lost Ark* (1981), in which the Nazis quite ill-advisedly open the Ark, unleashing the wrath of the Lord.

ARMIES The name used in *Paradise Lost* by John Milton for one of the choirs of angels. The term is also rich in symbolism, as it represents the often military bearing of the angels, in the fulfillment of their appointed tasks by the Lord to resist and even expel evil from heaven or especially the earth. While not precisely synonymous, the term can be argued to be equatable with the traditional title heavenly hosts, which is bestowed upon the entire body of angels in heaven. The two orders or choirs of angels that can be said traditionally to evince an attitude and atmosphere of the military are the angels and archangels, the two lowest orders, the ones most often painted wearing armor and bearing weapons, and those celestial beings most often thought to have direct dealings with humanity.

ARMISAEL An angel who should be called upon to assist in easy childbirth. According to the teachings of the Talmud, a woman could improve giving birth by reciting nine times Psalm 20: "The Lord answer you in the day of trouble! The name of the God of Jacob protect you! May he send you help from the sanctuary, and give you support from Zion! May he remember all of your offerings, and regard with favor your burnt sacrifices! . . ." Should this fail (or should one be unable to remember all of it), the next step was to seek the aid of Armisael with the suitable ritual invocation.

ARSYALALYUR Also Asuryal, an angel mentioned in the apocryphal First Book of Enoch. He was said to have been sent to Noah, son of Lamech, with the famed warning: "And the Deluge is about to come

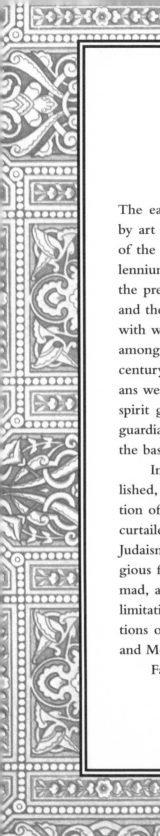

ANGELS IN ART

The earliest depictions of angel-like beings are traced by art historians to the times of the Sumerian culture of the fertile crescent, dating to around the third millennium. They created stone carvings of winged beings, the precursors of the angels, to symbolize their deities and their servants. Other gods and mythological beings with wings and duties similar to the angels were found among the Assyrians in their genie, dating to the ninth century B.C. In succession to the Sumerians and Assyrians were the Babylonians, who advanced the notions of spirit guardians, protecting palaces and temples. These guardians were the keribu (see *Babylon*), who formed the basis of the later angels called the cherubim.

In the eras when belief in angels was firmly established, it is interesting to note that artistic representation of the members of the heavenly host was severely curtailed by the strict prohibitions found in Orthodox Judaism and also Islam against the depiction of religious figures, including the Lord, the prophet Muhammad, and angels. Fortunately Persian art had no such limitation, and consequently some of the finest illustrations of winged angels are found in Persian miniatures and Moghul art.

Far and away, however, the depiction of angels is

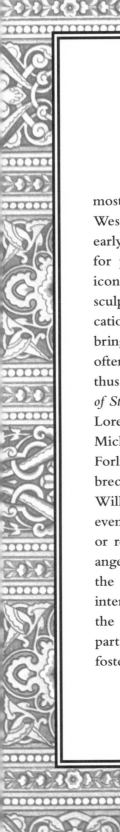

most fully and extensively expressed in Christian and Western art. Angels appeared in Christian art at an early time, remaining one of the most popular motifs for painters, sculptors, and illustrators and found in icons, illuminated manuscripts, paintings, reliefs, and sculpture. Expressing the faith of the time, giving edification and spiritual encouragement to the viewer, and bringing to life some event in Scripture, the angel was often used by the foremost artists in history. There are thus angels by Giotto, Raphael (including the *Liberation of St. Peter* in the Vatican), Roger van der Weyden, Gian Lorenzo Bernini, Leonardo da Vinci, Fra Angelico, Michelangelo, Rembrandt, Brunelleschi, Melozzo da Forlì, Jan and Hubert van Eyck, Hans Memling, Albrecht Dürer, Pieter Brueghel, Gustave Doré, and William Blake; there are also the countless lesser or even unknown artisans whose work, while not famous or renowned, nevertheless contributed to the place of angels in the hearts and minds of humanity throughout the ages. Today these masterworks are joined by new interpretations by contemporary artists, many part of the renaissance in angelology of the past years, others part of the ongoing New Age movement that has also fostered the study and appreciation of the angelic.

upon all the earth; and all that is in it shall be destroyed. And now instruct that he may flee, and his seed shall be preserved for all generations."

🧿 **ART, ANGELS IN** See box on pages 30–31.

🧿 **ASAPH** The angel who is said to have made a direct contribution to the Bible by authoring twelve of the Psalms of the Old Testament. The Psalms were number 50 and from 73 to 83. His skill in composing hymns to the Lord apparently earned him the honorific post of chief or director of the heavenly hosts, ceaselessly giving praise to God; his authority, however, extends only over the night, the songs of the choir under the command of the angel Jeduthun.

🧿 **ASCENSION, ANGELS OF** The two angels mentioned in the Acts of the Apostles (1:10) as appearing to the apostles at the moment of Christ's Ascension into heaven: "And while they were gazing into heaven as he went, behold, two men stood by them in white robes, and said, 'Men of Galilee, why do you stand looking into heaven? This Jesus who was taken up from you into heaven, will come in the same way as you saw him go into heaven.' " These were only two of the many angels who appeared on earth during the period of Christ, as recounted in Scripture and Christian tradition.

🧿 **AT-TAUM** An angel whose name means "the twin" who is credited in the lore of the Manichaeans with giving the religious leader Mani the revelations that were to form the foundation for his subsequent teachings.

🧿 **AUPIEL** Another name used for the angel Anafiel. (See *Anafiel* for details.)

🧿 **AUTHORITIES** An alternative name used for the choir of angels known as the virtues or powers. Among experts on angels over the years, however, there has been speculation that the choir of authorities should be considered a distinct and separate body.

🧿 **AUZA** One of the so-called sons of God, also called Oza, who fell from heaven and journeyed to earth to engage in carnal union with

AZRAEL

A young man was walking one day in Jerusalem when he looked up and, to his abject horror, was staring into the pale, frightening eyes of Azrael, the angel of death. Screaming and running for his life—because he knew that no one encounters the angel who is not marked for death—he begged to be received by the mighty and wise King Solomon to implore his advice. The king agreed to hear his remarkable tale and, after pondering the man's problem, counseled him to flee from Jerusalem, as the angel was said to be required to go to an appointed place and there find the soul who was to die. By departing Jerusalem, the man might be able to avoid death altogether, having been blessed with the good fortune of seeing Azrael just before the expected time. The man rode desperately out of the gates of Jerusalem and went straight to Damascus. Much relieved upon entering the city, he went suddenly white with fear, for there in his path was Azrael. Now unable to escape, the man cried to the angel that he had avoided death in Jerusalem. "You see," Azrael said cheerfully, "I was supposed to meet you here in Damascus, so I was quite surprised to find you in Jerusalem." With that, the angel reached out and snatched the soul from the astonished mortal.

mortal women. This event, touched upon in the Book of Genesis, resulted in the birth of the anakim, also known as the nephilim.

🏵 **AVATAR** Ten angel-like beings who appear in Hindu lore and are the human or animal incarnation of a deity, taking such a form in order to combat evil or perform some significant act of goodness. The avatars (Sanskrit *avatara*) are best known as the ten incarnations of Vishnu. Obviously the most famous of the avatars is Krishna (Krsna), the divine cowherd. Kalki (or Kalkin) is an avatar still to come, supposedly riding a white horse with wings to destroy the world at the end of the four ages. The other avatars are Buddha, Matsga, Narasimha, Varaha, Kurma, Parasurana, Vamana, and Rama. Krishna, in some regions, is actually considered a god, his brother Balarama serving as an avatar. The avatar demonstrate the worldwide prevalence of angelic beings intervening in the affairs of humanity.

🏵 **AVENGING ANGEL** See *Destruction, Angels of.*

🏵 **AZAZEL** One of the fallen angels, also known as Iblis. (For the list of fallen angels, see under *Fallen Angels*.)

🏵 **AZAZIEL** A seraph who figured in Lord Byron's poem "Heaven and Earth." Azaziel fell in love with Anah, granddaughter of Cain. To save her from the coming of the Great Flood, which covered the earth, the angel snatched her up and, tucking her beneath her wings, carried her to safety on another planet. (See also *Poetry*.)

🏵 **AZBUGA YHWH** Also Asbogha, a prominent angel in Hebrew lore, ranked as one of the eight princes of the throne of judgment. He is even more powerful than the dread angel Metatron. According to some Jewish legends, Azbuga has the task of welcoming the truly worthy into heaven (some being considerably more worthy than others) and covering them with righteousness.

🏵 **AZRAEL** The much-feared angel of death in both Islamic and Hebrew lore, whose name means "whom God helps." Among the Muslims, Azrael possesses four thousand wings and seventy thousand feet. Most important, he was given a supply of eyes and tongues exactly equal to the number of people inhabiting the world. Each time Azrael blinks one of his eyes, it signifies that another person has died. He came to the task by virtue of a surprisingly difficult job given to the angel by God. The Lord commanded that Michael, Gabriel, and Israfel journey to the earth and return with seven handfuls of dirt with which God planned to create Adam. The earth, however, refused to give up its treasure, moaning that mankind should not be created because they would turn against God and bring only sadness. As the three angels returned empty-handed, the Lord chose a fourth, Azrael. Far more determined, Azrael wrenched from the earth the dirt and brought it before the heavenly throne. As a reward, God made Azrael the angel responsible for separating the human soul from the body at the moment of death. Aside from his blinking eyes, Azrael also keeps track of the dying by scribbling ceaselessly into a mighty book. He writes into the book the births of the living and just as often erases other names—those who have died.

Azrael does not know, though, when each person is to die. In fact, he learns it when a leaf, bearing the name of the soon-to-be-deceased, falls off one of the branches of the incomparable tree below the throne of God. Azrael reads the name and knows that he is to separate the soul forty days later. Not surprisingly, some mortals resist departing the world. To entice them, Azrael places beneath their noses an apple plucked from the tree of life; this proves more than sufficient. In some Islamic legends Azrael is actually to be identified with Raphael, the archangel most closely associated with the life of humanity. (See also box on page 33; see also *Death, Angel of.*)

AZZA A fallen angel who is condemned to suffer a unique punishment for his sins. According to Jewish lore, Azza was bitterly opposed to God's plan to reward the patriarch Enoch with elevation to angelic status (Enoch was transformed into the angel prince Metatron). Expelled from heaven, Azza was hung upside down between earth and paradise. Ever plunging but never actually crashing, he is forced uncontrollably to open one eye so that the full horror of his predicament is driven home. Prior to his fall, Azza was listed as a ministering angel (in the Third Book of Enoch) and is said to have been responsible for teaching the famed King Solomon many secrets of heaven.

BAAL A deity that was worshiped regularly throughout much of the ancient Near East, particularly by the Canaanites. The name is derived from the Semitic word meaning "possessor" or "lord" and was used as a common noun with many applications; over time, however, Baal was adopted as the chief fertility god, a master of the world, and the lord of rain, whose benevolence in supplying moisture was essential to the flowering of crops. By the time of the Israelites' arrival in the land of Canaan, the worship of Baal— most so on a local level—was firmly established. The still-formative Israelites not surprisingly assumed many characteristics of Baal worship, and it even came to be understood as representing the Lord of Israel. Their assimilation of Canaanite custom was bitterly opposed by a number of prophets, as recorded in the Old Testament, who denounced it as idolatry and heathenism. This strong reaction, dating to the eighth century, had its start in the ninth century during the time of Jezebel, wife of King Ahab of Israel. She introduced the Phoenician practices of worshiping Baal.

In angel lore, Baal figures in several ways. First, as written in the Old Testament Book of Wisdom, King Jair succeeded Abimelech as ruler of Israel and declared that Baal should be worshiped. When opposed by seven faithful men, Jair ordered them thrown into a fire. The seven were rescued by the angel Nathanael, the so-called Angel of the Furnace, who not only secured their escape but roasted Jair along with one thousand of his troops and courtiers. Baal was also the foundation of the later names used for several evil beings, including Beelzebub and Belphegor.

🦋 **BABYLON** The ancient city and empire that flourished in Mesopotamia from around the second millennium B.C. until its conquest by the Assyrians in 772 B.C., after which it served as the basis for the neo-Babylonian empire. The Babylonians had a major influence in the development of the lore and understanding of angels through their art, mythology, and especially their conquest and domination of the Jewish people, the so-called Babylonian Captivity (the exile of the Jews to Babylon from 597 to 538 B.C.). During that period, the Jews were introduced to a number of Babylonian traditions relating to spirit guardians and beings that were probably to serve as the foundation for angels. For example, there were the keribu, huge stone guards that stood at the entrances to temples and palaces; they were carved with the bodies of winged bulls, sphinxes, or eagles and had the faces of men or lions. They would serve as the foundation of the cherubim. The Babylonians and Assyrians also had a belief in the sukallin, which were a foreshadowing of the subsequent personification of the angel as a divine messenger in the Old Testament. (See also *Nebo*.)

🦋 **BALLATON** An angel whose name is used by sorcerers when drawing the potent pentagram of Solomon, a symbol used for summoning spirits and conducting esoteric rites. Ballaton's name, as noted in the much-read *Lemegeton* by occultist Arthur Edward Waite, appeared in the surrounding or external circle of the pentagram.

🦋 **BARACATA** An angel who figures in the ancient and very arcane rites of magic associated with King Solomon. Baracata may not be precisely considered an angel, but traditionally it takes a sorcerer of considerable powers to summon him.

🦋 **BARADIEL** One of the princes of the seven heavens mentioned in the Third Book of Enoch. Baradiel is one of the "seven great, beautiful, wonderful, and honored princes." Each angelic prince has command "over a heavenly host, and every one of them is attended by 496,000 myriads of ministering angels." The prince in charge of the third heaven, Baradiel is also one of the princes (or angels) who guide the progress of the world. His area of authority here is as an angel of hail (other angels are of earthquakes, comets, the stars, wind, fire, etc.).

🦋 **BARAQIEL** One of the seven great angels in control of the seven heavens. Baraqiel is one of the "great, beautiful, wonderful, and honored princes" listed in the Third Book of Enoch, that extensive compendium of angelic lore. As an angelic prince, he is "attended by 496,000 myriads of ministering angels," and his specific heaven is the second. As additionally one of the princes who guide the world, Baraqiel is counted as the angel of lightning, joined by such other angels as those of the sun, hail, earthquakes, snow, etc. It is possible that Baraqiel is also to be identified with the fallen angel Baraqyal. This angel is also considered one of the angelic beings—with Uriel and Rubiel—to whom one should turn when in need of success at cards or gambling. Getting his attention and a favorable response to the invocation are, of course, another matter.

BARAQYAL An angel who belonged to the so-called Watchers, who descended from heaven to cohabit with mortal women. The angels took the women as wives and raised children from the union, the giants, or anakim (also nephilim). The event of the coming of the angels to earth is mentioned in the Book of Genesis and in the two apocryphal (or pseudepigraphical) works of the First Book of Enoch and the Book of Jubilees. In Enoch, Baraqyal is listed among the two hundred fallen angels and was ranked among the chief of ten, the divisions of the evil unrepentant angels. As a demon, Baraqyal is able to teach those who summon him the secret arts of astrology.

BARATTIEL One of the great angelic princes listed in that famed compendium of angelic lore, the Third Book of Enoch. Barattiel has a specific place in the angelic hierarchy presented in that work, being situated between the angelic princes Tagas and Hamon. When Tagas sees Barattiel, he falls upon his face prostrate and removes his princely crown. Likewise, when Barattiel beholds Hamon, he falls down prostrate and removes his own crown. Barattiel has the special post or power of literally holding the highest heaven—called in this tradition the Arabot—on the tips of his spread fingers.

BARTHOLOMEW, GOSPEL OF ST. An apocryphal writing (meaning that it was not accepted into the canon—the list of sacred writings—of the New Testament) dating to the third century A.D. and much influenced by the teachings of the Gnostics (the heretical Christian sect that flourished in the first few centuries of the Church). Rich in symbolism and vivid descriptions, the Gospel of St. Bartholomew purports to be an account of the descent of the risen Christ into hell, the

Annunciation of Mary, the terrible vision of the abyss, and the answers to questions on hell, sin, and the angels.

The Gospel, while quite apocryphal, is full of fascinating angel lore. According to the work, Bartholomew is able to extract from the demon Beliar—bound by fiery chains and held by 660 angels—answers to a variety of questions. Beliar speaks of the creation of the first angels, including Michael, Gabriel, Uriel, Raphael, Nathanael, and six thousand others. He tells as well of such angels as those of hail, snow, thunder, and the winds.

BARUCH A popular figure of legend among the Hellenistic Jews, Baruch was probably an assistant to the well-known Old Testament prophet Jeremiah. He is the reputed author of several notable works, ranked in the type of literature called pseudepigraphical, meaning that it was composed by some writer in a style that strives to be similar to actual and accepted scriptural writings, using the name of some notable personage to add to an air of authenticity. Baruch is thus the supposed writer of the Book of Baruch; the (Syriac) Apocalypse of Baruch (also 2 Baruch); 3 Baruch (the Greek Apocalypse of Baruch); and 4 Baruch ("The Rest of the Words of Baruch"). The 5 Baruch and 4 Baruch are frequently interchanged. The writings range in date from the first century to the second century A.D.

As is often the case with apocryphal and pseudepigraphical works, Baruch's writings are laced with intriguing lore and tales of angels and the heavens they occupy. Two Baruch, for example, contains a prophecy by the angel Ramiel, who declares the coming of the Messiah, the bright lightning. Even more specific is 3 Baruch, in which Baruch is supposedly taken by an angel, named in the text as Phanuel, on a tour of the seven heavens, although the surviving manuscripts contain only the account to his description of five of the seven heavens.

BAT QOL Also Bath Qol, an angel, often spoken of as female, whose name means "heavenly voice." The angel is said among the Syrians to have the voice heard by Cain asking "Where is thy brother, Abel?" after Cain murdered his brother. Bat Qol is also said to have visited the famous second-century A.D. rabbi Simion ben Yohai (the supposed author of the Jewish mystical work the Zohar) while he was imprisoned. In the sense of Bat-Kol, the angel can represent the divine voice that announces the will of God. It was also understood to have an oracular meaning, serving as a kind of omen. When a diviner sought the meaning of an event or undertaking, the words *bat qol* were called out, and the very next words heard were considered the expected response, although these would naturally be subject to some interpretation.

BEATRICE In full, Beatrice Portenari, a woman of a noble Florentine family of the thirteenth century to whom the great Italian poet

Dante Alighieri dedicated much of his poetry and who appeared as a crucial angelic being in Dante's *Divine Comedy*. Beatrice was beheld by Dante when he was only nine years old, and according to the poet, he never ceased to love her. She died at the age of twenty-nine in 1290, but Dante was still deeply in love with her at the time of his own passing in 1321. He wrote ebulliently about her beauty in *La Vita Nuova* (c. 1293; "The New Life"), concluding this work with the promise that he shall write of her as "hath not before been written about any woman." This he does in the *Divine Comedy*. Here, Beatrice achieves the full splendor of the angelic, intervening on

Beatrice, the great love of Dante, as she appears in the *Divine Comedy;* by Gustave Doré.

Dante's behalf in the *Inferno* and serving as his guide in *Paradiso*. Her arrival in *Purgatorio* (XXX:32–38) is suitably magnificent:

> *A virgin in my view appear'd, beneath*
> *Green mantle, robed in hue of living flame:*
> *And o'er my spirit, that so long a time*
> *Had from her presence felt no shuddering dread*
> *Albeit mine eyes discern'd her not, there moved*
> *A hidden virtue from her, at whose touch*
> *The power of ancient love was strong within me.*

Later, in *Paradiso* (XXX:16 ff.), he writes:

If all, that hitherto is told of her,
were in one praise concluded, twere too weak
To furnish out this turn. Mine eyes did look
On beauty, such, as I believe in sooth,
Not merely to exceed our human, but
That save its Maker, none can full Enjoy it.

Her beauty is such that it continues to dazzle him even in the midst of heaven, but, as his guide, she faithfully takes him to the Empyrean, the abode of God and the angels. While technically not an angel, Beatrice stands as a magnificent symbol of Dante's spiritual love and a perfect means for him to enter the realm of the angelic and the divine. (See also *Dante.*)

BEBUROA An Angel mentioned in the apocryphal book the Revelation of Esdras. Beburoa is ranked as one of the nine angels who will come and reign over the end of the world.

BENE ELOHIM Also bene Elim, a group of angels who belong to the order or choir of thrones. Meaning "sons of God," the bene Elohim are considered a part or division of the thrones, receiving the duty of forever singing the ineffable praise of God. As the sons of God, they are sometimes counted as the beings mentioned in the Book of Genesis (6:2) who save the daughters of men "and took to wife such of them as they chose." The result of this union were the giants, the anakim, "the mighty men that were of old, the men of renown." The bene Elohim are also thought to be the angels called the ischim.

BETHOR A powerful angel, one of the seven angelic beings ruling the 196 divisions of heaven. To assist him in his work, Bethor commands some 29,000 legions of angels. His area of authority also extends to everything related to the planet Jupiter, part of the ancient belief of each planet, star, and phenomenon of nature having its own angelic patron or ruler.

BIBLE See box on page 43; see also *New Testament, Old Testament,* and *Revelation, Book of.*

BIRD OF GOD A colorful name used by Dante in his *Divine Comedy* for angels. It captures the winged flight of the angels and their origins by the will of God. The task of this otherwise unnamed angel is to act as pilot of the ferry transporting the souls belonging to purgatory from their embarkation point on the Tiber to their painful but temporary purgatorial respite. In *Purgatorio* (II), Dante beholds the bird of God:

> As more and more toward us came, more bright
> Appear'd the bird of God, not could the eye
> Endure his splendor near: I mine bent down.
> He drowv ashore in a small bark so swift
> And light, that in its course no wave drank.
> The heavenly steersman at the prow was seen,
> Visibly written "Blessed" in his looks.
> Within, a hundred spirits and more there sat.

Longfellow, in his poem "The Celestial Pilot," used Dante's imagery for the ferryman of souls, calling this pilot "the bird of God." (See also *Pilot Angel.*)

BLACK ANGELS A name used, especially in Islamic lore, for the fallen angels. Black angels are generally considered demons. The two most famous fallen angels by this appellation are Nakir and Monker.

BLAKE, WILLIAM English poet, painter, engraver, and mystic (1757–1827) who made significant contributions to the lore of angels through his poetry and especially his illustrations; aside from Albrecht Dürer and Gustave Doré, Blake is considered one of the foremost interpreters of angels. While largely unappreciated in his own time, Blake is today recognized for his genius and his visionary skill. His association with angels was said to be a lifelong one; he saw and communicated with them, noting in the preface to his work *The Jerusalem:* "I am not ashamed to tell you what ought to be told—that I am under the direction of messengers from heaven, daily and nightly." His angel illustrations often fulfilled both the practical purpose of illuminating a work of literature and expressing Blake's own deep spiritual outlook. Among his illustrations were those for such works as Dante's *Divine Comedy, Milton, The Marriage of Heaven and Hell, Songs of Innocence,* and assorted biblical pieces. Blake also wrote of angels, hardly surprising given his attested connections to them and his eclectic literary and poetic pursuits. He once commented, "It

BIBLE

Among the many literary sources for information on angels, the greatest and most enduring has been the Bible. Interestingly, the Old and New Testaments actually name only three angels, Michael, Gabriel, and Raphael (the latter appearing in the Book of Tobit, which some faiths do not accept in their books of the Bible), but the word *angel* is used at least 292 times. Scholars point out, however, that those are references specific to the term *angel,* and not included are the uses of other synonyms that denote angels or angelic beings. There are thus also terms and names ranging from the very specific to the vague: seraphim, cherubim, ministering spirits, chariots of God, powers, authorities, morning stars, heavenly bodies, sons of God, princes, thrones, and elders.

Angels appearing in the Old and New Testaments assume a variety of incarnations. There are the "men" who appeared to Abraham and Lot just before the obliteration of Sodom and Gomorrah; the fearsome cherub who was placed at the east gate of Eden with his flaming sword; and the mind-boggling angels beheld by Ezekiel. Throughout, however, angels fulfill clear duties for the Lord, be they messengers bringing the joyous news of Christ's coming or the impending doom of the Sodomites, or angels of vengeance and destruction. (See also *New Testament* and *Old Testament.*)

is not because angels are holier than men or devils that makes them angels, but because they do not expect holiness from one another, but from God alone."

BLINDED ANGEL The term used by Pope John Paul II for the devil, Satan. The pontiff implies that the devil has chosen to blind himself to the light and beauty of God and so exists in perpetual darkness, the blackness of sin. (See also *Fallen Angels.*)

BOAMIEL An angel mentioned in the obscure Jewish mystical work the Book of the Angel Raziel and ranked as one of the angels with authority over the four divisions of heaven.

BODHISATTVA An extremely special individual in Buddhist teachings who has achieved enlightenment and thus earned entrance into Nirvana but who chooses to postpone personal salvation, out of love for humanity. The bodhisattva returns to the earth and is born into the early cycles once more in order to assist others toward enlightenment and ease the sufferings of life. The bodhisattvas are considered by some to be like angels in that they exist to serve and assist humanity, bringing to earth a compassion equal to their wisdom. Also as with angels, there is theoretically no limit to the number of bodhisattvas. Many Buddhists teach that any person, of any religion, can become one of these individuals whose very essence is *bodhi* (enlightenment), and the bodhisattvas have long been revered as figures of great salvation. Individual bodhisattvas include Ksitigarbba, Manjusri, and Avalokitisvara.

BOEL One of the foremost angels occupying the first heaven (of the seven heavens), according to the lore of the Zohar (the book of Jewish mysticism that forms the basis of Qabalah). Boel has possession of the four keys of the four corners of the earth. He thus has the keys that can, if he is so instructed by God, open the gates of the Garden of Eden, which were locked after the fall of humanity and which had two very stern cherubim placed as guards. As a ruler or guardian of one of the planets, he has authority over Saturn.

BOTTOMLESS PIT, ANGEL OF THE The angel who has authority over the abyss, the bottomless pit, often also called hell. This angel is usually identified as Abaddon (or Appolyon). The bottomless pit is closed and locked by a great key, described in the Book of Revelation (20:1). Abaddon holds the key and also has the duty (or perhaps pleasure) of binding Satan for one thousand years. There has been some debate over the centuries concerning whether the angel of the bottomless pit is good or evil; for example, John Bunyan in his *Pilgrim's Progress* (1678) considers the angel to be Satan himself. This is naturally not compatible with Revelation or other traditions, for the angel is said to carry a chain with which will be bound Satan. In his biting satire on the medical profession, writer-director Paddy Chayefsky in *The Hospital* has a deranged murderer performing acts of divine retribution upon various hospital officials (they had managed to murder God through incompetence and neglect) by assuming the role of "wrath of the Lamb and the Angel of the Bottomless Pit." In England during the political ascendancy of William Pitt the Younger (1759–1806), that prime minister was affectionately called the "bottomless Pitt" because of his remarkable thinness.

BURNING BUSH, ANGEL OF THE The famous angel of the event recorded in the Book of Exodus (3:2) in which Moses beheld the burning bush: "Now Moses was keeping the flock of his father-in-law, Jethro, the priest of Midian; he led his flock to the west side of the wilderness, and came to Horeb, the Mountain of God. And the angel of the Lord appeared to him in a flame of fire out of the midst of a bush; and he looked, and lo, the bush was burning, yet it was not consumed." It was through this bush that God spoke to Moses and set him the task of leading the Jewish people out of Egypt. Some scholars prefer to say that the burning bush was not really an angel, but God assuming this memorable form. In one Jewish tradition, the name of the angel of the burning bush was Zagzagel.

CAMAEL A notable angel whose name means "he who sees God," also known as Chamuel, Kemuel, and Camiel; he appears in a variety of legends and is honored with a number of titles, appearing in some occult lore as a denizen of the infernal legions of hell. In the legends describing Camael as an angel, he is credited with having authority over a mighty force of the so-called Angels of Destruction; he is also honored as the chief or one of the ruling princes of the angelic choir or order of powers, with such notables as Gabriel and, before his mighty Fall, Satan. In the famous occult work *The Magus,* by Francis Barrett (1801), he is listed as one of the seven truly powerful angels who have the great honor of standing in the very presence of God. Two other notable titles are borne by Camael. He is often declared to be the otherwise unnamed dark angel who wrestled with the Old Testament figure Jacob (see *Dark Angel* and *Jacob*), although candidates for this renowned wrestling match have been Uriel, Peniel, Michael, and Metatron. He is also thought in some tales to be the angel of the garden of Gethsemane, another usually nameless angelic visitor (most regularly said to be Gabriel) who gave comfort and encouragement to Jesus in Gethsemane in the terrible hours just prior to the Lord's arrest and the beginning of the Passion leading to his Crucifixion. There is still one more legend relating to Camael. In this, found among the Jews, he chose for whatever reason to prevent the reception by Moses of the Torah (the Pentateuch, the first five books of the Old Testament: Genesis, Exodus, Leviticus, Numbers, and Deuteronomy). This ill-ad-

vised act caused God to permit Moses the extremely unusual privilege of actually destroying Camael in retribution. His function prior
to this unfortunate incident was, according to Jewish custom, to serve
as the mediator, taking before the angelic princes residing in the seventh heaven the righteous prayers of Israel. It is possible that the "destruction" of Camael by Moses signaled his fall from grace, for there is
a tradition that he is now one of the high-ranking personages of hell.
It is said that when a sorcerer summons Camael, the fiend appears as a
spotted leopard sitting upon a large, smooth rock.

CAPHRIEL One of the angels who have rulership over the days of
the week; Caphriel is ruler of the seventh day, the important day of
the Sabbath.

CAPTAIN OF THE HOST OF THE LORD Also commander of the
army of the Lord, the angel who appeared suddenly to Joshua, near
Jericho, giving the mortal the instructions of the Lord as to how the
Israelites should capture the city. "When Joshua was by Jericho, he
lifted up his eyes and looked, and behold, a man stood before him
with his drawn sword in his hand; and Joshua went and said to him,
'Are you for us, or for our adversaries?' And he said, 'No; but as commander of the army of the Lord I have now come.'" There followed
the famous destruction of Jericho's walls by the shouts and trumpet
blasts of the Israelites. It is generally accepted that the captain was the
archangel Michael, the angelic warrior so often associated with leading the heavenly hosts.

CARDINAL VIRTUES Also called the natural virtues, four of the
seven traditional values: justice, fortitude, prudence, and temperance.
The other three, however, known as the theological virtues, are faith,
hope, and charity. The cardinal virtues are called the four virtues of
human morality; to these are related all of the other virtues. During
the Middle Ages—called the golden age of angelology, when there
was conceived an angel for virtually everything in nature—theologians postulated that the virtues were represented or embodied by actual angels, named, appropriately, justice, fortitude, prudence, and
temperance. This angelic embodiment was also depicted in art with
angels, painted often in rich symbolic imagery, representing the cardinal virtues. (See also *Art, Angels in.*)

CASSIEL A high-ranking angel who has figured rather prominently in the writings of occultists, such as Francis Barrett's interesting work *The Magus*. According to this occult tradition, Cassiel (or Kafziel) is one of the leaders of the choir of angels called the powers; he is also the angel of tears and temperance and one of the angels who has rulership over Saturday (each day of the week having its own ruling or patron angels). In Barrett's book is a handy table denoting the angels of the week. Under Saturday is listed Cassiel, complete with his sigil (or symbol) and his proper zodiacal sign. Illustrations of Cassiel depict a fearsome man with beard and crown, holding a feather arrow or dart, astride a dragon.

CATHOLIC CHURCH One of the most important sources for the traditions and lore of the angel; the Catholic Church has a clear and long-established teaching on angels, made most manifest in the pronouncements of its councils and especially in the writings of its foremost saints and theologians, most notably St. Thomas Aquinas. The Church teaches that angels were created before humanity and that they are beings of pure spirit knowable only through revelation. God made the angels as a deliberate act of will, and they continue to exist at his personal desire. They were made out of nothing, but in the image and likeness of their Creator. St. Thomas Aquinas thus wrote, "The Angel is the most excellent of all creatures because among all creatures he bears the greatest resemblance to his Creator." They were sanctified and, according to St. Augustine, given a chaste love, whereby they adhered to the Lord, receiving grace from God even while he was creating them. Nevertheless, they possessed free will for a time, a kind of probationary period during which their grace was not absolutely confirmed and the beatific vision—the glimpse of the very face of God—was denied them. It was during this time that some of the angels chose to sin, falling from heaven and becoming the forces of darkness that have for so long plagued the world. The Church makes clear, however, that the devil and his demons were created initially good by God, but they deliberately chose to enter into sin. This was the choice given to all the angels. Central to this decision was what Aquinas termed its irrevocable nature. Once an angel decided to embrace evil or goodness, their choice was made forever and is immutable, irrevocable, and eternal. The evil angels were driven from heaven by the good angels, led by St. Michael the archangel. The good angels then were granted the beatific vision and entered fully into the service of God and completely into his love. Theologians point out that this entire probationary period was actually quite short because of the heightened abilities of angels and their inherently decisive nature.

The choirs or orders of angels have been much speculated upon by members of the Church. There have generally been acknowledged by the so-called Fathers of the Church nine choirs of angels, the specific order concretized by the sixth-century theologian Dionysius the Areopagite; other lists were drawn up by St. Ambrose, St. Jerome, and Pope St. Gregory I the Great. Dionysius' list, however, remains the one most used, with its nine orders of seraphim, cherubim, thrones, dominations, virtues, powers, principalities, archangels, and angels.

One of the most enduring and significant traditions of the Church relating to angels is that of the guardian angel. Although not formally defined and thus not required to be believed by all Catholics as a necessity of their faith, the acceptance of the guardian angel is a part of long-standing teaching, especially that all children have their own angel caring for them. This is based on the words of Christ: "See that you do not despise one of these little ones; for I tell you, their angels in heaven always behold the face of my Father in heaven" (Matthew 18:10). St. Jerome added, "Great is the dignity of souls that each of them has an angel assigned for its protection from the moment it is born." There is various opinion, of course, as to how a guardian angel actually functions. For example, does the angel remain with a person when he or she sins? Aquinas answered in the affirmative, assuring believers that their angel never abandons them, remaining by their side in the perpetual hope that they will not sin and, in the event that they do, that they will seek to make penance. The Church also accepts the idea of guardian angels for places, cities, churches, and even entire nations. (See also *Art, Angels in; Choirs; Fallen Angels; Guardian Angels; Dionysius the Areopagite;* and *Thomas Aquinas, St.*)

CELESTIAL HIERARCHY A name used for the listing or organization of angels into orders or choirs. For details on the history of the choirs, see *Choirs;* see also table on choirs. "Celestial hierarchy" was first used as the title of the extremely influential work by theologian Dionysius the Areopagite (or Pseudo-Dionysius). Through this book he helped establish firmly the concept of the nine choirs in the Christian tradition, although credit for the probable first creation of such a list for the Christian Church generally goes to St. Ambrose in the fifth century; Ambrose and Pseudo-Dionysius would be joined over the next centuries by numerous theologians such as Pope St. Gregory I the Great, St. Jerome, Isidore of Seville, and John of Damascus, as well as Dante and even Billy Graham. There was also a long tradition in Jewish religious culture of organizing the angelic orders into a hierarchy, much of which was later borrowed by Christian writers.

CERVIEL One of the leaders of the angelic choir of principalities. Cerviel was supposedly sent (according to one tradition) by God to assist the young and seemingly overmatched David in his fight with Goliath. Cerviel clearly provided the future king with both strength and inspiration, not to mention a keen eye. The angel, as often was apparently the case, did not receive any credit in the biblical account.

CHALKYDRI Also khalkedras, angelic beings described in the Second Book of Enoch (one of the great sources of angelic lore). The chalkydri inhabit the fourth heaven, along with phoenixes and such angelic notables as the seraphim and cherubim. According to the account of these "strange and wonderful" creatures, they were shaped like lions, with the head of a crocodile. They had a multicolored appearance, with wings like angels, but they possess twelve wings each. Following any command of the Lord, they normally accompany the sun ceaselessly, running with it, carrying both heat and dew as willed by God. A song is ever bursting from their throats. Some scholars consider the chalkydri to be brass serpents, equated or associated with the cherubim. They may, as serpents, thus be placed under the authority of the archangel Gabriel, who in some sources is said to have command over the Garden of Eden, serpents, and the cherubim.

CHAMUEL One of the seven mighty archangels in many lists; his name means "he who seeks God" or "he who sees God." Often identified with the archangel Camael, Chamuel is one of the leading princes (or leaders) of the angelic choir of powers, ranked with such heavenly greats as Gabriel and, before his Fall, Lucifer (Satan). Chamuel took part in some famous biblical events. He was probably (but not necessarily) identified with the dark angel, the man or angel who spent an entire night wrestling with Jacob. (See *Dark Angel.*) Other candidates for the dark angel of Genesis (30:24–30) have been

Michael, Uriel, Samael, and even the grand Metatron. Chamuel is also listed by angelologists as one of the two possible angels—along with Gabriel—who visited Christ in the garden of Gethsemane in Jerusalem, giving him comfort in the terrible hours before Christ's arrest and crucifixion. The angel, be it Chamuel or Gabriel, is said to have given encouragement to Jesus, reminding him of the promise of the Resurrection.

CHARIOTS OF GOD The term used for the angels or hosts of angels, as found in the Book of Psalms (68): "With mighty charitry [Chariots of God], twice ten thousands, thousands upon thousands, the Lord came from Sinai into the holy places." The image of angels as chariots was first used by the Hebrews in a more specific sense for the angelic order of ophanim. These angels are equated with the cherubim in later hierarchies of angels; the name *chariot* is probably derived from the description of the ophanim (cherubim) by some accounts as wheels. Throughout the Old Testament they are described as the bearers of God's throne or his chariot. The latter image forms an important element of the obscure mystical society among the Jews called the Merkabah (meaning "Chariot"). Flourishing from the first century A.D., the Merkabah sought to use esoteric magical incantations or rites to ascend the seven heavens (called *hekhalots*). In the highest heaven was to be found the throne of God, resting upon a truly magnificent chariot.

CHAYDIEL See *Hayliel YHWH.*

CHERUB A shortened version of cherubim, one of the most powerful of the choirs or orders of angels. Over the centuries the cherub has developed at times a far more benign and approachable image, in large measure because of art. Today, the *cherub* epitomizes a small, chubby, exceedingly happy little angel, with tiny, adorable wings, more like a winged baby than one of the truly awesome servants of almighty God. This image can be dated to the magnificent creations of artists, especially in the Baroque and Rococo periods, with paintings and sculptures of sweet angels, such as the putto (pl. putti) found all over Europe's grand ceilings. (See *Cherubim* for other details.)

CHERUBIM (Choir) The second of the nine accepted choirs of angels, placed second as well in the first triad of the angelic hierarchy (with the seraphim and thrones) devised by the sixth-century theologian Dionysius the Areopagite. The cherubim are some of the most powerful and awe-inspiring of all angels, standing below only the seraphim in direct closeness to God; they thus are second only to their seraphic brethren in the degree to which they emanate the love of God and possess knowledge and wisdom. Their illuminative knowledge and wisdom are thus so great as to be utterly incomprehensible to the mortal mind, blinding the blessed human who has the honor of actually beholding them in this world.

In Islamic lore, the cherubim were supposedly created out of the tears shed by the archangel Michael for all of the sins of humanity, but their historical origins can probably be traced to Babylon and Sumeria, for there were to be found the keribu, the fearsome stone statues guarding the entrances to temples and palaces. They had the bodies of a winged bull, an eagle, or a sphinx and the faces of men or lions. So impressive were they that the Hebrews who had been brought to Babylon as part of the so-called Babylonian Captivity (the enforced migration of the Jews to Babylon by King Nebuchadnezzar II, lasting from 597 B.C. to 538 B.C.) adopted them as suitable for their own developing conception of angelic beings. The cherubim are thus the first angels to be encountered in the Old Testament, being posted in the Book of Genesis in the east of Eden to ensure that no one entered after the expulsion of Adam and Eve and to guard the tree of life with a flaming sword. They appeared again in Exodus (25); two cherubim were carved in gold upon the Ark of the Covenant. Later in 1 Kings (6:23), there were two carved cherubim, of olive-wood and ten cubits high, placed in the temple of Solomon. However, the most vivid and interesting description of the cherubim was provided by Ezekiel when they appeared to him at the river Chebar (see box on page 54).

As is clear from Ezekiel's hair-raising encounter, the cherubim possess four wings and four faces, symbolizing their eternal vigilance and knowledge, which reaches to every direction of Creation. They are also often presented with peacock feathers bearing a host of eyes, again a reference to their all-seeing omniscience. Their chief task in the celestial hierarchy is to sing the praises of God, but they are also declared in occult lore to have the responsibility of driving the chariot of the Lord, a key symbol of heaven in such mystical traditions as the Merkabah; the thrones, interestingly, are frequently thought of as

Four members of the mighty choir of cherubim give praise to Christ; from a
Florentine church (COURTESY ART RESOURCE).

the wheels of the chariot. The cherubim are additionally given the arduous task of maintaining the records of heaven and seeing to the
myriad details that must be fulfilled to maintain the heavenly host.
Dionysius declared them to be guardians of the fixed stars.

By the Hebrews they were called *kerub,* a name that may mean
"one who intercedes"; Dionysius claimed that it meant "knowledge,"
a reference to their incalculable intelligence. The angels have also
been considered synonymous with other angelic beings in Jewish
lore, such as the hayyoth and, less appropriately, the ophanim. Their
chiefs are named as being Cherubiel (Kerubiel), Ophaniel, Gabriel,
Uriel, Raphael, and Zophiel. (See also *Cherub, Choirs,* and *Ofanim.*)

CHIEFTAINS The name given to certain angels who act as guardians
or chieftains of assorted countries or nations in the world. The chieftains are found in the lore of the Qabalah and were said to number
seventy.

EZEKIEL'S CHERUBIM

❦

As I looked, behold, a stormy wind came out of the north, and a great cloud, with brightness round about it, and fire flashing forth continually, and in the midst of the fire, as it were gleaming bronze. And from the midst of it came the likeness of four living creatures. And this was their appearance: they had the form of men, but each had four faces, and each of them had four wings. Their legs were straight, and the soles of their feet were like the sole of a calf's foot; and they sparkled like burnished bronze. Under their wings on their four sides they had human hands. And the four had their faces and their wings thus: their wings touched one another; they went every one straight forward, without turning as they went.

As for the likeness of their faces, each had the face of a man in front; the four had the face of a lion on the right side, the four had the face of an ox on the left side, and the four had the face of an eagle at the back. Such were their faces. And their wings were spread out above; each creature had two wings, each of which touched the wing of another, while two covered their bodies. And each went straight forward; wherever the spirit would go, they went, without turning as they went.

(Ezekiel 1:4–12)

CHILDREN AND ANGELS One of the most common associations both in lore and art; angels are traditionally said to appear most often to children, and many children are supposedly able to see angels. The special relationship of angels and children can perhaps best be expressed by Christ, who once declared: "See that you do not despise one of these little ones; for I tell you, their angels in heaven always behold the face of my Father in heaven" (Mt. 18:10). Angels appear to children because, some say, they are still innocent and closer to God; they are also still in possession of the wonder of new life, uncorrupted by the material world and thus able to look beyond to see Creation in all of its possibilities. Most of all, children are defenseless and thus in need of special care and protection. The angels, who have the important task of assisting humanity, thus take it upon themselves to aid the littlest ones. For more jaded grown-ups who dismiss such speculation as nonsense, it might be useful to take note of the many children who describe seeing their guardian angel during times of prayer, while at play, or especially in times of danger or crisis. Quite memorable, for example, is the case of St. Gemma Galgani (d. 1903), who swore that she saw her own guardian angel every time she prayed. Even more remarkable was her sincere astonishment when she learned that everyone else did not. (See also *Guardian Angels*.)

CHOIRS The name used for the orders of angels, a method of organization that proposes a kind of celestial hierarchy for the entire angelic realm. The term *choirs* is probably derived from one of the most central roles of all angels, the singing of praises to God so that all of heaven and Creation reverberate with the joyous sound. The underlying principle of the angelic choirs is rooted in the metaphysical understanding of varying degrees of angelic perfection or the extent to which each order reflects the perfect light of God's illuminative love. According to this thinking, there is, logically, a descending series of creations that reflect levels or grades of spiritual perfection owing precisely to their proximity to the Creator, that which is utterly, absolutely perfect. The most perfect of all angels are found, obviously, standing closest to God or the throne of God; as succeeding or other angels were created, they were farther away from the throne and hence reflected, in spiritually minute terms, lesser degrees of spiritual perfection. However, as the great philosopher and writer Mortimer Adler has pointed out, the sense of lesser perfection is to be considered not moral, but what he calls in *The Angels and Us*

(1982) "a perfection in mode of being, in the created nature of being."

There are two other ways of conceiving the descending order of angels. The first, as expressed by Mortimer Adler, is the sense of the grades of angels being determined by their relative distances from the Lord. Similar to this is the intriguing and rather beautiful notion of angels as reflectors of the divine light of the Lord. According to this, each angel is a reflection or channel of the burning glory of God. Some angels are better vessels or prisms of that light than others. The greatest channelers of divine love are thus the highest-ranked angels, as they come closest to pouring forth the glory of God; there is a natural descending order of degrees of reflection, although some might argue that this is merely another, albeit more expressive, way of saying degrees of perfection.

Several angels from the heavenly host; presented by Pietro Cavallini, from a detail of the Last Judgment in S. Cecilia in Trastevere, Rome
(COURTESY ART RESOURCE).

Throughout the ages, humans have contemplated this potential heavenly organization, expressing it regularly in terms that sought to give credence and respect to the notion of descending perfection or proximity to the throne of God. The two principal sources for such orderings are those of Judaism and Christianity; Islam does not adhere to such a system. The Old Testament was actually of only limited help in this undertaking, despite the hundreds of direct and implied references to the angelic. There are generally accepted only two angelic orders mentioned in the Old Testament: angels and archangels. Nevertheless, Jewish scholars, assisted by traditions and the so-called apocryphal writings (works not accepted into the canon or body of writings of the Hebrew Bible), were able to place the vast universe of angels into a series of orders. They used a variety of titles that were identical in many respects to the lists drawn up by the theologians of the Christian Church, which was assisted by the extra books of the

New Testament. Jewish lists contain angelic orders with names such as the elohim, ophanim, hashmallim, and tarshishim. The New Testament, meanwhile, especially the writings of St. Paul, helped considerably to flesh things out for the Christians. St. Paul mentions, for example, powers, principalities, and dominations.

While lists were created by St. Jerome (who had seven orders, omitting the virtues and principalities) and St. Ambrose (who had all nine), far and away the most important and influential was that appearing in the *celestial Hierarchy,* attributed to the sixth-century theologian Dionysius the Areopagite (Pseudo-Dionysius). He proposed nine orders: seraphim, cherubim, thrones, dominations, virtues, powers, principalities, archangels, and angels. Central to the wide acceptance of his list was the exceedingly high repute in which his writings in general were held throughout much of the Middle Ages. Thus, St. Thomas Aquinas gave it his endorsement and used it to serve as the basis of his exposition on angels in his mammoth work on Christian thought, the *Summa Theologica.* St. Thomas additionally advanced the belief that not only were the angels divided into nine choirs, they were also separated into three triads, each possessing three choirs. According to this, the angels of the first triad (the seraphim, cherubim, and thrones) take as their particular object the contemplation of the glory and perfection of God, knowing divine providence in itself, and can be called the angels of spiritual perfection or perfect love; the angels of the second triad (dominations, virtues, and powers) are preoccupied not with God himself, but in the plurality of universal causes, meaning they are taken up with the ordering of all Creation and can thus be termed the angels of Creation; the angels of the third triad (principalities, archangels, and angels) know not the order of divine providence in itself or even the general causes of things, but rather the specific causes, meaning that they are involved in the minute details of the universe, the most central of concerns being humanity's welfare. Through Dionysius and St. Thomas, the nine choirs of angels were adopted as fact by virtually every theologian and writer, including Dante Alighieri and John Milton, who utilized it for their *Divine Comedy* and *Paradise Lost* respectively. While some might question the logic of the entire system, pointing out numerous inconsistencies in angel lore, the entire structure of this angelic organization remains one of the most popular aspects in all of angelology, known even to the most casual follower of angels and their rich and colorful history. (See individual choirs and *Orders, Angelic.*)

🜨 **CHRISTMAS** The Christian feast day celebrating the birth of Christ. Aside from being one of the most important holidays in the world, both in terms of religious and social significance, Christmas is the main time of the year in which angels figure most prominently and public appreciation of their activities, beauty, and service to God is at its height. Angels are today a mainstay of Christmas decorations and Christmas spirit, appearing as tree ornaments, in the shape of baking pans, on the covers of Christmas cards, and as statues, candles, candies, wrapping paper, costumes (the handy wings, halo, and harp), glasses, stationery, and cookware. Angels are also seen on television, through the much-anticipated airing of old classics such as *The Bishop's Wife* and *It's a Wonderful Life*. There is also the quaint custom of the snow angel, the making of the shape of an angel in the snow by slumping backward into a snow bed and flapping the arms and legs.

Lost in much of this often crass material exploitation are the true meaning of the holiday and the major role angels had in it. The birth of Christ was predicted or "announced" to Mary by the angel Gabriel in the Annunciation, an event that anticipates and sets in motion the glorious (from the Christian perspective) events of the Nativity. On that night the angels were said in Scripture to be so overjoyed by the birth of Jesus that they appeared to shepherds and declared in triumph that something wondrous was happening that very night in Bethlehem. Their bringing glad tidings (see *Nativity, Angels of the*) has been the source of numerous expressions in art, poetry, and especially music. Among some of the Christmas carols with references to angels are "Angels from the Realm of Glory," "Angels We Have Heard on High," "Hark! The Herald Angels Sing," "It Came upon a Midnight Clear," "O Come, All Ye Faithful," "O Come, Little Children," "Sleep, Thou Little Child," "What Child Is This?" and "While Shepherds Watched Their Flocks by Night."

🜨 **CLARENCE ODDBODY** With the possible exception of the angel Dudley, perhaps the most famous angel in all of film history, appearing as a pivotal and delightfully memorable character in the 1946 Frank Capra film *It's a Wonderful Life*. Clarence was first brought to life in the form of the nameless angelic being who comes to aid George Pratt in the short story "The Greatest Gift" (1943) by Philip Van Doren Stern. Here, the angel gives to the despondent George his wish: he was never born. George, of course, comes to regret his wish, and the story ends with George understanding that the greatest gift is his life. In the Frank Capra film (with Jimmy Stewart as George Bailey and Henry Travers as Clarence), the angel turns out to be a junior angel still struggling, after 292 years, to earn his wings and move up from his lowly status as an "angel second class." Bumbling, sincere, and painfully well intentioned, Clarence succeeds both in convincing George of the preciousness of his life and in earning his wings. Clarence's triumph is signaled at the end of the movie by the ringing of a little bell ornament on the Baileys' Christmas tree; upon hearing it, George's daughter points to the ornaments announcing that anytime a bell rings, an angel receives a pair of wings. Clarence says good-bye to George with the simple

Henry Travers as Clarence Oddbody, the probationary angel "second class"; from *It's a Wonderful Life* (1946).

note declaring: "Remember, no man is a failure who has friends. Clarence." Disheveled, disorganized, and distinctly unangelic, Clarence is nevertheless a charming example (in the best tradition) of an angel intervening on behalf of humanity.

CONFUSION, ANGELS OF A group of quite unique angels whose function—as commanded by God—is to descend to earth and cause, as their name might indicate, confusion and chaos. While some could argue that the angels of confusion have been working hard in human affairs, especially in the modern era, they have been dispatched with probable certainty at least twice. Once was perhaps recorded in the Book of Genesis (11:7), when the Lord journeyed down to have a look at the mighty tower that was being built "with its top in the heavens." As such arrogance was intolerable, God chose to scatter the people: "Come, let us go down, and there confuse their language, that they may not understand each other's speech." The angels of confusion are credited with carrying out the Lord's bidding. A second incident was recounted in the famous collection *The Legends of the Jews*

THE CREATION
OF ANGELS

Psalm 148 in the Old Testament declares: "Praise the Lord! Praise the Lord from the heavens, praise him in the heights! Praise him, all his angels, praise him, all his host! . . . Let them praise the name of the Lord! For he commanded that they were created." This passage reveals the fundamental truth concerning the origins of the heavenly host: every angel, from the mightiest seraph and cherub to the humblest guardian angel, was created by God. They continue to exist, function, and serve the Lord entirely at his will and pleasure; without his eternal consent, the angels would disappear, a fact noted by theologians throughout much of Christian history, from St. Thomas Aquinas to Billy Graham.

On these facts virtually every major religion accepting the presence of angels agrees, although there is considerable room for disagreement as to exactly when and how the choirs of angels were brought into existence. Some argue that angels were around before the Creation of the world, seemingly supported by the declaration in the Book of Job (38:7): "Where were you when I laid the foundation of the earth? . . . when the

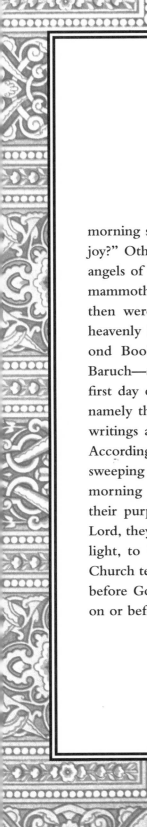

morning stars sang and all the sons of God shouted for joy?" Others amend this to state that the seven great angels of Creation were made first to assist God in the mammoth creative work of the cosmos. These angels then were joined by the remaining members of the heavenly host. Some Jewish sources—such as the Second Book of Enoch, the Book of Jubilees, and 3 Baruch—assure us that all the angels were made on the first day of Creation. Other works give different days, namely the second, fourth, and fifth. Still other Jewish writings and traditions posit a radically different view. According to these, the angels were not made in one sweeping gesture, but rather come into existence every morning through the breath of God; after fulfilling their purpose, especially in singing the praises of the Lord, they are reassumed into the fire of God's eternal light, to be reborn the next morning. The Catholic Church teaches that all the angels were created at once, before God made the world and humanity, most likely on or before the second day.

by Louis Ginzberg. Here the angels were dispatched by God to the court of the Persian emperor Xerxes (486–465 B.C.), who appears in the Bible under the name Ahasueras. The angels were to bring confusion and thus end the king's merrymaking. Jewish legend puts the number of angels at seven.

CREATION, ANGELS OF The group of seven angels who are said to have been in existence before the Creation of the world. That angels may have been created before the birth of the world is attested to by this passage in Job (38): "Where were you when I laid the foundation of the earth? Tell me, if you have understanding, Who determined its measurements—surely you know! Or who stretched the line upon it? On what were its bases sunk, or who laid its cornerstone, when the morning stars sang together, and all the sons of God shouted in joy." While this might imply that all the angels had been created, there is a tradition that only seven angels had yet been made: Michael, Gabriel, Raphael, Orifiel, Zachariel, Anael (or Haniel), and Samael (who later joined the fallen angels). According to the Second Book of Enoch, a useful source for angelic lore, the seven angels reside in the sixth heaven: "Their faces were more radiant than the radiance of the sun, and there was no difference between their faces or in their dimensions or in the style of their clothing . . . [they] carry out and carefully study the movements of the stars, and the revolution of the sun and the phases of the moon, and the well-being of the cosmos." There remains, however, serious discussion among angelologists as to when God created the angels. (For a discussion of this, please see *Creation of Angels*.)

CREATION OF ANGELS See box on pages 60–61.

DAATH A term found in Jewish mysticism and in the Qabalah for wisdom. In the concept of the divine emanations—as expressed in the ten sefiroth—there are ten holy emanations (with corresponding unholy sefiroth). Daath represents or unites the second and third holy sefiroth: chachmah (or chokmah), which represented the highest good or wisdom, and binah, representing understanding. Chachmah also represented the male aspect and binah the female. In qabalistic teaching, the sefiroth took the form of angels, so Daath can be said to epitomize an angelic being, one way in which angels have been used to epitomize or embody such concepts as wisdom, fortitude, courage, and compassion.

DAEMON Also daimon, a Greek term used for certain supernatural powers or spirits, often representing the active or intervening aspect of the deity. The daemon was thus used to explain sudden, unexpected, or peculiar happenings; it was eventually looked upon as a kind of benevolent spirit or was even seen as interchangeable with God himself. Individuals were said to have their own daemon, as in the case of Socrates, whose spirit guide offered advice, inspiration, and counsel when he was in need. The daemon is considered one of the bases for the later understanding of angels as messengers of God and the direct, physical way he intervenes in human affairs, but they also assisted in the speculation and development of evil beings, the fallen angels. Christian theologians and philosophers used the daemon to blame the wicked or anti-Christian activities of the increasingly defunct pagan gods, described as fallen angels; the daemon thus came to be considered exclusively evil, the demon of modern parlance.

🌸 **DAEVAS** See under *Devas.*

🌸 **DAIMON** A variant spelling of daemon.

🌸 **DANIEL (1)** The prophet of the Old Testament whose name means "God has judged." Daniel's story is recounted in the Book of Daniel, which describes his experiences—along with his three companions, Shadrach, Meshach, and Abednego—under King Nebuchadnezzar and several other kings, as well as his successful interpretation of the Persian king's dreams; also an important part of the story is the series of visions granted to Daniel. He emerged out of the book as one of the foremost prophets of the Jewish people, whose visions were to form the foundation of the prophecies contained in the Book of Revelation.

The Book of Daniel is also considered one of the more notable sources in Scripture for information about angels. While initially thought to have been composed in the sixth century B.C., it is now recognized to have been written around 167 B.C., during the persecution and suffering of the Jews under the Syrian king Antiochus IV Epiphanes—an event that explains its grim apocalyptic tone and the assistance rendered by angels, the emissaries of God to his Chosen People, on behalf of Daniel and his friends. Most dramatic of all was the intervention by the (aptly named) angel of the furnace, who saved Shadrach, Meshach, and Abednego from the fiery furnace. Next came the episode, now legendary, of the lion's den, in which Daniel is hurled by a reluctant King Darius the Mede into a pit, to be consumed by lions. To everyone's surprise, of course, Daniel was spared, after which he noted to the astonished ruler: "My God sent his angel and shut the lions' mouths, and they have not hurt me, because I was found blameless before him; and also before you, O King, I have done no wrong."

The book is further distinguished by its mention, for the first time in the Old Testament, of two actual names of angels. They are Gabriel and Michael, and they help Daniel to interpret his dreams, going so far as to make clear the future of the Jewish people. From this work, Michael and Gabriel were chosen as guardians of the nation of Israel. These two would remain the only angels actually designated in the Hebrew Old Testament, to be joined later in the apocryphal Book of Tobit by Raphael.

🙙 **DANIEL (2)** An angel whose name means "God is my Judge," not to be confused with the renowned Jewish prophet of the same name (see *Daniel (1)*). The angel Daniel is variously associated with good and evil, being ranked among the holy and fallen angels. As a good angel he is grouped with the order or choir of principalities and is held to be an angel of considerable repute. Unfortunately he is also said in some traditions to be distinctly evil; in one source, the First Book of Enoch, he is actually listed among the fallen angels and is a leader of a group of wicked angels. There is moreover a custom that holds Daniel to be the cruel overlord of the nether regions of the numerous damned souls who in life were lawyers.

🙙 **DANTE** In full, Dante Alighieri, foremost of the Italian poets (1265–1321), one of the greatest writers of the Middle Ages, and author of *The Divine Comedy (La Comedia Divina),* generally considered a masterpiece in all of literature. Dante was born in Florence to a local noble family, grew up in the city, and ultimately participated in the often rancorous and raucous Florentine political life. A member of the political faction of the Guelph party (the group that supported the papacy during its long struggle with the Holy Roman Emperors), Dante helped to govern the city from 1295 to 1301; his period of public service ended abruptly, however, with the ascendancy of a rival faction—the Black Guelphs—who came to power in 1301. Especially targeted by the Black Guelphs, Dante was exiled from Florence, thereafter living as an exile in several Italian cities where a welcome could be secured. He finally settled in Ravenna, where he would die, never having the opportunity to return to his beloved Florence.

Poet, philosopher, and prose writer, Dante was the author of a large body of writings, including *De Vulgari Eloquentia* (1304–1305), which helped establish Italian as the language of literature in place of Latin; *De Monarchia,* espousing his conception of Christian political life; and *Il Convivio* (c. 1304–1307), which presented a kind of "feast of learning." Influencing much of Dante's life was his deep and abiding spiritual love for Beatrice Portinari (d. 1290), whom Dante first beheld when he was nine years old and with whom he was still entranced at the time of his own passing. Dante celebrated his love for Beatrice in the verse and prose masterpiece *La Vita Nuova* (c. 1293),

DANTE'S DIVINE COMEDY: THE NINE CHOIRS

Musing awhile I stood: and she [Beatrice], who saw
My inward meditations, thus began:
"In the first circles, they, whom thou beheld'st,
Are seraphim and cherubim. Thus swift
Follow their hoops, in likeness to the point,
Near as they can, approaching; and they can
The more, the loftier their vision. Those
That round them fleet, gazing the Godhead next,
Are thrones; in whom the first trine ends. And all
Are blessed, even as their sight descends
Deeper into the truth, wherein rest is
For every mind. Thus happiness hath root
In seeing, not in loving, which of sight
Is aftergrowth. And of the seeing such
The meed, as unto each, in due degree,
Grace and good-will their measure have assign'd.
The other trine, that with still opening buds

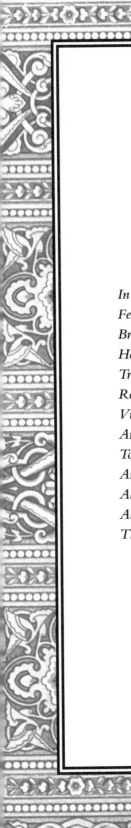

In this eternal springtide blossom fair,
Fearless of bruising from the nightly ram,
Breathe up in warbled melodies threefold
Hosannas, blending ever; from the three,
Transmitted, hierarchy of gods, for aye
Rejoicing; dominations first; next them,
Virtues; and powers the third; the next to whom
Are princedoms and archangels, with glad round
To tread their festal ring; and last, the band
Angelical, disporting in their sphere.
All, as they circle in their orders, look
Aloft; and downward, with such sway prevail,
That all with mutual impulse tend to God.

(TRANSLATED BY HENRY FRANCIS CARY,
1946 EDITION)

and his adoration reached a stunning zenith in the *Divine Comedy,* in which Beatrice served as his guide in *Paradiso.*

The *Divine Comedy* begins, "In the midway of this our mortal life, I found me in a gloomy wood, astray . . ." From here, Dante presents the tale of his journey to the three realms of Hell (*Inferno*), Purgatory (*Purgatorio*), and Heaven (*Paradiso*). His guide in Hell and Purgatory is the Roman poet Virgil; his guide in Heaven, of course, is Beatrice Portinari, whom Dante has elevated nearly to the rank of angel (see *Beatrice*). Beyond the wonders of Paradise, with its saints and philosophers of great renown (such as St. Thomas Aquinas), Dante beheld the Empyrean and, in Canto XXVIII, the nine orders of angels in full assembly, with color commentary from Beatrice (see box on pages 66–67).

DARK ANGEL The mysterious being, almost certainly an angel, who wrestled with the Hebrew patriarch Jacob, in an episode detailed in the Book of Genesis in the Old Testament. Jacob had taken his family

Jacob wrestles with the stranger, identified as the dark angel; by Gustave Doré.

to the ford of the Jabbok and sent them across the spring with all of his possessions. "And Jacob was left alone, and a man wrestled with him until the breaking of the day. When the man saw he did not prevail against Jacob, he touched the hollow of his thigh; and Jacob's thigh was put out of joint as he wrestled with him. Then he said, 'Let me go, for the day is breaking.' 'But I will not let you go, unless you bless me.' And he said to him, 'What is your name?' And he said, 'Jacob.' Then he said, 'Your name shall no more be called Jacob, but Israel, for you have striven with God and with men, and have prevailed.' Then Jacob asked him, 'Tell me, I pray, your name.' But he said, 'Why is it that you ask my name?' And there he blessed him. So Jacob called the name of the place Peniel, saying, 'For I have seen God face to face, and yet my life is preserved' " (Gen. 32:24–30). There has long been question as to which angel was sent to wrestle Jacob. Among the angels suggested in the role are Michael, Uriel, Chamuel, Peniel, and Metatron; it has also been suggested that the dark angel was God or the Holy Spirit. Acclaimed horror writer Meredith Ann Pierce authored a 1982 horror novel, *The Darkangel,* about a vampire on the moon that acts in a manner most unangelic.

DARKNESS, ANGEL OF A feared angel, equated with the prince of darkness. The angel of darkness is often said to be Satan or the fallen Lucifer, or one of several possible demons or devils, such as Belial or Beliar.

DEATH, ANGEL OF One of the universally feared angels, known and dreaded in every major religion of the world; the angel of death is found all over the earth, throughout all of history, existing as the spiritual embodiment of the great mystery of passing into the next world. Not surprisingly, however, there is considerable question as to his exact attributes, and his nature, origins, and even his designated activities are subject to considerable variation depending upon the source and the faith in question. Interestingly, most of the religions tend to agree (with some discrepancies and contradictions) that the angel of death is not by inclination one of the fallen angels. Rather, he is the appointed servant of God, with the task of bringing an end—at the appointed time—to the lives of humans. He goes about his business with considerable dispassion, rarely expressing remorse at his relentless task, although the idea that he might tire of gathering souls is presented in the famous tale "Death Takes a Holiday," with its numerous variations in film, literature, and television (see box on pages 70–72).

In the Jewish tradition, the angel of death appears under a number of incarnations and names. Among the well-known candidates for this arduous task are Bebriel, Metatron, Samael, Adriel, Azrael, and Hemah. Jewish legend, such as the collection of tales in Louis Ginzberg's *The Legends of the Jews,* tells of the angel actually being overcome in a struggle with the prophet Elijah; he would have been destroyed had the Lord not intervened and permitted his continued existence. Another account reports that the leader of the Israelites, Aaron, was able to trap or incarcerate the angel within the tabernacle containing the holy of holies; one can only presume that such an imprisonment was merely temporary, as the angel was unable to make his appointed rounds and so death ceased for the world, at least for

DEATH GOES TO
THE MOVIES

As might come as little surprise to the reader, the figure of the angel of death, or simply Death, has been the source of considerable enthusiasm on the part of filmmakers and screenwriters who recognize the dramatic and visual potential of the subject. Thus a large number of films and television programs have been devoted to the activities of Death, from the renowned film *The Seventh Seal* by Ingmar Bergman to comedic episodes of the *Twilight Zone* or moments in *Monty Python's The Meaning of Life* (in which Death shows up at a dinner party, his arrival prompting one guest to observe, "Well, that put a spot of gloom on the evening!"). Following are a few of the more memorable films offering up interpretations of the angel of death:

Bill and Ted's Bogus Adventure (1991), starring Keanu Reeves, Alex Winter, Joss Ackland, George Carlin, and Bill Sadler. This sequel to *Bill and Ted's Excellent Adventure* features the two leads journeying through heaven and hell and

Death (Fredric March) converses with a mortal in *Death Takes a Holiday* (1934).

meeting Death (splendidly played by Bill Sadler). To avoid being taken away by him, Bill and Ted challenge him to assorted games of wit, ultimately defeating him in tense games of Battleship and Twister; the grim reaper then acts as their guide to the netherworld. The scenes with Death are funnier than one might think.

Death from Ingmar Bergman's masterpiece *The Seventh Seal* (1957).

Death Takes a Holiday (1934), starring Fredric March, Katherine Alexander, Gail Patrick, and Evelyn Venable. Death assumes human form, to wander for a time among the living. Occasionally melodramatic, but well acted and considered a classic.

Death Takes a Holiday (1971), starring Melvyn Douglas, Myrna Loy, and Yvette Mimieux. A made-for-television remake of the 1934 film; the original is vastly superior.

Devil Rides Out, The (also *The Devil's Bride*) (1968), starring Christopher Lee, Charles Gray, and Nike Arrighi. A film version of the Dennis Wheatley novel, this production by Hammer Films (best known for their Dracula, Frankenstein, and Mummy movies) offers up some fun performances, especially by Gray, as a sorcerer tries to snare the soul of a young woman. The angel of death makes a somewhat anticlimactic arrival astride a winged horse.

Death (John Cleese) brings "a spot of gloom on the evening" in *Monty Python's The Meaning of Life* (with Eric Idle, Michael Palin, Graham Chapman, Terry Jones, and Terry Gilliam; 1983).

Masque of the Red Death (1964), starring Vincent Price, Patrick Magee, Hazel Court, and Jane Asher. One of Roger Corman's best films, this version of the Edgar Allan Poe classic features a finale in which Death stalks across a palace, massacring the inhabitants. At times gruesome, but one of Vincent Price's finest roles.

On Borrowed Time (1939), starring Cedric Hardwicke, Lionel Barrymore, and Beulah Bondi. A delightful classic in which a stubborn old man chases Death up a tree to prevent the grim reaper from fulfilling his duties.

Seventh Seal, The (1957), starring Max von Sydow, Bibi Andersson, and Gunnar Bjornstrand. The classic Ingmar Bergman masterpiece about a knight who plays chess with Death with his very life at stake. Considered Bergman's finest film, it also boasts a superb performance by von Sydow. (See also *Films*.)

the moment. In the Old Testament, the work of this angel can be considered virtually synonymous with the labors of the angels of destruction and even God, at whose will, of course, all angels continue to exist. Thus there are the wholesale massacre of the Assyrian army of 185,000, the obliteration of Sodom and Gomorrah, and the descent of death upon the Egyptian firstborn, which led to the granting of freedom to the Israelites under Moses.

As is seen in each of these instances, the Hebrew Bible does not mention the angel of death by name, nor does it even make obvious that there is such a being, relying instead upon a kind of personification. It was in later Jewish literature that Death assumed a clearer description. He is said to appear as a bird with twelve wings or as an angel of light, manifesting himself before the terror-stricken eyes of his next

The angel of death stalks the land of Egypt, slaying the firstborn; by Gustave Doré.

client. Perhaps the most vivid of his incarnations was as a horror-inducing angel of fell visage who stands at the head of a dying person with his sword drawn, its tip over the mouth of the poor soul struggling to cling to life. A drop of poison falls from the tip into the mouth of the gasping human, whose struggle in this world is then at an end. Sammael (or Samael) is often listed as the angel of death, and some scholars suggest that his name may be derived from the Hebrew word *sam* ("poison"), a reference to the poisonous liquid on the tip of his sword, for which there is no antidote. The image of an angel with a drawn sword is supported in Scripture by the terrible angel who slew seventy thousand Israelites as punishment for King David's pride; as written in 1 Chronicles (21:16): "And David lifted his eyes and saw the angel of the Lord standing between earth and heaven, and in his hand a drawn sword stretched out over Jerusalem."

Christian lore is noted for its angel of death, although there is more unanimity as to his identification. St. Michael is frequently named as the angel responsible for carrying to heaven the souls of the dearly departed. The destinies of the souls not headed to the blessed realm are not in Michael's hands; they are left to other, less benevolent beings.

During the Middle Ages, the figure of the angel of death was transformed into a simple but equally feared embodiment of Death itself. In art, for example, there was the grim reaper, the bringer of death to all. The spread of the Black Death in the mid–fourteenth century served only to reinforce this image, with artists painting the so-called Dance of Death, a sickle-wielding skeleton leading rulers, popes, merchants, and serfs into the great beyond without regard to rank, status, or wealth. This vision of Death is the one that has largely endured into our own day.

Islamic lore, meanwhile, presents the most well-known angel of death. Although not specifically named in the Qur'an, the bringer of death is Azrael. He became the focus of a large number of tales and legends. (For details, see *Azrael*.)

DEMIURGE Originally a Greek name meaning "artisan" or "craftsman" (*demiourgos*), used by Plato in his work *Timaeus* for the Creator or Maker of the world; it was subsequently adopted by Platonists for the spirit or being who made all of material creation. In the later teachings of the Gnostics (the heretical Christian sect of the early centuries A.D.), Demiurge was understood to be an emanation of the Supreme Being, distinct from the Godhead, responsible for the creation of all material things; this thus permitted an explanation for the evil nature of the earthly environment, an important element in Gnostic thinking, which saw the universe divided into light and darkness, the holy spiritual world and the sin-filled material world. The precise understanding of Demiurge, however, varied considerably according to the individual Gnostic sects that flourished in parts of the Roman Empire. One view held that Demiurge was one of the great archons who assumed the guise or persona of Yahweh, the God of the Old Testament. In this form, the archon (at times identified with Ialdabaoth) created Adam, but the false God is inherently evil and so grows jealous of the first man, creating Eve to compel Adam to become more humble. The first humans are aided by the so-called

Pistis Sophia, the feminine principle of wisdom. She assists Adam and Eve, has them bite the forbidden fruit, and so teaches them of the virtue of heaven. Demiurge in punishment expelled them from Paradise to the earth, where he hoped that they would forever after be preoccupied with the sinful state of earthly existence. His long-term plans were ultimately defeated by the incarnation of Christ, who assists souls on earth to reach the higher spiritual world. The Gnostic figure of Demiurge as the impostor God Yahweh was the result of the deep-seated resentment and mistrust of the Gnostics for the Old Testament and its spiteful, vengeful God, and their pervasive anti-Semitism. Throughout, Demiurge is assisted by the archons, considered evil by the Gnostics because they reside and partake in the world. They are opposed by the true God and the holy angels, who reside in the high holy realm of light and goodness.

DEMONS See under *Fallen Angels.*

DEPUTY ANGELS The name given to certain angels who, in Jewish lore and magic, act as spirit servants. They could be summoned by a powerful enough sorcerer or magician using the appropriate spells. Once brought to the material world, the deputy angel is required to perform the task given to it. By custom, the angels are reputed to be evil, although the famed Jewish scholar Eleazar of Worms (d. 1238) declared them to be entirely good.

DESTROYING ANGEL Another name for the angel of destruction, also analogous to the angel of death. "Destroying angel" has been used in several other contexts. In the Utah territory of the mid–nineteenth century there arose a group of violent, secret assassins who called themselves "the Destroying Angels." They belonged to the extreme religious body known as the Danites, and their predations, occurring in the region inhabited by the Mormons (who had settled in Utah, in the area around Salt Lake), caused the Mormons to be terribly stigmatized and accused of crimes they did not commit. The Danites were eventually wiped out and faded from history. They had taken their name from the Danites, a Hebrew line that claimed descent from the biblical figure Dan. A type of mushroom, the *Amanita verna,* is known as "the Destroying Angel," deriving its name from the similarity of its cap and fruiting to the wings of an angel.

Found mostly in wooded areas, it is the world's most deadly mushroom.

🦪 **DESTRUCTION, ANGELS OF** A fearsome type of angel appearing regularly in Jewish writings, the angels of destruction customarily serve two functions. The first is to descend to the earth and inflict terrible suffering upon those among the living who are wicked and in need of punishment. The second is to inflict even worse punishment upon damned souls in hell; in the latter roles they act as purifiers. As was written in the Third Book of Enoch (32:1): "When the Holy One, blessed be he, opens the book half of which is fire and half flame, the angels of destruction go out from his presence moment by moment to execute judgment against the wicked with the unsheathed sword of God, the brilliance of which flashes like lightning and passes through the world from end to end, as it is written. For by fire shall the Lord execute judgment, and by his sword, against all mankind."

An angel of destruction massacres an entire army of Assyrians; by Gustave Doré.

The leader of these angels is described in one Jewish account as Qemu'el (or Kemuel), but other sources name Samkiel. The latter angel is described by Enoch with a fellow destroying angel, Za'apiel, as bringing down from "the presence of the Holy One" those wicked souls who are to go to Sheol, the Hebrew land of the dead. Samkiel has control over those who are to be purified of their sins, and Za'apiel has the gruesome duty of torturing his unrepentant souls "with fires in Gehinnon [Gehenna], with rods of burning coal." Another leader of the angels—at least the commander of a great number of them—is the angel of silence, named Duma, who supervises the brutalities upon the wicked. A terrible vision of the angels at work in the underworld was given in Jewish legends concerning Moses and by Dante in the *Inferno,* part of his *Divine Comedy.* In one

Two angels of destruction (played by Peter O'Toole) warn Lot (Gabriele Ferzeti) of the fiery end that is coming to Sodom and Gomorrah, in *The Bible* (1966).

story Moses was taken on a tour of Gehenna and there beheld the sinful in a state of abject torture. Dante's imagery in depicting the suffering of lost souls at the hands of their tormentors was especially poignant.

Over the years there has been question among scholars as to whether the angels of destruction are exceedingly holy or whether they are evil or even whether they are permitted to inflict destruction at the express will of God. Whether they are good or evil, these angels have accomplished some truly epic feats of vengeance or annihilation. In the forms of avenging angels, they appear regularly in the Old Testament: two angels destroyed Sodom and Gomorrah, an angel massacred 70,000 people (2 Kings 24:16) to punish the pride of King David, and in 2 Kings (19:35) is told the account of one angel who wiped out an Assyrian army of some 185,000.

DEVAS Also daeva, a type of celestial being that appears in both Persian mythology and Hinduism. Named after a Sanskrit word meaning "god," the deva emerged in Hindu teachings as a spiritual being, serving the supreme beings. Devas were benevolent and were considered builders and helpers. While ranked at times as being less than humankind, the devas were once classified as one of the two groups of gods (along with the asuras). Over time, Indian lore described the devas as powerful spiritual beings, greater than the asuras, who were ever after evil. In Persian lore, however, the deva was the equivalent of a demon, a dreadful spirit, opposed in the Zoroastrian cosmology by the ahuras, the Persian equivalent of the Hindu asuras (only here they were beings of goodness). The deva is often cited as a precursor of an angel.

Siva and Parvati Enthroned on the Bull Nandi with celestial musicians, an example of the universal appearance of angelic beings; from the Victoria and Albert Museum, London (COURTESY ART RESOURCE).

DEVILS See *Fallen Angels.*

DIONYSIUS THE AREOPAGITE Also called Pseudo-Dionysius and Dionysius the Pseudo-Areopagite, a probably sixth-century Christian theologian who had a major influence upon the development of Christian thought and who was largely responsible for formulating the current system now used for our understanding of the angelic choirs or orders. Dionysius is a figure of considerable mystery, for his exact identification remains unknown. Almost certainly from Syria and probably a monk, he is known virtually only through the body of writings attributed to his pen. This did not, however, prevent the efforts of scholars and writers to make some kind of direct connection between Dionysius and historical figures. One identifies him as the Dionysius mentioned in the New Testament book Acts of the Apostles (17:34) who was converted by St. Paul on his second missionary journey; in another source he was listed as the first bishop of Corinth or the first bishop of Athens.

The writings of Dionysius first gained notoriety in the sixth century, and from around the time of Pope St. Gregory I the Great

(r. 590–604), they were viewed as possessing nearly unquestioned theological authority; Sts. Thomas Aquinas, Albertus Magnus, Bonaventure, and other profound theologians made use of them in the course of their work. While eventually subjected to intense scrutiny in the sixteenth century and determined to possess no origin dating to the apostolic age (the earliest period of the formative Church), the writings—in four treatises—nevertheless had exercised a lasting effect on medieval and Church thought. One of the most significant of the treatises was entitled the *Caelestis Hierarchia* or *De Hierarchia Celesti,* the *Celestial Hierarchy.* This work was the first great study of angels, presenting extensive details on the nature, attributes, and especially the organization of the angelic realm, and was based loosely upon some of the lists that had been organized previously (such as the ones by Sts. Jerome and Ambrose of Milan) and the writings of St. Paul (who had supposedly converted the author).

At the heart of Pseudo-Dionysius' work was a comprehensive listing of the angelic orders or choirs. So clear and well structured was his list that it was accepted wholesale throughout the Western world and serves even today as the near universally recognized celestial organization of angels. An idea of the credibility given to Dionysius' structure can be seen in the *Divine Comedy* by Dante. He criticizes quite harshly Pope St. Gregory I for committing a nearly unpardonable sin against Dionysius. His crime: the pope had organized his own angelic ordering and had reversed the placement of the virtues and principalities. In a biting measure, Dante actually has Pope Gregory admit to the poet in heaven that he had erred.

Dionysius divides all angels into nine choirs (or orders), which are further subdivided into three groups or triads, thusly:

First triad:	seraphim, cherubim, and thrones.
Second triad:	dominations, virtues, and powers.
Third triad:	principalities, archangels, and angels.

Each choir possesses its own purpose, powers, and characteristics, the subject of intense speculation and debate over the centuries. (See also *Choirs.*)

DIVINE COMEDY See *Dante.*

🦋 **DJIBRIL** The Arabic name for the archangel Gabriel. (See *Gabriel* for other details.)

🦋 **DOMINATIONS** (Choir) One of the nine accepted orders or choirs of angels, called also the dominions and the lords and termed in the Hebrew the hashmallim. In the celestial hierarchy as organized by sixth-century theologian Dionysius the Areopagite, the dominations belong to the second triad, with the virtues and powers, and are ranked fourth overall among the angelic choirs. The chief or ruling princes of the order are said to be Hashmal, Zadkiel, Muriel, and Zacharael. The name is derived from St. Paul's Letter to the Colossians (1:16), in which he wrote ". . . for in him all things were created, in heaven and on earth, visible and invisible, whether thrones or dominions or principalities or authorities—all things were created through him and for him." Similarly, the Second Book of Enoch declares the armies of archangels, the bodiless forces and dominions, and authorities, cherubim, seraphim, and the many-eyed thrones.

According to Dionysius, the dominations have the duty in the heavenly host of regulating the tasks of the angels, and "through them the majesty of God is manifested." Through the efforts of the dominations—who are naturally seen only rarely by mortals—the very order of the cosmos is maintained. They handle the minute details of cosmic life and existence, designating tasks to the lower orders of angels. By custom they are believed to wear green and gold, and their symbols are the sword and scepter, denoting their lordship over all created things. In turn, the dominations receive their instructions from the cherubim or thrones. (See *Choirs.*)

🦋 **DORÉ, GUSTAVE** In full, Paul-Gustave Doré (1833–1883), a brilliant and intensely imaginative book illustrator, best known for the magnificent woodcuts used to illustrate such works as those of Balzac, Rabelais, and especially Dante; other illustrations were created for Cervantes's *Don Quixote,* Coleridge's *The Rime of the Ancient Mariner,* Alfred Lord Tennyson's *Idylls of the King,* and a folio Bible. Perhaps the most remarkable of Doré's work was his interpretation of the *Divine Comedy.* In this, as in his major undertakings, he was assisted by a set of forty engravers he assembled and who he felt were reliable enough to assist him. He began the illustrations for the *Divine Comedy* in 1857, starting with the *Inferno.* These exquisite pieces were published by Doré himself in 1861 and remained unquestionably the author's

DUBBIEL AND GABRIEL

According to Jewish legend, the angel Dubbiel was once able to replace the mighty archangel Gabriel as prime minister of heaven. It seems that the Lord once grew so angry at Israel that Gabriel was ordered to orchestrate the complete destruction of the Jews, first by raining down burning coals upon them and then by ensuring that the stunned survivors were wiped out by the Babylonians. Taking pity upon the Israelites—and probably at the plea of Michael, guardian angel of Israel—Gabriel picked the most lazy angel in heaven to assist him; it took the angel so long to hand him the coals that they were nearly cool by the time the archangel hurled them to earth. This caused little destruction. Next Gabriel was able to convince the Babylonians not to massacre the Jews, merely force them to migrate to Babylon in the so-called Babylonian Captivity. Furious at Gabriel, the Lord supposedly demoted him from the post of prime minister, replacing him with the scheming Dubbiel. Dubbiel thus promoted his own people, the Persians, at the expense of the Jews and just about everyone else in the Near East. Gabriel, however, bided his time, waiting patiently behind the curtain that ever surrounds the throne room of God. Finally, one day while the Lord was having a conference with his foremost angels, Gabriel stuck his head into the room and made some brilliant observation. So delighted was the Lord that Gabriel was immediately restored to his office. Dubbiel probably did not take this well, which no doubt advanced his path to the status of fallen angel.

favorite work. The other parts of the *Comedy, Purgatorio* and *Paradiso,* were begun in 1868. Throughout Dante's epic poem, Doré included a host of angels, both holy and fallen. Some of the most memorable are the devils, Virgil and Lucifer (from the *Inferno*), the celestial pilot, the gates of purgatory, Beatrice (in the *Purgatorio*), and the glorified souls and Empyrean (in the *Paradiso*). Also ranked as significant and noted for its superb illustrations of angels is Doré's Bible. Here he included such memorable pieces as the angel appearing to Joshua, the angel (see *Dark Angel*) wrestling with Jacob, the New Jerusalem shown to St. John, the three angels appearing to Abraham, and (perhaps most vivid and moving) the expulsion of Adam and Eve from the Garden of Eden.

DRAGON One of the world's great mythological beings, described most often as a fabulous winged serpent or crocodile. The dragon is found in myths of cultures all over the world, including China— where it has retained a noble and beneficent nature; the Near East— such as Chaldaea, where, in the Babylonian creation epic, Tiamat the dragon helped create the gods and was the embodiment of chaos; and northern Europe, where the Norse revered the dragon as one of the most essential elements in the formation of the world. The dragon represented eternal rebirth and the powers of the elements, both for good and evil. Over time, however, the darker, sinister, and more malevolent characteristics came to predominate in the imaginings and teachings of such peoples as the early Hebrews, who saw the dragon as the very essence of evil, with no redeeming qualities. Christianity continued and elaborated this outlook, proclaiming the dragon to be the symbol of all that is sinful and wicked. In the Book of Revelation, for example, Satan is termed as the "ancient serpent"; in fact, the New Testament book is full of dragon imagery, such as the "great red dragon, with seven heads and ten horns, and seven diadems upon his heads" (Revelation 12:3). Not surprisingly, Christian art found the dragon a superb motif in demonstrating the triumph of the faith over evil. Saints, such as St. George, St. Margaret, and St. Martha (who slew the dragon Tarasque), were depicted overcoming or step-ping on dragons, thus fulfilling the declaration in the Book of Psalms (91:13): "You will tread on the lion and the adder, the young lion and the serpent you will trample under foot." Just as pervasive in art are the triumph of Mary over the dragon—an image again reinforced by the vivid descriptions in Revelation—and the victory of St.

Michael the Archangel. Considered a precursor or foreshadowing of St. George, St. Michael is the definitive dragon slayer, leading the heavenly host in its victory over the forces of the devil. (See also *Michael.*)

DUBBIEL An angel who was ranked among the Jews as one of the national angels—that is, angels who were said to act as guardians over the seventy nations. Dubbiel was counted as the protector of Persia and as such defended its interests against its enemy Israel, a role that naturally put him at odds with the Chosen People and their special patron, St. Michael the Archangel. Dubbiel's favor for Persia was apparently so corrupting that he, like the other guardian angels of the nations—save for Michael of Israel—fell and were ever after counted among the evil angels. (See box on page 81; see also *Guardian Angels* and *Nations, Angels of the.*)

DUDLEY The charming and extremely helpful angel in the delightful 1947 film *The Bishop's Wife* (based on the 1928 novel of the same name by Robert Nathan), starring Cary Grant as Dudley, Loretta Young as Julia (the title character), and David Niven as the much-harassed Anglican bishop praying desperately for divine assistance to build his coveted cathedral. As he

Cary Grant as the ever-helpful angel Dudley; from *The Bishop's Wife* (1947).

is a good man, his prayer is answered, and Dudley arrives to aid him. Naturally the guidance the bishop receives is not what he expects—with comical consequences. Dudley is one of the most memorable of all film angels, although he is probably a distant second in popularity to Clarence Oddbody of *It's a Wonderful Life* fame. (See also *Films.*)

🙾 **DUMA** Also Dumah, the angel of Egypt and the angel of silence. Duma, whose name in Aramaic means "silence," is often cited as the angel recorded in Jewish legend who appeared and terrified the Israelites as they departed Egypt under the leadership of Moses. As the patron angel of Egypt, Duma made certain that no lasting harm came to the nation under his authority. As Jewish lore declares that all of the seventy guardian or patron angels of the nations fell—with the obvious exception of Michael, archangel and patron of Israel—it is possible to count Duma among the fallen angels. In one Jewish tradition (that of the Zohar), he is now prince of hell, with command over a host of angels of destruction and a great number of demons and authority over the punishment of wicked souls. (See also *Destruction, Angels of,* and *Egypt, Angel of.*)

🙾 **DÜRER, ALBRECHT** German artist and printer (1471–1528) who was one of the foremost figures of the Renaissance in Germany; Dürer is also ranked as one of the premier angel artists in history, along with such brilliant masters as Doré, Fra Angelico, William Blake, and others. A native of Nürnberg, he lived most of his years there, but he also made a number of influential trips, most importantly to Italy in 1494–1495 and 1505–1507. He was also in the service of the Holy Roman Emperor Maximilian. Among his great works are portraits, altarpieces, and a large number of religious paintings and engravings. He is perhaps best known, however, for his woodcuts, which tend more than his other creations to retain the Gothic style; Dürer gradually abandoned this motif in his other media as he came increasingly to appreciate the Renaissance, particularly after his journeys to Italy. The woodcuts present a sumptuous variety of angels and remain one of the foremost sources for angelic images. Just a few notable pieces are *St. Francis Receiving the Stigmata,* c. 1502 (with a representation of a seraphim); the *Annunciation,* c. 1500–1501; the *Angel with the Key Forcing the Dragon into the Abyss,* c. 1498; *St. Michael and the Dragon,* c. 1498; and the famous *Pillared Angel from the Book of Revelation,* c. 1498. Stark and even discomforting, the woodcuts of Dürer continue to evoke strong emotion in the observer and do much to stress the awe-inspiring nature of the angelic realm. (See also *Art, Angels in.*)

🙾 **DYNAMIS** One of the celestial beings known as aeons (the first created entities), who were also thought to be divine emanations from

God. Among these eternal beings who were equated with the sefiroth (see *Sefiroth*) and ranked as angelic beings right up to the sixth century A.D., Dynamis was considered one of the most significant. While under the rulership of Abraxas, Dynamis is still honored as the very embodiment of power. Among the Gnostics (an early heretical branch of Christianity), Dynamis is the male personification of power, while his counterpart, Pistis Sophia, is the female embodiment of wisdom. (See *Aeon* for other details.)

EARTH, ANGELS OF THE In the stories and legends of angels, there are said to be certain angels who make as their focus the guidance and oversight of the world. They concern themselves with the well-being of humanity and also watch that the earth continues to go along its proper path in the heavens. According to the seventeenth-century angel expert Thomas Heywood, in his *Hierarchy of the Blessed Angels* (1635), there are four angels of the earth, the famous Michael, Raphael, Uriel, and Gabriel. Each angel has control over one of the four cardinal points of direction: north (Gabriel), south (Uriel), east (Michael), and west (Raphael). In the Jewish tradition, there are seven angels of the earth: Ariel, Yabbashael, Azriel, Arhiel, Arciciah, Horobael, and Admael.

EDEN, GARDEN OF The earthly Paradise that was the first abode of Adam and Eve until their expulsion from the garden, an event recorded in the Old Testament Book of Genesis: "And out of the ground every tree that is pleasant to the sight and good for food, the tree of life also in the midst of the garden, and the tree of knowledge of good and evil. . . . The Lord God took the man and put him in the garden of Eden to till it and keep it. And the Lord God commanded the man, saying, 'You may freely eat of every tree of the garden; but of the tree of the knowledge of good and evil you shall not eat, for in the day that you eat of it you shall die' " (2:8–9, 15–17).

Deriving its name perhaps from the Sumerian word *eden,* meaning "plain" (or perhaps from a word denoting "pleasure"), Eden was supposedly located in the Near East, close to Israel, its precise locale narrowed by the position of four rivers that formed out of the river that flowed out of Eden and nourished the garden: the Pishon, the Gihon, the Tigris, and the Euphrates, rivers that would seem to place the garden in the fertile crescent. Attempts to locate the garden, however, have (not surprisingly) proven unsuccessful.

The expulsion of Adam and Eve from Paradise; by Gustave Doré.

The first days of Adam and Eve in the garden were truly joyous, as God walked with them in the evening, and they enjoyed an abiding spiritual intimacy with their Creator and the angels. All of this changed, of course, with the arrival of the serpent and the successful temptation of the first family. After consuming the fruit of the forbidden tree, Adam and Eve were expelled: "He [God] drove out the man; and at the east of the garden of Eden he placed the cherubim, and a flaming sword which turned every way, to guard the way to the tree of life" (Genesis 3:24).

Beyond the fearsome cherubim (listed often as Metatron or Jophiel), there are a number of associations between angels and the garden. For example, the famed archangel Raphael is said to be the angel responsible for guarding the tree of life; this angel was also named by John Dryden in his poem "State of Innocence, or the Fall of Man," as being the very angry angel who tossed Adam and Eve out of Paradise. In *Paradise Lost* by John Milton, however, this task was given to the archangel Michael:

> *In either hand the hastening angel caught*
> *Our living parents, and to the eastern gate*
> *Led them direct, and down the cliff as fast*
> *To the subjected plain; then disappeared.*

They looking back, all the eastern side beheld
Of Paradise, so late their happy seat,
Waved over by that flaming brand, the gate
With dreadful faces thronged and fiery arms:
Some natural tears they dropped, but wiped them soon;
The world was all before them, where to choose
Their place of rest, and providence their guide.
They hand in hand with wandering steps and slow,
Through Eden took their solitary way.
(Book XII)

EGYPT, ANGEL OF The angel who is charged with the special protection and guardianship of Egypt. Ranked as one of the guardian angels of nations (see *Guardian Angels*), this angelic patron has been given various identifications, including Samael (a chief angel of the fallen angels), Mastema (the accusing angel), and Duma. The latter angel is most often considered the proper angel of Egypt. He was most vociferous in defense of his charges, going so far in legend as to empower the accomplished wizards of Egypt to perform the same feats of magic as Moses when the Lawgiver arrived at the court of the pharaoh and tried to impress him enough that the Israelites should be freed from their bondage (an event recorded in the Old Testament Book of Exodus). The angel of Egypt, however, could not long resist the will of God, and Moses—after the great plagues were imposed upon the Egyptians—led the Israelites out of the country. According to legend, recounted in Louis Ginzberg's *The Legends of the Jews,* the angel descended to the land of the Nile to give succor to his people upon the departure of the Jews, stopping long enough to put a fright into the Israelites by an impressive demonstration in the air. As Jewish custom declares all of the guardian angels of nations to have fallen (save, of course, for the ever-redoubtable St. Michael), the angel of Egypt joined the denizens of the hoary netherworld; it is unclear whether the Lord ever appointed a successor. (See also *Duma, Mastema,* and *Samael.*)

EIAEL The very helpful angel who is able to teach secrets in occult arts and science. Eiael can be summoned by competent sorcerers, but the person invoking him must be certain to recite the fourth verse of Psalm 36: "He plots mischief while on his bed, he sets himself in a way that is not good; he spurns not evil."

ELDERS The collective name given to a group of twenty-four beings who sit upon thrones encircling the throne of God, as described by St. John in the Book of Revelation: "At once I was in the Spirit, and lo, a throne stood in heaven, with one seated on the throne! And he who sat there appeared like Jasper and carnelian, and round the throne was a rainbow that looked like an emerald. Round the throne were twenty-four thrones, and seated on the thrones were twenty-four elders, clad in white garments, with golden crowns upon their heads." The elders make comment to John throughout the text and several times fall down prostrate, at one point bowing before the Lamb of God while holding a harp and a golden bowl of incense (Revelation 4:2–4; 5:5–10). It is often

The twenty-four elders described by Dante in the *Divine Comedy* and appearing in the Book of Revelation; by Gustave Doré.

believed by scholars and interpreters of Revelation that the elders are, in fact, to be counted as great angels, perhaps a secret or distinct order of angelic beings. They appeared in Dante's *Divine Comedy* (*Purgatorio,* Canto 29) in an apocalyptic vision while the poet was touring Purgatory:

> *Beneath a sky*
> *So beautiful, came four and twenty elders,*
> *By two and two, with flower-de-luces crown'd.*

Their image was presented in striking fashion by the French illustrator Gustave Doré in his work on the *Divine Comedy*. Another remarkable depiction of St. John and the twenty-four elders was created by Albrecht Dürer. It is unclear where exactly the elders reside, although the Second Book of Enoch lists them as inhabiting part of the first of the seven heavens; here they act as "rulers of the stellar orders."

ELIJAH The ninth-century Hebrew prophet who, with the patriarch Enoch, was one of only two Old Testament figures to be translated to heaven while still living upon the earth; aside from being one of the most revered of all Jewish religious leaders, Elijah is also declared in legend to have been transformed, like Enoch, into an angel. Appearing in the Old Testament Books of Kings, Elijah stands forth as the great defender of the worship of Jehovah by the people of Israel against the idol-worshiping cults of the Canaanites and Phoenicians. Much as he appeared suddenly to the Israelite king Ahab, so too was his departure one of the most memorable in all of Scripture.

"When they had crossed [the river Jordan], Elijah said to Elisha, 'Ask what I shall do for you before I am taken from you.' And Elisha said, 'I pray you, let me inherit a double share of your spirit.' And he said, 'You have asked a hard thing; yet, if you see me as I am being taken from you, it shall be so for you; but if you do not see me, it shall not be so.' And as they still went on and talked, behold, a chariot of fire and horses of fire separated the two of them. And Elijah saw it and he cried, 'My father, my father! the chariots of Israel and its horsemen!' And he saw him no more" (2 Kings 2:6–12).

On the basis of this fiery exit, Elijah became the source of a host of tales and traditions. He was, it was said, transformed into an angel and given a large place in the celestial hierarchy. The name most associated with his angelic persona is Sandalphon, the twin brother of Metatron (the onetime Enoch) and one of the tallest angels in heaven. In Jewish lore he stands at the crossroads of paradise, waiting eagerly to direct the holy to their places of eternal bliss; he also is reported in the Talmud to act as the recording angel, keeping track of all deeds by the living. Finally, he is nicknamed the "bird of heaven" in recognition of his constant flight from heaven to earth to mediate or participate in earthly affairs.

One of the most central elements in the place of Elijah in tradition is his role of serving as the herald or announcer of the coming of the Messiah, as declared in the Book of Malachi (4:5), the last words of the Old Testament: "Behold, I will send you Elijah the prophet before the great and terrible day of the Lord comes." Thus, in the Gospel of St. Luke, Elijah appeared with Moses at the side of Christ in the Transfiguration. The sense of anticipation in the Jewish faith continues in the custom at the Passover seder table of leaving a place empty for Elijah, filling a cup of wine for him, and opening the door that he might enter.

Several stories exist to explain how Elijah might have managed to escape death. One has Elijah actually being the incarnation of an angel, in the same way that Isaac was supposedly always an angel. His elevation to heaven was thus more of a return than a transportation. The other tale has him engaged in a fascinating struggle with Death itself. His journey to heaven was apparently opposed by the angel of death, and the Lord gave his permission for the angel to stop Elijah before reaching the gates of heaven. The two grappled, and to the angel's surprise, Elijah gained the upper hand. The prophet would have finished off Death entirely had God not intervened. The angel stepped aside, and Elijah went on to become Sandalphon, an angel most concerned with the welfare of humanity. (See also *Manna*.)

ELOHIM The Hebrew name for God (Yahweh), the plural of eloha, meaning "god"; while technically a plural word, the singular Elohim was used and understood as the Hebrew conception of the God of Israel, the One True God. In Hebrew texts of the Old Testament, the word Elohim was used variously with other words or conjunctions such as *ha-* to make entirely clear that this is "the" God and not some other deity or personage. This grammatical addition was considered essential because elohim had also been used for other earlier goddesses—its root, in fact, came from the Canaanite word *el*—and for such beings as angels. The application of elohim (perhaps to be defined as "sons of God") has been given to angels in the sense that they represent God as messengers and thus are equatable or synonymous with God himself. It can be argued, however, that the elohim might constitute their own order or choir, as was maintained by the fifteenth-century scholar Pico della Mirandola. When he compiled his own list of the angelic choirs, he placed the elohim in ninth place.

EMMANUEL Also Immanuel, in the common understanding of the Hebrew word for "God is with us," which was used by the prophet Isaiah for the child whose eventual birth he predicted (Isaiah 7:14). To Christians, Isaiah's prophecy was fulfilled by the birth of Christ, the Messiah long predicted: "Behold, a virgin shall conceive and bear a son, and his name shall be called Emmanuel." "Emmanuel" is also used for several angels. In the lore surrounding the angel of the furnace—the angel who appeared with the condemned Jewish princes Shadrach, Meshach, and Abednego in the fiery furnace (which did not consume them, to the amazement of their Babylonian captors)— Emmanuel is used as a possible identification for the otherwise nameless angel. French poet and dramatist Alfred de Vigny (1797–1863) used "Emmanuel" for the son of an angel born by union with a mortal woman and also another angel in his poem *"Le Deluge."* (See also *Furnace, Angel of the.*)

EMPYREAN The fifth and final heaven of the celestial organization first enunciated by the famed astronomer Ptolemy in the second century. This heaven, deriving its name from the Greek *empuros* ("fire"), is said to be composed of fire and unapproachable light and is the place where resides the throne of God. It is thus the abode of the Lord and his angels. A beautiful description of the Empyrean was made by John Milton in *Paradise Lost* (Book III):

The Empyrean; by Gustave Doré.

> *Now had the almighty father from above,*
> *From the pure empyrean where he sits*
> *High throned above all height, bent down his eye,*
> *About him all the sanctities of heaven*
> *Stood thick as stars, and from his sight received*
> *Beatitudes past utterance . . .*

ENOCH The seventh-named patriarch of the Old Testament Book of Genesis and one of the best-known figures in the field of angelology because of his reputed authorship of the Books of Enoch and his supposed transformation by God into the mighty angel Metatron. One of the so-called antediluvian patriarchs (the patriarchs prior to the Flood of Noah fame), Enoch was the son of Jared and was himself the father of Methuselah, who would live to be 969 years old. Said to be exceedingly pleasing to God, Enoch received the high honor of being taken to heaven: "Enoch walked with God; and he was not, for God took him" (Genesis 5:24), and "By faith Enoch was taken up so that he should not see death; and he was not found, because God had taken him" (Hebrews 11:5).

Despite these relatively brief mentionings in Scripture, Enoch (called Idris in the Qur'an and honored as a "truthful man, a prophet" by the Muslims) became the basis of a large body of legends. He is the supposed author of 366 books, collectively termed the Enochian literature. The most famous writings bearing his name are the First, Second, and Third Books of Enoch, ranked among the large body of literature termed apocryphal and pseudepigraphical, meaning that they are noncanonical (not accepted into the body of recognized books of the Bible) and are—in the case of the pseudepigrapha—attributed to some person of note and written in the style of genuine biblical books.

Most interesting of all the legends is the one in which Enoch was transported to heaven and there transformed into the angel Metatron. Similar to the legends related to other patriarchs (most notably Elijah, who was taken to heaven in a fiery chariot and turned into the angel Sandalphon; see *Elijah*), Enoch was supposedly taken into the sky. Some sources speak of a fiery chariot, à la Elijah, but others proclaim his journey to be undertaken by the angel Anafiel (or Anfiel), an event described in the collection *The Legends of the Jews* by Louis Ginzberg. Once there, he was, with a divine flourish, made into Metatron, the angel of the face, high priest of the heavenly temple, and one of the supreme angels in all of the celestial hierarchy—not to mention the tallest of angels, with 36 wings and 265,000 eyes. (See *Metatron*.)

ENOCH, BOOKS OF Three so-called pseudepigraphical works that were supposedly written by or under the influence of the antediluvian patriarch Enoch, who was taken up to heaven by the Lord, an event described in the Book of Genesis (5:24); pseudepigraphical writings are those that are noncanonical (meaning not accepted into the body of biblical books) and were composed in a style intending to resemble or appear as authentic biblical literature, often assuming the title of some personage known to the audience. In the case of the Books of Enoch, the actual writers or compilers chose a figure who was the source of many legends and tales, the most notable being his transformation by God into the truly powerful angel Metatron. While decidedly uncanonical, the three books remain fascinating and colorful reading, as well as treasures of detail and fanciful images concerning angels.

1 ENOCH Known also as the Ethiopic Book of Enoch from the fact that the only surviving complete manuscript of it is in Ethiopic, this is the oldest of the three Enoch books, dating to the mid–second century B.C., although it actually comprises various sections, each dated differently: "The Book of Noah"; "Similitudes"; "The Dream Visions"; "Apocalypse of the Weeks"; and "The Book of the Heavenly Luminaries." Aside from material on Gehenna and heaven and the nature of evil, the text is full of stories and accounts of angels. The writer covers the fall of angels, the names of the archangels, and the fire of the luminaries of heaven. The reader thus encounters such angelic personages as Raguel, Uriel, Gabriel, Raphael, Michael, and Saraqael.

2 ENOCH Known also as the Slavonic Book of Enoch because the only extant version is a Slavonic translation of the Greek original text, this specific edition dates to the seventh century A.D., although it is based on a much older Jewish text of the first century A.D. While similar in some ways to the First Book of Enoch and perhaps using it as a source, the Slavonic Enoch details Enoch's journey through the seven heavens, the life of Enoch's successors, especially Methuselah, and then gives a forecast of the Great Flood that encompassed the world in later generations. There are descriptions of angels residing in the heavens.

3 ENOCH Also called the Hebrew Apocalypse of Enoch, this is a Jewish writing dating probably to the second century A.D. It was supposedly written by the noted Rabbi Ishmael, a brilliant scholar of Palestine during the early second century A.D. He reputes to recount his journey to heaven, where he beheld the very throne of God, along with the hosts of angels. His information was granted to him by the archangel Metatron, the onetime patriarch Enoch. This work remains perhaps the single greatest compendium of angelic lore, including a comprehensive assemblage of angels, archangels, and holy creatures, such as the watchers and holy ones.

EPHEMERA A very unusual type of angel (plural ephemerae) that has a divinely appointed life span of barely a day or even a few hours. The ephemera (whose name means "short-lived") comes into existence at the start of the day. It has but one purpose: to chant the *"Te Deum,"* the great song of praise to God. Once completing this chant of glorious adoration, the ephemerae are snuffed out of existence, being subsumed or reassumed into the divine light. These angels are similar to many other angels appearing in lore whose sole—and honored—duty is to chant or sing ceaselessly in praise of God. (See *Singing, Angelic.*)

ERELIM The Hebrew equivalent of the angelic order or choir of the thrones. The name *erelim* means "the valiant (or courageous) ones." (See *Thrones* for details.)

ESERCHIE An angel (although some say this stands for God) who appeared in the legends surrounding Moses. According to these stories, Eserchie was called upon by Moses to assist him in inflicting at least two of the plagues sent by God upon the Egyptians. The first was the turning of the waters of the Nile into blood, and the second was the plague of frogs. Both events are recorded in the Old Testament Book of Exodus (7:20–24; 8:1–15), although Scripture does not mention Eserchie. As it was, neither plague proved sufficient to convince the pharaoh to permit the Jews to depart Egypt, in part because the gifted court magicians themselves were able to perform the same remarkable feats. In angel lore, this episode is especially interesting because the magical acts by the Egyptian wizards were accomplished by the so-called Angel of Egypt, the guardian of Egypt who was ever working for the interests of the people whose angelic patron he was, even if that meant working against God's Chosen People or a fellow angel. (See also *Moses.*)

ETHNARCHS The name given to those angels who have authority as guardians or protectors of the nations of the world. (For details, see under *Guardian Angels.*)

EXAEL One of the ten angels mentioned in the First Book of Enoch who descended to earth and took wives. They also taught mortals about "magical medicine, incantations, the cutting of roots, and . . . plants."

EXOUSIA The original Greek name for angels—in the New Testament. Exousia is translated variously as virtue or power, leaving open as to which exact angelic order it refers, as both powers and virtues are considered angelic choirs. St. Paul, for example, wrote about the angels, whom he called powers (exousia).

FACE, ANGELS OF THE Also at times known as the angels of the presence, a group of revered angels who appear in the rabbinic lore of the Jews. Their exact number is unclear, but there were probably around twelve of them. They are so honored because they enjoy the incomparable honor of beholding the very face of God, residing ever in the divine presence. They thus share in the beholding of the so-called beatific vision. Among the angels of the face are Michael, Uriel, Zagzagel, and the powerful Metatron.

FALLEN ANGELS The collective name given to those angels who, for whatever reason, chose to rebel against God and so "fall" from the ranks of the heavenly host. The fallen angels have been called devils, unclean spirits, demons, and denizens of the hoary underworld, declared to reside in Gehenna, hell, the abyss, or the bottomless pit. They are the profound—some say unredeemable—enemies of the Lord and all of his Creation, especially humanity. They struggle against all that is holy, sacred, and good, seeking ever to corrupt the innocent, destroy the beauty of the cosmos, plunge the universe into chaos, and snuff out the perfect and unapproachable light of God's love. For all of these endeavors, and because they are now the twisted and perverted caricatures of their angelic brethren, the fallen ones are especially opposed and countered by the angels of God, under the command of Michael.

How the angels of heaven actually fell from grace and the presence of God is one of theology's and spiritual history's great mysteries. Fortunately, there is no want for theories as to what may have occurred aeons ago. One of the most common stories is that God informed the angels that he intended to create humanity and that the angels should bow down before this new species. This some of the angels refused to do, counting themselves superior to mankind. The chief of these rebellious angels was Satan (later incorrectly identified with Lucifer), one of the foremost of all angels, beloved of God, and a chief of the seraphim. His pride would not permit his submission or his apology to God. Joined by a host of other angels, said in some accounts to number nearly one-third of the entire heavenly army, Satan launched a war against God, even though he knew that victory was utterly impossible. Driven from heaven by Michael and the angels of light, Satan and his minions, now grotesque and twisted in form and spirit, fell from the firmament and entered into the dreadful darkness of hell.

This explanation is supported to a large degree by the speculation of such eminent theologians as St. Augustine and St. Thomas Aquinas that God initially made the angels with free will, permitting them to be open to accept or reject his grace, the means by which they would be linked to him for eternity. As God had made angels with natures that made them eternally decisive, their decision one way or the other was, according to Thomas, irrevocable. Some of the angels chose to sin and so rejected what God offered them; their probationary period, so to speak, ended with their eternal damnation. Those who embraced the love of God and his grace were given the full measure of his love, the beatific vision, a glorious union with their Creator, which would make rebellion or sin literally unthinkable. Connected to the free will argument are the writings of Origen, the third-century controversial theologian and biblical expert whose unorthodox views were condemned by the leaders of the Christian Church. He argued that God created spiritual beings in possession of both intelligence and free will. They exercised their free will and, albeit without necessarily sinning, drifted away from the source of the creation. The degree of their movement away from the Prime Mover determined their place in the celestial hierarchy of all things. Thus those closest to God exist in the ethereal realms, while the next level of drifted spirits became the angels. Those who went farther descended to the earth and became the basis of humanity. The most extreme of moved beings degenerated badly and became the demons. Interestingly, in the Origenist scheme, angels can continue to fall, becoming humans, but conversely, humans are able to return toward the

Creator and thus reassume their higher nature. Such a redemption is possible even for the demons.

The nature of angelic sin has prompted another theory, one that stresses the rather human hubris of some of the angels. This idea asserts that a group of angels, called variously the watchers and the sons of God, descended from heaven to take part in the project of the world. They taught humanity many useful things, but they also fell prey to lust, pursuing mortal women with whom they copulated with divine abandon. The result of their sin was the race mentioned in the Old Testament Book of Genesis, the nephilim. So troublesome were the giants that the Flood was necessary to cleanse the world. Even worse, the angels taught secrets of the universe to mortals, knowledge that should have remained the exclusive purview of the divine. For their crimes, the fallen angels were bound up and cast into eternal damnation by the Lord. They thus became the

The fall of the sinful angels from heaven in *Paradise Lost;* by Gustave Doré.

demons who escaped from their confinement and returned to the world to continue to tempt humanity. These fallen angels were said in the First Book of Enoch to number two hundred under the leadership of Semyaza, Azazel, Tam'el, Baraqyal, and others.

To give some reasonable explanation as to how angels, supposedly beings of pure spirit, were able to reproduce, some theologians proposed that the watchers were a special tenth choir of angels, made of spirit and body. (See *Watchers.*) Other, heretical writers surmised that angels might possess the ability to assume human form and substance and, while in this shape, can be led into sin.

A more complicated explanation of the fallen angels is given in some Jewish legends concerning the so-called Accusing Angel. This concept advances the notion that all evil occurs with the purpose of

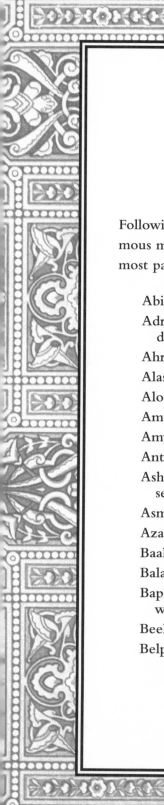

FALLEN ANGELS

Following is a list of a few of the most famous and infamous members of the hierarchy of hell. They all, for the most part, once belonged to the angelic choirs.

Abigor (grand duke of hell)

Adramelech (president of the high council of demons)

Ahriman (Persian devil)

Alastor (the executioner)

Alocer (commands thirty-six legions of demons)

Amducias (grand duke of hell)

Amy (demon hoping to return to heaven)

Antichrist (the great enemy of humanity)

Ashtoreth (appeared at Loudun in the seventeenth century)

Asmodeus (demon of lust and anger)

Azazel (standard-bearer of hell)

Baalberith (secretary of hell)

Balan (a king of hell)

Baphomet (bearded demon; supposedly worshiped by the Knights Templar)

Beelzebub (prince of hell)

Belphegor (tempter)

Cagrino (Gypsy demon)

Dagon (Phoenician demon)

Devil (the evil one)

Friar Rush (a bartender in hell and tempter of monks)

Furfur (count in hell)

Incubus (seducer of women)

Keteb (the noonday demon)

Leviathan (a sea demon)

Lilith (Adam's first wife and a fearsome demoness)

Lucifer (the fallen light-bearer)

Malphas (grand president of hell)

Mammon (master of avarice)

Mephistopheles (the tempter of Faust)

Nebiros (field marshal of hell)

Old Scratch (a form of the devil)

Rabdos (the strangler)

Satan (the great fallen angel)

Succubus (seducer of men)

Zaebos (grand count of hell)

tempting the faith of humanity. Thus the wicked angels, such as Samael, serve a vital function in the ordering of the cosmos.

Regardless of how they departed the blessed realm, the fallen angels (or whatever their appellation) have been one of the central elements in religions throughout the world. Writers and occultists have developed for them an organization that is of such diabolical complexity and fiendish rigidity that it stands in marked contrast with the relative simplicity of the celestial hierarchy. Hell has a massive bureaucracy, with a horrific aristocracy that jealously and cruelly protects its rights and prerogatives, all the while scheming to secure the undoing of both heaven and their fellow damned souls. There are the seven princes of hell (to rival the seven archangels), dukes, archdemons, archdevils, devils and demons (the two constituting *very* different species with individual lines of descent, something that both—devils more so because they come from better, angelic stock—are at some pains to point out), and a host of incubi, succubi, imps, fiends, vampires, larvae, and fell spirits. The list of individual demons and devils is a truly long one, entries most noted for their old positions in the heavenly host (it seems that the bulk of the fallen angels came from the angelic choirs of the powers and principalities) and their new offices in the infernal realms. Their names are familiar to any who have even a passing familiarity with the occult, while others are known only to the most ardent students of demonology or sorcery. How many fallen angels there are is anyone's guess, but one medieval cardinal estimated it to be 133,306,668; it is, of course, possible that the ranks of the demons and devils have increased over the ages by the addition of many truly wicked souls who were "promoted" by Satan to a higher rank in the legions of Hades. Such a transformation would give the evil soul certain powers and abilities—to increase the torment of other damned souls—but it also serves to add exponentially to the unspeakable horrors endured by the souls in question, especially as it brings them into contact with beings higher up in the breathtakingly evil pecking order of the netherworld, once angels of incomparable dread and unrivaled imagination when it comes to inflicting pain and misery upon all who are weaker than they. This was brilliantly presented in the 1951 short story "Hell-Bent" by Ford McCormack. The master of hell, of course, remains, as it has since time immemorial, the devil, known under a host of names, as is fitting for one called the "Father of Lies": Satan, Samael, Beelzebub, Mastema, Lucifer, the evil one, the prince of evil, Beliel, Duma,

Azazel, Mephistopheles, Old Scratch, Mr. Hobbes, Lusty Dick, Old Horney, and, to the Muslims, Iblis. His individual history is so long and so terrible that perhaps no chronicle could possibly do justice to the tale.

The list offered under "Fallen Angels" (see box on pages 100–101) is of the major potentates of hell; it would be impossible (and perhaps distasteful) in a book about angels to give all-encompassing detail about the enemies of light. This list thus includes additional information only when useful.

FEAST DAYS Those days devoted to honoring angels or a specific angel. Angel feast days are celebrated in the Catholic Church and the orthodox churches. These days were expressions of the special place of honor reserved for angels in the liturgical calendar of the Church, although it was always pointed out that angels, like the saints and the Virgin Mary, are not worshiped but given veneration. One of the most significant of the feasts is on October 2, in honor of the guardian angels. The Church also today celebrates September 29 as the feast day of Michael, Gabriel, and Raphael. Prior to the extensive reforms of the Roman calendar in 1969, each of the angels had his own day, Michael on September 29, Gabriel on March 24, and Raphael on October 24. In the orthodox churches of Egypt and Ethiopia, the Christians celebrate July 28 in honor of the archangel Uriel. (See also *Michaelmas.*)

FEMALE ANGELS Those angels who are held or honored as females (see also *Gender of Angels*). While most scholars and theologians are of the view that angels do not possess a specific gender owing to the fact that they are entirely spiritual beings, there is a custom in some cultures of naming some angels to be females. In Islamic lore, for example, female angels are called the daughters of God, revered personages because of their nearness to God and because they represent the female aspect of Creation. Perhaps the greatest of the female angelic spirits is the Pistis Sophia, the female aspect of Creation, the aeon or celestial power revered in Gnosticism. The male equivalent is Dynamis. Angels in art appear at times to possess distinctly feminine qualities or attributes, although this is realistically the androgynous nature of angels as presented by the great artists who have combined the finest aspects of both the male and the female. Such a representation is consistent with the principal theological view in the Christian tradition, in which angels combine the spiritual qualities of both genders, creating a pure, whole spiritual being. In those famous accounts of angelic visitations, the vast majority of disguised angels have been taking the outward or earthly appearance of males. There would, theoretically, be no limitation upon an angel so empowered from assuming female shape. The possibilities of a female angel have actually been explored in film, most notably in the tepid television remake of *It's a Wonderful Life,* starring Marlo Thomas and Cloris Leachman, and the 1987 comedy *Date with an Angel,* starring Emmanuelle Beart as an angel who loses her wings.

FIERY FURNACE, ANGEL OF THE See *Furnace, Angel of the.*

FILMS As a mysterious, popular, and even beloved being, the angel not surprisingly has been featured in many films, although critics of film and television will point out that disappointingly few of them have been either well crafted or memorable. When, however, a film featuring an angel has succeeded, it has tended to become a classic. The two most popular are *It's a Wonderful Life* (1946) and *The Bishop's Wife* (1947). Another brilliant work is director Wim Wenders's *Wings of Desire* (1988). As is obvious with *It's a Wonderful Life* and *The Bishop's Wife,* angels have often appeared in films concerned with the Christmas season, bringing joy, hope, and promise into the lives of ordinary people, normally poor mortals struggling with some crisis or at some emotional or spiritual crossroads. Such an undertaking is one of the most important of all angelic missions, and films have made the most (or often the least) of the dramatic potential of human lives touched by the divine. This theme is not limited to films, of course, as television over the years has offered its own angel programs, beyond even what some might complain is the *ad nauseam* airing of Christmas favorites like *It's a Wonderful Life.* Actor-director Michael Landon (d. 1991) helped create one of the most popular of all angels in Jonathan, the compassionate but wistful being in the TV series *Highway to Heaven,* which ran for many years on NBC. Recently CBS has aired the program *Touched by an Angel,* and the continuing public fascination with all things angelic guarantees that other productions will be forthcoming. The table below offers some of the more notable (or eminently forgettable) films featuring angels over the years. (See box; see also "Death Goes to the Movies" under *Death, Angel of,* for films presenting the angel of death.)

ANGEL FILMS

All That Jazz (1974) Cast: Roy Scheider and
   Jessica Lange.

Almost an Angel (1990) Cast: Paul Hogan, Linda
   Kozlowski, and Elias Koteas.

Angel Levine, The (1970) Cast: Zero Mostel and
   Harry Belafonte.

Angel on My Shoulder (1946) Cast: Paul Muni,
   Anne Baxter, and Claude Rains.

Angel on My Shoulder (1980) Cast: Peter Strauss,
   Richard Kiley, and Barbara Hershey.

Angel Who Pawned Her Harp, The (1954) Cast:
   Diane Cilento and Felix Aylmer.

Angelic Conversations (1985) Cast: Paul Reynolds
   and Philip Williamson.

Angels in the Outfield (1951) Cast: Paul Douglas,
   Keenan Wynn, and Janet Leigh.

Angels in the Outfield (1994) Cast: Danny Glover
   and Christopher Lloyd.

Barbarella (1968) Cast: Jane Fonda, John Phillip
   Law, and Milo O'Shea.

Bible, The (1966) John Huston, Peter O'Toole,
   George C. Scott, and Ava Gardner.

Bishop's Wife, The (1947) Cast: Cary Grant,
   Loretta Young, and David Niven.

Cabin in the Sky (1943) Cast: Eddie Anderson
   and Ethel Waters.

Charley and the Angel (1973) Cast: Fred
   MacMurray, Cloris Leachman, Harry Morgan,
   and Kurt Russell.

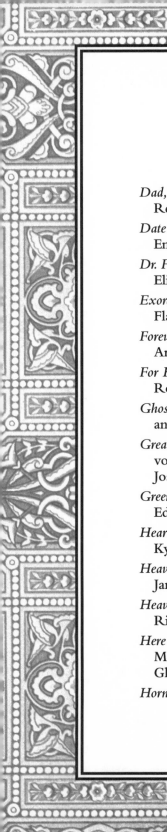

Dad, the Angel and Me (1994) Cast: Judge
Reinhold and Carol Kane.

Date with an Angel (1987) Cast: Phoebe Cates,
Emmanuelle Beart, and Michael E. Knight.

Dr. Faustus (1967) Cast: Richard Burton and
Elizabeth Taylor.

Exorcist III (1990) Cast: George C. Scott, Ed
Flanders, and Brad Dourif.

Forever Darling (1956) Cast: Lucille Ball, Desi
Arnaz, and James Mason.

For Heaven's Sake (1950) Cast: Clifton Webb,
Robert Cummings, and Edmund Gwenn.

Ghost (1990) Cast: Patrick Swayze, Demi Moore,
and Whoopi Goldberg.

Greatest Story Ever Told, The (1965) Cast: Max
von Sydow, Charlton Heston, Telly Savalas,
Jose Ferrer, and Angela Lansbury.

Green Pastures (1936) Cast: Rex Ingram and
Eddie Anderson.

Heart and Soul (1993) Cast: Robert Downey, Jr.,
Kyra Sedgwick, and David Paymer.

Heaven Can Wait (1978) Cast: Warren Beatty,
James Mason, Buck Henry, and Dyan Cannon.

Heavenly Kid, The (1985) Cast: Lewis Smith,
Richard Mulligan, and Jane Kaczmarek.

Here Comes Mr. Jordan (1941) Cast: Robert
Montgomery, Claude Rains, and James
Gleason.

Horn Blows at Midnight, The (1945) Cast: Jack

Benny, Alexis Smith, Dolores Moran, and John Alexander.

I Married an Angel (1942) Cast: Jeanette MacDonald, Nelson Eddy, and Edward Everett Horton.

It Happened One Christmas (1977) Cast: Marlo Thomas, Cloris Leachman, Wayne Rogers, and Orson Welles.

It's a Wonderful Life (1946) Cast: Jimmy Stewart, Henry Travers, Donna Reed, and Lionel Barrymore.

Jesus of Nazareth (1976) Cast: Robert Powell, James Farentino, James Mason, Anne Bancroft, and Rod Steiger.

Kid with the Broken Halo, The (1982) Cast: Gary Coleman, Robert Guillaume, and June Allyson.

King of Kings (1961) Cast: Jeffrey Hunter, Robert Ryan, Siobhan McKenna, and Hurd Hatfield.

L'Ange (The Angel) (1982) Cast: Animated.

Made in Heaven (1987) Cast: Timothy Hutton, Kelly McGillis, Maureen Stapleton.

Montana Mike (1947) Cast: Robert Cummings, Brian Donlevy, and Marjorie Reynolds.

Oh, Heavenly Dog (1980) Cast: Benji, Chevy Chase, Jane Seymour, and Omar Sharif.

One Magic Christmas (1985) Cast: Harry Dean Stanton, Mary Steenburgen, and Arthur Hill.

Sodom and Gomorrah (1963) Cast: Stewart Granger, Stanley Baker, and Pier Angeli.

Stairway to Heaven (1946) Cast: David Niven, Roger Livesey, and Kim Hunter.

Ten Commandments, The (1956) Cast: Charlton Heston, Yul Brynner, Cedric Hardwicke, and Anne Baxter.

Two of a Kind (1983) Cast: John Travolta, Olivia Newton-John, Beatrice Straight, Charles Durning, and Oliver Reed.

Wholly Moses! (1980) Cast: Dudley Moore, John Houseman, Laraine Newman.

Wings of Desire (1988) Cast: Bruno Ganz, Peter Falk, and Solveig Dommartin.

Yolanda and the Thief (1945) Cast: Fred Astaire, Lucille Bremer, Mildred Natwick, and Frank Morgan.

🍃 **FIRE, ANGEL OF** An angel who has been given a number of identifications and has been the source of inspiration both in art and music. One of the most fearsome angels of fire was mentioned in a legend concerning the Israeli king Jair, who was a devoted worshiper of the pagan god Baal. This ruler constructed a sanctuary to Baal and commanded his people to make sacrifices. When seven men were unwilling to do so, he ordered them burned alive. "And when they [Jair's servants] had put them in the fire, Nathaniel [Nathanael], the angel who was in charge of fire, came forth and extinguished the fire and burned the servants of Jair. But he let the seven men escape in such a way that none of the people saw them, because he had struck the people with blindness. And when Jair came to the place, he was burned with fire, and before he burned him up, the angel of the Lord said to him, 'Hear the word of the Lord before you die.' And these words the Lord says: 'I have raised you up from the land and appointed you leader over my people, but you rose up and corrupted my covenant and deceived and sought to burn my servants with fire, because they chastised you. Those who were burned with corruptible fire, now are made alive with a living fire and are freed; but you will die,' says the Lord, 'and in the fire in which you will die there you will have a dwelling place.' And afterward he burned him up, and he came to the pillar of Baal and demolished it and burned Baal along with the people who stood by, that is a thousand men" (Pseudo-Philo 38). Aside from Nathaniel, the archangel Uriel is often called the flame of god (his name means this). In the Book of Revelation reference is made to "the angel who has power over fire."

The angel of fire was the subject additionally of art, music, and literature. Russian composer Sergei Prokofiev (1891–1953) wrote the *L'Ange de Feu (The Angel of Fire)* from 1919 to 1927. Based on the novel by Valerie Brusoff, the opera tells of the angel of fire named Madiel. Finally, the renowned painter Marc Chagall in his painting *Descent of the Red Angel* presents the harrowing arrival of the angel of fire into the world.

🍃 **FLAMES** A choir or order of angels that appears in a certain aspect of Jewish lore, as noted by Voltaire in one of his works, "Of Angels, Genies, and Devils." An angelic choir by the name of flames is not normally counted among the traditionally accepted orders of angels (see *Choirs*). They can perhaps be equated with one of the recognized choirs of angels, although it would be a matter of speculation as to which one.

🙿 **FOOD** The nourishment taken by angels. Although entirely spiritual beings, angels have been the source of much speculation by theologians and scholars as to what they might eat. There has been nearly unanimous agreement among saints and experts, based upon passages in the Bible, that angel food is the famous sustenance from heaven, manna. Manna is described in the Book of Exodus—sent down to feed Moses and the house of Israel—as being "like coriander seed, white, and the taste of it was like wafers made with honey." The name *manna* is from the Aramaic, meaning "What is this?"—the words uttered by the Jews following Moses in the desert when they first encountered it as it rained down upon them from heaven after their departure from Egypt.

That manna is food for angels is taken from several beautiful passages in the Old Testament. In Psalm 78, it is written: "And he [the Lord] rained down upon them manna to eat, and gave them the grain of heaven. Man ate the bread of the angels; he sent them food in abundance." The prophet Elijah was also fed by an angel, given their food as commanded by the Lord: "And he lay down and slept under a broom tree; and behold, an angel touched him, and said to him, 'Arise and eat.' And he looked, and behold, there was at his head a cake baked on hot stones and a jar of water. And he ate and drank, and lay down again. And the angel of the Lord came again a second time, and touched him, and said, 'Arise and eat, else the journey will be too great for you.' And he arose, and ate and drank, and went in strength of that food forty days and forty nights."

One of the dissenting opinions concerning that angelic diet was offered in the delightful 1971 short story "A Very Old Man with Enormous Wings" by Gabriel García Márquez. In that tale, a battered, storm-tossed angel, with "huge buzzard wings, dirty and half-plucked," lands in a startled mortal's backyard. Uncertain as to what to feed the angel, the mortal is assured by a neighbor that angels eat only mothballs. In the end, however, the tattered angelic visitor consumes nothing but eggplant mush—not manna, but nourishing enough.

🙿 **FORCES** An angelic choir or order first identified or named by the Greek theologian and doctor of the Church St. John of Damascus (d.c. 754). According to the saint, the forces are to be identified with the choirs of powers or virtues and are only one of a variety of alternative angelic choirs proposed over the centuries.

🕸 **FOUR ANGELS** The name given to the four otherwise nameless angels who appear in the Book of Revelation: "I saw four angels standing at the four corners of the earth, holding back the four winds of the earth, that no wind might blow on earth or sea or against any tree" (7:1). These angels should probably not be confused with the angels of the four winds usually identified with Michael, Uriel, Gabriel, and Raphael, although they may appear in Revelation with specific, albeit anonymous, tasks. In the Old Testament Book of Zachariah is told the vision of the prophet Zachariah relating four chariots riding forth from two mountains of bronze, the chariots interpreted as spirits or angelic guardians: "The first chariots had red horses, the second black horses, the third white horses, and the fourth chariot dappled grey horses. Then I said to the angel who spoke with me, 'What are these, my Lord?' And the angel answered me, 'These are going out to the four winds of heaven, after presenting themselves before the Lord of all the earth. The chariot with the black horses goes to the north country, the white ones go toward the west country, the dappled ones go toward the south country.' When the steeds came out, they were impatient to get off and patrol the earth" (6:1–7)

The four angels on their chariots, as described in the Book of Zachariah; by Gustave Doré.

Another important group is that of the gathered four archangels, the four leading figures of their choir and some of the most important angelic princes both in angelology and in the grand scheme of heaven. The exact list of the four angels tends to vary, however, depending upon culture or source. Commonly, the archangels are listed as Michael, Gabriel, Raphael (or Suriel), and Uriel. In Islamic lore the four are Michael, Gabriel, Azrael (the angel of death), and Israfel (the angel of the end of the world).

The four angels of the winds: Raphael, Gabriel, Michael, and Uriel; by Albrecht Dürer.

🙟 **FOUR WINDS, ANGELS OF THE** The name given to those angels who guard or preside over the four winds of the earth. It might perhaps be more appropriate to call them the archangels of the four winds, as each belongs to the order of archangels. The four are Raphael (the west), Gabriel (the north), Michael (the east), and Uriel (south, with the aid of Raphael). At times they are to be equated with the four angels of the Book of Revelation. (See also *Four Angels.*)

🙟 **FRAVASHI** The spirits of the dead in Zoroastrian belief. The fravashis are thought to be the eternal aspect of a person, continuing on after the physical body has ceased to function. The significance of the fravashi is its activity in caring for the soul of the individual on earth, a division existing between the soul and the spirit. It is thus possible to equate the actions of the fravashi to those of a guardian angel or spirit. It is believed by some scholars that the Zoroastrians taught that the fravashi entered into this caretakership or guardianship in order to advance the vital cause of goodness—as epitomized or rooted in Ahura Mazda—in the world.

🙟 **FURNACE, ANGEL OF THE** The otherwise unnamed angel who was sent to the aid of Shadrach, Meshach, and Abednego, who were thrown into a furnace by the Babylonian king Nebuchadnezzar after they refused to worship before a great image of gold. The event, recorded in the Old Testament Book of Daniel (3), declares that the infuriated Babylonian ruler ordered the three recalcitrant princes cast into the "burning fiery furnace," which had been prepared for any who might refuse to worship. The three were bound and tossed into the flames. To the amazement of Nebuchadnezzar and his court, however, the princes remained untouched in the heat (which had apparently burned several soldiers who had approached it), and even more amazing, they were joined by a fourth figure. The king exclaims: " 'Did we not toss three men bound into the fire?' They [the court] assured the king, 'True, O king.' He answered, 'But I see four men bound loose, walking in the midst in the fire, and they are not hurt; and the appearance of the fourth is like a son of the gods.' " Freeing the three prisoners, Nebuchadnezzar states: "Blessed be the God of Meshach, Shadrach, and Abednego, who has sent his angel and delivered his servants, who trusted in him, and set at nought the king's command, and yielded up their bodies rather than serve and worship any God except their own God." While not named in the Bible—and disappearing before any identification could be made—the angel of the furnace has been called Emmanuel ("God is with us") in Jewish lore.

GABRIEL An archangel whose name means "God is my strength" and who is one of the most beloved of all members of the heavenly host. Gabriel is also one of the highest ranked of all angels and is only one of two (or three) actually named angels in the entire Bible, with Michael and Raphael (who is mentioned in the often termed apocryphal Book of Tobit). Gabriel is revered by Christians, Jews, and Muslims and with Michael has been the subject of artists, theologians, and poets.

Gabriel appears four times in the Old and New Testaments. In the Old Testament he explains the dreams of Daniel and is described thusly: "The man Gabriel, who I had seen in the vision at the first, came to me in swift flight at the time of the evening sacrifice" (Daniel 9:21). In the New Testament he foretells the birth of John the Baptist and, most famous of all, makes the Annunciation to the Virgin Mary, for which he is termed the angel of the Annunciation.

Among the Jews, Gabriel's power and strength—as implied by his very name—were frequently noted in legends and tales. He has been called the angel of the power of God and also the angel of judgment and has been equated with thunder and majesty. In the role of judgment angel he will supposedly appear on the last day and blow the final trumpet that will call all of the living and the dead to come forth and face the final, irrevocable judgment of the Lord. A number of colossal achievements have additionally been attributed to him, some of which are also credited to otherwise nameless angels (or angels of destruction), such as the obliteration of Sodom and Gomorrah, the massacre of the Assyrian army of 185,000, the wrestling episode with Jacob (see *Dark Angel*), and the burial of Moses. Elsewhere in Jewish lore he is reputed to be the angel of justice and one of the archangels, as noted in the First Book of Enoch, where he is declared the guardian of the Garden of Eden and chief of the angelic

choir of the cherubim, a post that would rank him among the foremost of all angels in the celestial hierarchy. He is declared in the Third Book of Enoch to be a prince of heaven, in charge of the sixth heaven, although other sources state his realm to be the first heaven. Regardless, he stands ever at the side of God and is the prime minister or chief minister of heaven. This is supposedly proven by the old Babylonian legend that states that Gabriel once fell out of favor and was replaced for several weeks by Dubbiel. His absence made possible the cruel oppression of the Jewish people by the Persians (whose patron angel Dubbiel happened to be), but after making a brilliant suggestion about some matter, Gabriel was restored to his position and permitted to enter once more beyond the heavenly curtain that surrounds the throne of God. (See *Dubbiel*.)

The archangel Gabriel; by Melozzo da Forlì, the Uffizi, Florence
(COURTESY ART RESOURCE).

Among Christians, Gabriel is honored for his role in the Annunciation and is foremost of all angelic messengers. The special veneration of the angel, however, probably dates to around the tenth century. He was a figure of high repute during the Middle Ages and was even mentioned by St. Joan of Arc as one of the heavenly visitors who gave her the courage and inspiration to visit the king of France and so begin the momentous events that culminated in her rescue of Orléans in 1431 from the English during the Hundred Years' War. Christian art has made Gabriel one of its favorite subjects, especially as concerns his role in the Annunciation, with works by such masters as da Vinci, Barbieri, Martini, and Raphael. Gabriel's symbol is the lily, and there is a tradition that he is the angel of birth, carefully spending the nine months of pregnancy watching over each unborn child and instructing it on the necessary knowledge of heaven that is an inherent part of all people. Just before birth, though, he touches the baby on the upper lip to make it unable to remember all of the information about heaven until it returns to the spiritual state at death; the sign of Gabriel's touch is the cleft just below the nose. On the basis of this close involvement with conception and birth, some scholars (such as Malcolm Godwin in his delightful 1990 work, *Angels*) have suggested that this angel is actually female. Unfortunately, this ignores the wide writings of theologians that angels are entirely spiritual creatures devoid of gender, referred to in the masculine purely for a common, albeit somewhat sexist, ground for reference.

Known in the Arabic as Jibril, Gabriel has a prominent role in Islamic teachings, for he is believed to have dictated the entire Qur'an, surah by surah, to Muhammad and is called the angel of truth and the chief of the four favored angels. He supposedly had the honor of carrying Muhammad to paradise, transporting him there on Al-Borak. This magical beast had the face of a man but the cheeks of a horse, the wings of an eagle, a body of radiant light, the voice of a man, and eyes like stars. In *Paradise Lost,* Gabriel is the guardian of the earthly Paradise who dispatches angels across the world to hunt for Satan when the evil one descends to the earth and begins the temptation of Adam and Eve.

GADIEL An angel who lives in the fifth of the seven heavens. His name was supposedly used as a word of power among sorcerers and was carried upon or within charms and amulets in the ancient world. Gadiel himself was apparently invoked as a means of repelling evil.

GALGALLIM A Hebrew name meaning "spheres" or "wheels" that is generally accepted as the equivalent of the choir or order of thrones as understood in the Western tradition; also, the other Hebrew term for the order ophanim. In the sense of being wheels, the galgallim are often described as the actual wheels of God's chariots or as chariots themselves. (For other details, see under *Thrones.*)

GARDEN OF EDEN See *Eden, Garden of.*

GAVRIEL An alternative spelling for Gabriel.

GAZARDIYA Also Gazardiel, an angel who in some Jewish legends is responsible for making certain that each day the sun rises and sets as it should and always at the appropriate time. According to another tradition, Gazardiya helps to send the prayers of the faithful upward so that they might be heard by God.

GEHENNA The Hebrew place of eternal suffering, equated with hell. Deriving its name from the Valley of Hinnom (Ge Hinnom), Gehenna was originally a site near Jerusalem where the early Israelites made sacrifices to Baal and Moloch, often children to the latter deity. It was later a dreadful place used to deposit garbage and waste, considered an area of fire and stench because of the perpetual fire maintained there to burn the refuse. Gehenna eventually became the name of the dread underworld, a place of unceasing fire where those deserving punishment were sent. Originally the Jews accepted the belief in Sheol, the grim underworld where all souls of the dead existed in a cheerless eternity. Some Jews, however, conceived of Gehenna as a fell land of punishment. Here were sent the wicked or failing Jews and all Gentiles. In the case of the Jews, though, such time in Gehenna was purgatorial, a period of cleansing after which they enjoyed the fullness of heaven. All Gentiles, unfortunately, spent eternity in this kind of hell. This thinking is clearly rooted in the purpose of the original Gehenna—as a fire-filled place of cleansing. In some legends about Gehenna, the tormented souls were tortured by demons and devils, but other traditions place the duty of punishment at the hands of remorseless angels. The name given to these angelic tormentors was angels of destruction. (See *Destruction, Angels of,* for other details; see also *Hell.*) Gehenna's imagery of hellfire and suffering was continued in the New Testament, becoming part of accepted Christian eschatology (the study of the so-called last things: heaven, hell, death, and judgment).

GENDER OF ANGELS See box on pages 118–119.

GENIUS A Latin term found in the religion of ancient Rome (pl. genii) for a king or guardian spirit or angel-like intelligence who acted as guardian over an individual, a house, or even an entire nation. The genius thus had a variety of understandings, but perhaps the most common was as a guardian spirit of the male (called a genius) head of a house or family and of the female (the juno) matron or house mother. The genius was also honored as the embodiment of the higher self, as well as of one's appetites or even desires and incli-

GENDER OF ANGELS

Angels are generally described by theologians as beings composed entirely of spirit, existing in a spiritual state and assuming corporeal form only through the express command and will of God, normally in order to accomplish some task or needed intervention in earthly affairs. There is no apparent limitation as to their form or appearance, and angels have been reported in the guise of men, women, and children. As beings of spirit, however, angels are of no specific gender or sex; they exist in a sexless state without the need to procreate and derive their fullness of being through a closeness to God, in whom they give their total love. That angels have no need for marriage or family life is deduced by Christ in the Gospel of Matthew (22:28–30) when he observed that angels neither marry nor are given in marriage.

Despite this genderless life, angels have, over the years, been presented in Scripture, art, and literature as possessing at least the appearance of men. The Bible itself, for example, uses masculine terms to describe angels and gives masculine names to the angels Gabriel, Michael, and Raphael. Such nomenclature can be explained by the necessity of giving angels understandable and familiar form for the reader; the writers of the books of the Bible chose the one closest to their own, presenting the angels in a male image, personifying male attributes. At work was also a cultural bias in favor of the male. The Qur'an (surah 53:27) would seem to support this tradition of male angels by the declaration "Surely those who believe not in the Hereafter name the angels with female names."

Against this male dominance are other customs, theories, and even some art. Female angels or angel-like beings are found in legend—such as the shekinah in Jewish lore and Pistis Sophia among the Gnostics—as well as in some Islamic tales, such as the huris. Female angels have also been depicted in art; for example, there are the Wilton Diptych of the late fourteenth century and the girl angel sculpted by Niccolo dell'Arca in the fifteenth century. Even more imaginative is the argument, included in the charming 1990 work *Angels* by Malcolm Godwin, that the archangel Gabriel was actually female.

While painting and sculpture heavily favor the depiction of male angels (with the noted exceptions), there are also to be found many works in which the gender of angels is uncertain or difficult to determine. This indeterminacy implies neither a hermaphroditic tendency nor a personal ambivalence on the part of the angels. Rather, it denotes a proper androgyny, in which the very best aspects of woman and man are combined to create a noble, pure being of the divine. (See also *Appearance, Angelic; Gabriel;* and *Female Angels.*)

nations. So pervasive was the belief in the genius that one's birthday was celebrated in terms not of honoring oneself, but in giving reverence to the genius who was guardian over one's life. Some of the more interesting genii were those of places or buildings, known as genii loci (geniuses of place). The genii loci were said to exist for palaces, homes, associations or guilds, and the Roman state itself (the genius populi Romani). Just as the genius and juno can be compared to the guardian angel, so can the genius loci be said to equal the patron or guardian angel of places or nations. The genius was derived largely from the Greek daimon or daemon. In this way it can be considered one of the foreshadowings of the angels in later thinking, minus the tendency or custom of giving such beings actual worship with offerings, prayers, sacrifices, and small shrines or temples. In later Christian teachings, the worship of angels was strictly forbidden, as such adoration was limited exclusively to God. Angels—like saints—should be revered rather than worshiped.

The Roman genius: Venus and Mars on a Pompeiian wall painting; Museo Archeologico Nazionale, Naples (COURTESY ART RESOURCE).

🜨 **GERMAEL** An angel whose name means "majesty of God." According to legend, he was one of the angels sent by God to create Adam from the earth, a task also ascribed to several other angels, including Gabriel, Michael, and Israfel. In one tale Germael, with his fellow angels, failed in the undertaking because the world would not surrender its dust, fearing as it did that humankind would turn away from God. In the place of these angels God sent forth from heaven the angel Azrael; this hardfisted angel did not fail.

🜨 **GETHSEMANE, ANGEL OF** The angel who came to Christ in the garden of Gethsemane to give comfort and fortification during the terrible doubt-filled hours before Jesus' arrest and the start of his Passion, culminating in his Crucifixion. As was written in the Gospel of St. Luke (22:43–44): "And there appeared to him an angel from heaven, strengthening him. And being in agony, he prayed more earnestly; and his sweat became like great drops of blood falling down upon the ground." While the angel of Gethsemane remains unnamed in Scripture, lore declares that it was probably the famed archangel Gabriel, although it is possible that the angel was actually the archangel Chamuel.

The angel of Gethsemane gives comfort to Christ in the hours before his Passion; by Albrecht Dürer.

GEZURIYA A member of the angelic choir or order of powers who has command over at least six other angels. One of them is Gazardiya, the angel who ensures the daily movement of the sun.

GLORIOUS ONES The name used in the Second Book of Enoch for the seven great archangels whom Enoch visited while on a tour of the heavens. He met them during his arrival at the sixth heaven. "And I saw there seven angels, grouped together, brilliant and very glorious." (See also *Archangels.*) Another use of the name occurs in some translation of the New Testament Letter of Jude (8), where it is written: "Yet in like manner these men in the dreaming defile in the flesh, reject authority, and revile the glorious ones."

GLORY, ANGELS OF A group of angels who, as written in the Third Book of Enoch, reside in the highest heaven, called arabot by the Hebrew tradition of Enoch. They are said to number 660,000, standing in the high, honorific place near the very throne of God. They thus lead the very heavens in endless praise of God. The angel Sandalphon, one of the great angelic princes, has also been called an angel of glory.

GNOSTICISM A heretical sect of Christianity that flourished in the first centuries A.D. It stressed the existence of two main worlds, a perfect and good spiritual one and an imperfect and wicked material one. The Gnostics also had a belief in angellike beings, such as the aeons and archons. (For details, see *Aeons, Archons,* and *Demiurge.*)

GOD, ANGEL OF The term used often interchangeably with the angel of the Lord to describe an angelic visitor who is fulfilling some mission. Under certain circumstances, however, the name has also been used to denote God himself. The latter understanding is especially appropriate when interpreting angel of God or angel of the Lord as it appears in the Old Testament. (See also *Lord, Angel of the.*)

GONFALONS Apparently, a group or even choir of angels who form part of the "imperial host" described by John Milton in his *Paradise Lost.* They are spoken of by the angel Raphael:

> *Of angels by imperial summons called*
> *Innumerable before the almighty throne*
> *Forthwith from all the ends of heaven appeared*
> *Under the hierarchs in orders bright*
> *Ten thousand thousand ensigns high advanced,*
> *Standards, and gonfalons twixt van and rears*
> *Stream in the air; and for distinction serve*
> *Of hierarchies, of orders, and degrees.*

GREAT AND WONDERFUL The name used by the archangel Michael in a legend recounted by Clara Erskine Clement in her 1898 work *Angels in Art.* According to the tale, Michael was sent to the earth to bring word to the Virgin Mary that her death was approaching. When he arrived, she looked up at him and asked his name. He replied merely, "I am Great and Wonderful." (See also *Michael.*)

GRIGORI The Hebrew name for the watchers. (For details, see under *Watchers.*)

GUARDIAN ANGELS Also called tutelary angels, the well-established and widely accepted belief that all people (as well as nations, cities, and churches) have a special angel who stays with them, watching over their lives and encouraging their spiritual well-being and happiness. Many deny that guardian angels (or any angels, for that matter) could possibly exist, but others state, with the support of Scripture, theological writings, and common sense, that they do live, even if mortals forget or obdurately refuse to acknowledge their presence. The idea of the guardian angel is found in Judaism, Christianity, and Islam, and the roots of the belief date to the earliest times. Among the Babylonians and Assyrians there were spirit guardians (the keribu) who stood watch over the gates of temples and palaces, and Nabopolassar, father of King Nebuchadnezzar II the Great (d. 562 B.C.) of Babylon, once proclaimed that Marduk (the Babylonian deity) had sent a minister of grace to assist him in all things and to permit all his undertakings to succeed. Plutarch, the neo-Platonists, and other philosophers of the ancient world readily accepted the notion of a helping spirit.

In the Old Testament are found numerous references to angels providing assistance to mortals, from the rescue of Lot from Sodom and Gomorrah to the aid given Daniel in the interpretation of his dreams. In Exodus (32:34), Moses is told, "My angel shall go before you," and in the Book of Tobit (which some faiths do not accept as canonical), the angel Raphael gives much-needed help to Tobias. Jewish lore teaches that each and every human being is assigned a guardian angel at birth, while the Talmud assures us that all people are attended by eleven thousand ministering angels. The Qabalah states that the chiefs of the guardian angels are Michael, Uriel, Gabriel, and Raphael.

Christian teaching, based in large part on the New Testament, is even more precise and organized. Christ speaks in the Gospel of Matthew (18:10) about the "little ones" each having a guardian angel who sees the face of God in heaven. Elsewhere, guardian angels give comfort to Christ in the garden of Gethsemane and rescue St. Peter from prison. Perhaps the most specific declaration is found in the Letter to the Hebrews (1:14): "Are they [the angels] not all ministering spirits sent forth to serve, for the sake of those who are to obtain salvation?" On the basis of these quotes, theologians throughout the history of the Church have developed a comprehensive teaching on guardian angels. These doctrines are not considered essential elements of the faith and are therefore not binding upon Catholics, but belief in these angels is considered valuable because, as St. Jerome put it, "How great the dignity of the soul, since each one has from his birth an angel commissioned to guard it." St. Thomas Aquinas, one of history's foremost experts on angels, stated that all people have guardian angels. They remain with one throughout life, staying ever at one's side even during sin. They foster good works and help to direct the soul to salvation, but only if the soul is so inclined to be led. They cannot influence the will, but they do act upon the senses and project themselves upon the imagination and intellect, discouraging evil acts. According to Thomas, the angels remain even after death, standing with the soul in heaven; there, however, it does not encourage salvation, but assists in the glimpsing of the final brightness of eternal bliss. All guardian angels are taken from the lowest ranks of the celestial hierarchy, namely the choir of angels. Pope Pius XI (r. 1922–1939) had such an unshakable belief in his guardian angel that he used him to settle important or troubling matters. Pius once said that anytime he was faced with a difficult situation, he would pray to his guardian angel and ask him to have a chat with the guardian angels of everyone else involved to make their mortal charges more receptive to what was proper or best for the Church. This apparently never failed to have the desired effect. The Church long celebrated October 2 as the Feast of Guardian Angels and taught schoolchildren this prayer:

> *Angel of God, my guardian dear*
> *To whom His love commits me here;*
> *Ever this day (or night) be at my side,*
> *To light and guard, to rule and guide.*

Among the Muslims, the guardian angel was embodied by the hafaza, the angel recorders who stood by each person in sets of pairs, protecting the living from harm by the roving spirits of evil. The hafaza also had the task of writing down every act, both good and evil, performed by the human in their keeping.

Another custom related to the guardian angels is that of the tutelary angels, or angels of the nations. Called also ethnarchs, these angels were assigned at the earliest time a kind of stewardship over the nations of the earth. There were thought to be seventy of them, including Michael (angel of Israel), Duma or Rahab (angel of Egypt), Dubbiel (angel of Persia), and Samael (angel of Rome). They apparently took to their jobs with considerable enthusiasm, for legends speak of their gradual biases in favor of their appointed people, so much so that Dubbiel and Duma became dedicated enemies of Israel. Unable to maintain their angelic purity because of their bias, the angels—with one obvious exception—all became corrupt and fell from grace. They were either destroyed or forced to join the ranks of the fallen angels in hell. The only exception was Michael, who remained among the blessed angels even though he may have shown excessive favor to Israel. This was acceptable to the Lord, given the fact that the Jews were the Chosen People. It is unclear whether the Lord appointed replacements to the fallen angels of the nations, but there is a tradition that all nations have an angel watching over them, much as there are supposed to be demons and devils who make certain countries their favorite targets for sin and temptation. William Blake touched upon this with his drawing of the angel of the United States. (See also *Patriarchs.*)

GUARDS A type of angelic sentinel mentioned several times by John Milton in *Paradise Lost.* It is unclear whether the guards according to Milton were their own angelic choir or were merely posted angels from some other choir and receiving duties as guards. In one passage they are under the authority of the archangel Gabriel:

> *Betwixt these rocky pillars Gabriel sat*
> *Chief of the angelic guards, awaiting night*
> *About him exercised heroic games*
> *The unarmed youth of heaven, but nigh at hand*
> *Celestial armory, shields, helms and spears,*
> *Hung high with diamond flaming, and with gold.*
> *(Book IV)*

Later, in Book XII, Michael is noted as their chief. He declares:

> *Let us descend now therefore from this top*
> *Of speculation; for the hour precise*
> *Exacts our parting hence; and see the guards,*
> *By me encamped on yonder hill, expect*
> *Their motion, at whose front a flaming sword,*
> *In signal of remove, waves fiercely round.*

HAAIAH An angel belonging to the angel order of dominations who was mentioned in angelic lore as recorded in the traditions of the Qabalah. Haaiah is credited with authority over the fields of diplomacy, working to guide the labors of representatives and ambassadors.

HABRIEL An angel who is a member of the choir or order of powers. He is considered a suitable angel or spirit for invoking or summoning in certain magical rites among the Hebrews.

HADARIEL Also called Hadarniel and Hadramiel, an angel who has a fairly prominent place in Jewish legend, serving traditionally as the much-feared and quite imposing keeper of the gates of heaven. Hadariel, whose name means "the Glory [or Greatness] of God," is one of the tallest beings in all of heaven, standing some sixty myriads of parasangs high, a distance calculated to exceed two million miles. Amazingly he is not the tallest of angels, still being dwarfed by the truly humongous Sandalphon. Nevertheless, Hadariel has a voice so dominating that when he shouts forth the proclamations of the Lord, the sound echoes through the two hundred thousand heavens, each word accompanied by twelve thousand flashes of lightning.

Hadariel figures in the legends surrounding Moses. When the Lawgiver visited heaven, the angel barred his way. Moses was much impressed but pleaded that the Lord had granted his blessing on the visit in order to give to him and the Jewish people the Torah (containing the Pentateuch, the first five books of the Old Testament). The

Lord himself soon intervened, and Hadariel was reduced to trembling before Moses when the Lawgiver uttered the supreme name of God. Hadariel thereafter served as Moses' guide through the celestial mansions.

HADRAMIEL See *Hadariel.*

HAFAZA A type of angel found in Islamic lore that can be considered the Muslim equivalent of the guardian angel. The hafaza, however, are not assigned one by one to each person. Rather, each living soul is guarded by four angels, two keeping watch during the day and two remaining vigilant during the night. Their protective duties are centered in defending the soul against the assaults of Satan and evil spirits, especially the jinn (the Islamic demon). Mortals should be most alert or concerned with their well-being at dawn and at sunset, for at those times the hafaza change their guard and thus the protective barrier they form is at its weakest. The person can thus be assured that at this crucial opportunity the jinn or other evil beings strike.

The hafaza have one other important task. They endlessly write down in great books every action—good and bad—committed by their ward. As there are four angels, the living can be assured that every little deed, no matter how small, will not escape their attention. When the person dies, the four present their books, which are kept until the final Day of Judgment, when they will be read and used to determine whether the mortal is deserving of admission into heaven. (See also *Guardian Angels.*)

HALO Also called the nimbus, a circular band or disk that surrounds the head of a holy person or an angel, most often seen in art. The halo is one of the classic symbols of holiness, perhaps derived from the long belief in the aura, the emanations of light that are seen surrounding all persons, but which are especially pronounced and extremely bright when seen around a great holy figure. The halo was used in assorted depictions by Hellenic and Roman artists in the pre-Christian period and even after, such as for the sun god Helios and also the Roman emperors; in the latter sense, they helped to present the emperor as more than human. The halo, more properly termed the nimbus (Latin for "cloud"), was to receive its fullest development in Christian art, with three main styles of presentation: a fish form, called the *vesica piscis,* in the rough form of a fish when showing

Angels with halos; from Benozzo Gozzoli, *The Savior and Angels,* S. Francesco,
Montefalco (COURTESY ART RESOURCE).

Christ (it encircled the entire figure); a radiating circle, similar to the
sun or a star; and the most common, a circle. In the case of the regular circular halo, there was a tradition that those of angels should be
decorated with a circle of small pointed rays, surrounded by a wider
circle of quatrefoils. The use of halos or nimbi for angels dates to at
least the fifth century and actually predates the similar adoption of
halos for the saints and even the Virgin Mary. The golden age of halo
painting was, of course, the so-called Age of Faith, the Middle Ages.
Gradually, however, as styles changed and artists moved toward the
naturalism of the Renaissance, there was a tendency to deemphasize
the halo as interfering with the proper expression of figures. The halo
nearly grew extinct as artists solved this dilemma by utilizing an emanation of light more in keeping with the aura than the nimbus. While
the halo followed certain set forms during the Middle Ages, there was
considerable room for variation, one of the most lovely being the
placement of "Sanctus, Sanctus, Sanctus" in a circle beneath the qua-
trefoil, representing the joyous utterances of the angels as they sing in
praise of God. Today, no angel costume is quite complete without the
halo; it is as important as the wings and the harp. (See also box, "Appearance of Angels," pages 20–21; see also *Art, Angels in.*)

🐚 **HAMON** A high-ranking and apparently powerful angelic prince mentioned in the Third Book of Enoch. In that compendium of angelic lore, Hamon is described as "the great, terrible, honored, beautiful, and dreaded Prince, who makes all the denizens of the heights when the time comes to recite [the endless praises of God], as it is written, 'At the voice of Hamon the peoples flee, when you arise, the nations scatter' " (18). In some traditions, and according to St. Jerome, Hamon can be considered or equated with the archangel Gabriel.

🐚 **HANIEL** Also Hanael and Aniel, an angel whose name means "the grace of God" and who is generally credited with the title of prince or chief of the angelic orders or choirs of the principalities and virtues. As such, he is honored as one of the seven great archangels in several lists, most notably that included in the 1635 work by Thomas Heywood, *The Hierarchy of the Blessed Angels.* Interestingly, his name does not occur in the most influential lists of the archangels, namely those of Dionysius the Areopagite, St. Gregory the Great, and the Third Book of Enoch.

🐚 **HARP** The most commonly associated musical instrument played by angels, today one of the essential identifying features in the attributes—or even the caricature—of the angel. Over the centuries angels have been depicted playing trumpets (the instrument long thought to be played at the end of the world by Gabriel or Israfel), horns, drums, and violins, or using their exquisite voices in songs of praise, but the harp remains the definitive form of angelic instrumental expression. The origins of this connection can probably be traced to the Old Testament and King David. That famed king and composer of many of the Psalms is traditionally credited with using a harp; if, presumably, it was good enough for him, then angels could use it with impunity. In an occult or spiritual sense, the harp's rough triangular shape represents the trinity (God, the Son, and the Holy Spirit) whom the angels serve. It also has ties to the ancient aeolian harps, kinds of instruments that caught and used the wind to create their sound (*aeolian* is from the Greek meaning "wind"), an expression of the celestial or heavenly nature that angels bring with them during their visits to the earth. The harp, however, does little to express the staggering and indescribably beautiful music that is thought to surround the throne of God, the so-called Music of the Spheres—the reverberation not merely of the joyous adoration of the angels for their Creator, but the very echoing of the music of the cosmos, the harmonious existence of all Creation bowing down before the One. (See also *Music.*)

HARUT AND MARUT Also Haroth and Maroth, two leading angels who appeared in both Persian and Islamic legend. Among the Persians, Harut and Marut were two very formidable angels who knew the incomparably powerful secret name of God. According to the Qur'an (surah 2:102), Harut and Marut were two angels who came down from heaven and taught certain secrets to humanity, interpreted variously as magic and sorcery or the workings of government. Islamic legend also tells the tale of Harut and Marut and how they joined the ranks of the fallen angels. They belonged to those angelic servants who were opposed to the special place given to the mortals created by Allah, ever speaking of them in derogatory terms. The Lord, however, replied to their lament about the sinful humans by stating that the angels, too, would have fallen into sin. Disputing their own Creator, the angels offered to send down representatives to test whether this was true. Harut and Marut were chosen, descending to the world with the express commands not to engage in pagan worship, drinking, and fornication. Not surprisingly, they took to drinking, lusted after a gorgeous woman, and then murdered a hapless man who had seen their crimes. For their failings, Harut and Marut were suspended by their feet in a dread pit in the land of Babel (or Babylon).

As an added wrinkle to this tale, the famed Persian Islamic poet Hafiz (d.c. 1390) spoke of the woman who was the object of the longings of Marut and Harut. Named Zuhrah, she was given by the angels the secret name of God during their frenzied longing; she uttered the name and was thereby caused to be elevated into the heavens, where she became identified with the planet Venus, the beautiful morning star in Islamic mythology.

HASHMAL Also known as Chasmal and Hasmal, the chief angel or leader of the angelic choir of the hashmallim (or hamshallim), the Hebrew equivalent of the later order or choir of dominations. Hashmal is said in Jewish lore to be the "fire-speaking angel" who is found near the holy throne of God. Aside from Hashmal, the chiefs of the dominations or hashmallim are said to be Zadkiel, Muriel, and Yahriel. (See also *Dominations* and *Hashmallim.*)

🌀 **HASHMALLIM** The Hebrew name given to one of the choirs or orders of angels; the hashmallim are considered the angelic equivalent of the later choir of dominations (or dominions). They are thus to be equated with the high order of angels occupying the fourth place in the nine choirs and the first place in the second holy triad of angels, with the virtues and powers. Also called the hamshallim, they are said to be under the command or leadership of Hashmal, Yahriel, Zadkiel, and Muriel. In Jewish lore the hashmallim reside in a realm under the care of the great Metatron. In that holy land are suspended the celestial letters of the holy name of God. (See also *Hashmal* and *Dominations.*) The hashmallim can also be considered analogous to the angels called the hayyoth, who carry or bear the throne of God and are under the authority of the dread angel Hayliel YHWH.

🌀 **HASTENING ANGEL** The name given to the archangel Michael by John Milton in the closing passages of *Paradise Lost* (Book XII), when the poet describes the tragic expulsion of Adam and Eve from the Garden of Eden:

> *The brandished sword of God before them blazed*
> *Fierce as a comet; which the torrid heat,*
> *And vapor as the Libyan air a dust,*
> *Began to parch that temperate climate; whereat*
> *In either hand the hastening angel caught*
> *Our lingering parents, and to the eastern gate*
> *Led them direct, and down the cliff as fast*
> *To the subjected plain; then disappeared.*

🌀 **HAYLIEL YHWH** A "great and powerful" angelic prince who is mentioned in the compilation of angelic lore assembled in the Third Book of Enoch. It is written there that Hayliel is a prince "noble and terrible," capable of swallowing the entire world in just one gulp. He is so called because he has authority over the creatures, whipping them with lashes of fire while extolling them to proclaim ever and always the song of praise: "Holy, holy, holy, and Blessed be the truly feared angels of the throne." (See also *Hayyoth.*)

🌀 **HAYY** The angel of medieval lore who supposedly served as a tutor to the great Islamic philosopher Avicenna (980–1037).

HAYYOTH Also called the chayyoth, a group of mighty angels who reside in the seventh heaven and are under the leadership of the frightful and imposing angel Hayliel YHWH. Impressive and imposing, the hayyoth are considered analogous to or can be equated with the cherubim of later angelic lore. Two descriptions are given for the hayyoth, the first in the Old Testament Book of Ezekiel (1:4–28), the second in the Third Book of Enoch, the apocryphal writing full of angelic lore. (For the Ezekiel account, see under *Cherubim.*) The hayyoth, according to Enoch, were four in number (other Jewish sources put the number at 36). "Each single creature would fill the entire world. Each one of them has faces within faces and wings within wings. The size of a face is 248 faces, and the size of a wing is 365 wings. Each creature is crowned with 2,000 crowns and every crown is like the rainbow; its brightness is as the brightness of the sun's orb and the rays which shine from each separate crown are as the rays which shine of the morning star in the east." Ezekiel beheld the hayyoth (cherubim) near the river Chabar, and his description is one of the most detailed and imaginative in the entire Old Testament, which is full of angelic references. The principal tasks of the angels are to bear or carry the throne of God (a mission identical to that of the hashmallim, with whom they are also closely identified) and to sing the endless praises of God. (See also *Cherubim, Hashmallim,* and *Hayliel YHWH.*)

HEAVEN See box on page 133.

HEAVENLY ACADEMY The name given to the rather uncompromising, objective, and hence pitiless (in an unemotional sense) committee or jury of angels that reportedly gathers each time a person dies, to render judgment upon the deceased based upon his or her actions in life. This academy appears in the lore of the Jews, receiving specific mention in the mystical book called the Zohar. If the decision of the angels is against the soul being judged, then the condemned must wait for a time until being led away—presumably by the much-feared angel of destruction—to eternal suffering or at least a temporary, purifying torment.

HEAVENLY HOST The broad collective name for all of the angels and archangels of heaven. While the term has rather distinct military connotations, the heavenly host does not necessarily imply the host in

HEAVEN

While it is common to think of heaven in the Christian sense of being the singular abode of the Lord, the saints, and the angels, there is also an ancient belief in the division of heaven into seven celestial mansions. Such a conception is based on an ascending order of heavens, culminating in the final, seventh heaven, the place of highest spiritual perfection. Also rooted in a multiplicity of heavens is the occult and mystical value placed on the seven, a number revered in faiths all over the world.

The seven heavens of Jewish tradition can be traced to the civilization of Sumeria, which existed in the fertile crescent of the Tigris and Euphrates valley from around the fifth to third millennia B.C. This was adopted by later Babylonian and Persian empires and came to influence the Jewish people during the so-called Babylonian Captivity. In Jewish writings, one of the best descriptions—and certainly one of the most colorful—was summoned up by the authors of the Books of Enoch. These accounts contain many stories about the angelic denizens of heaven. There are, additionally, angelic princes who govern the affairs of their appointed part of the seven heavens. (The princes are covered under *Heavens, Angels of the Seven.*) At the summit of the celestial mansions was the seventh heaven, the place where the throne of God was situated. Here the Lord was surrounded by the ever-chanting choirs of angels, the court of heaven, and the mightiest princes of the angelic choirs.

conflict or at direct war with the forces of evil. Rather, it denotes the angels as a whole, together chanting and giving endless adoration to God. One of the most enduring images of the heavenly host was presented by Dante in the *Paradiso* in his *Divine Comedy* (Canto 27), when the heavenly host was beheld by Dante, chanting joyously: "Glory to the Father, to the Son, And to the Holy Spirit," which "rang aloud Throughout all Paradise/that with the song My spirit reel'd, so passing sweet the strain." In the image of the host as a force ready for war, the term is most apt as embodied in the great war of heaven presented in Milton's *Paradise Lost,* in which the angelic legions of heaven utterly defeat the fallen angels and, under the leadership of St. Michael, drive Satan from the heavenly realm. A beautiful account of these angels was given in the Gospel of St. Luke in his description of the birth of Christ when a herald angel announced "news of great joy": "And suddenly there was with the angel a multitude of the heavenly host praising God and saying, 'Glory to God in the highest, and on earth peace among men with whom he is pleased!' " (2:13–14).

HEAVENS, ANGELS OF THE SEVEN The listing found in Jewish lore for the seven great angels who serve as the princes or ruling chiefs of the seven heavens. According to this list, the angels are

first heaven:	Gabriel
second heaven:	Raphael, Galizur, and Zachariel
third heaven:	Jabniel, Rabacyl, and Dalquiel
fourth heaven:	Michael
fifth heaven:	Samael
sixth heaven:	Sandalphon, Zachiel, and Sabaoth
seventh heaven:	Cassiel

In the lore of the Hechaloth, the traditions relating to the heavenly halls, there are additionally sixty-four angelic guards or wardens of the seven heavenly halls or palaces. There are few well-known or even familiar angels among the wardens, and their number includes such obscure figures as Zeburiel, Uzial, Tashriel, Shoel, and Arfiel.

HECHALOTH See *Sefiroth;* see also *Merkabah Angels.*

🌸 **HELL** See box on pages 136–137.

🌸 **HEMAH** A most unpleasant angel who appeared in Jewish lore. Ranked as a truly feared angel of wrath, Hemah was (according to the description given in the famous collection *The Legends of the Jews* by Louis Ginzberg) said to be made from chains of red-and-black fire and was, like his equally intemperate brother Af, five hundred parasangs tall; the parasang was a Persian unit of measure estimated to be around three and a half miles long (five and a half kilometers). In one legend, Hemah grew angry and attempted to swallow Moses with the assistance of Af. The Lord, however, compelled the angel to spit him out. In an unprecedented act of vengeance, Moses was permitted to slay the angel. (See also *Mashit.*)

🌸 **HEMAN** An angel who, with Asaph and Jeduthun, is one of the directors or choral leaders of those angels in heaven whose duty it is to sing in never-ending praise of God. While Asaph commands during the night and Jeduthun during the evening, Heman is the director during the hours of the heavenly morning. It is thought that overall direction is under the angel Jehoel. Like his colleagues, Heman may have been one of the music directors in the Great Temple of Jerusalem; they were supposedly brought to heaven to serve as conductors of the heavenly choirs, transformed into angels to be able to serve for eternity. Heman is actually mentioned in the Book of Psalms—presumably before his angelic rendezvous—where Psalm 88 begins: "A Song. A Psalm of the Sons of Korah to the choirmaster: according to Mahalath Leannoth. A Maskil of Heman the Ezrahite." (See also *Music.*)

🌸 **HERALD ANGEL** A colorful name given to certain angels who serve as triumphant announcers or declarers of some mighty event. By far the most famous historical moment of the herald angels came one night in Bethlehem when they proclaimed the birth of Jesus. As was written by Luke in his Gospel: "And in that region there were shepherds out in the field, keeping watch over their flocks by night. And an angel of the Lord appeared to them, and the glory of the Lord shone around them, and they were filled with fear. And the angel said to them, 'Be not afraid; for behold, I bring you good news of great joy which will come to all people; for to you is born this day in the city of David a Savior, who is Christ the Lord. . . .' And suddenly there

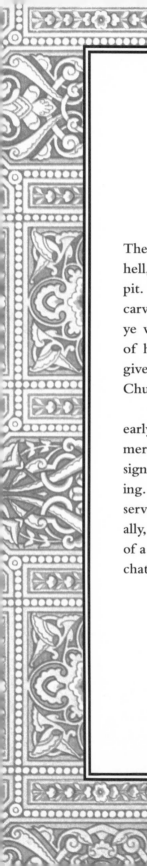

HELL

The most dreadful and feared place in all of creation is hell, called also Gehenna, the abyss, and the bottomless pit. Hell is a place so terrible that upon its gate is carved the heartrending command "Abandon hope, all ye who enter here." This visceral and enduring image of hell as a place of eternal, irredeemable woe was given its certification in the teachings of the Christian Church.

Hell, however, was not always so awful a place. In early Jewish teaching, for example, the underworld was merely a temporary realm where sinful souls were consigned for a period of purification and spiritual cleansing. In charge of this rehabilitation were angels who served the Lord, albeit in a gruesome fashion. Gradually, however, this original conception changed in favor of a far more brutal conception, the result of a stern eschatological outlook on the part of Christianity, in which members were given a stark contrast between the light of heaven and the impenetrable dark of hell.

Angels still had their part to play, however, supplying such remorseless beings as the angels of destruction, angels of wrath, avenging angels, angels of anger, and angels of torment to serve as masters and guardians of the abyss. They eventually lost their jobs, though, as belief in the fallen angels developed; hell became the home of devils and demons, who exist in their own torment and inflict endless punishments upon the damned souls given over to their wicked ministrations. Angels still supposedly keep watch over the gates of hell to ensure no wicked being or soul escapes its endless imprisonment. They can, theoretically, even enter hell should the Lord so choose to send them. (See also *Destruction, Angels of; Fallen Angels;* and *Gehenna.*)

was with the angel a multitude of the heavenly host praising God and saying, 'Glory to God in the highest, and on earth peace among men with whom he is pleased' " (2:8–14).

The herald angel is one of the more common artistic images of the Nativity, the source of great creativity and imagination by some of the foremost artists of all time. By custom (supported by art) the herald angel is named Michael, the famed archangel and commander of the heavenly host. That there is more than one herald, however, is implied by the beloved Christmas carol "Hark! The Herald Angels Sing!"

HERMES A Greek god, called in Roman mythology Mercury, son of the god Zeus and Maia and honored as the patron deity of messengers, flocks and shepherds, and travelers. Hermes was also revered as the revealer of secret knowledge, the caretaker of dreams (to whom the Greeks often gave a sacrifice before retiring), and the divine being who carries the deceased to Hades, the land of the dead. From his varied job description, Hermes is considered a prominent precursor to the angel of later understanding, especially in his labors as a messenger of the heavenly will, the bringer of aid to mortals, and the shepherd of the dead to the underworld. One other similarity was the description of Hermes in early Greek art as a bearded man in a tunic, his boots adorned with wings (a forecasting of the regular artistic representation of angels with wings). Given the name Hermes Trismegistos by the Greeks around the time of Herodotus, this new appellation added to Hermes' association with wisdom and arcane, occult knowledge or divine learning, an attribute frequently assigned to angels. So similar, in fact, was Hermes to the angels that his transformation into an angel in legend was inevitable. In Jewish lore he thus became the angel Hermesiel, one of the strongest of the heavenly body and the means for many of his gifts, powers, and activities to be incorporated into Jewish legends and customs concerning the angels.

HOCHMEL Also Hochmael, an angel whose name means "the wisdom of God." He is best known from medieval legend for supposedly inspiring the infamous Grimoire of Pope Honorius III, an utterly falsely attributed book of magic to Honorius III (r. 1216–1227), a supposed sorcerer of considerable prowess.

HOLY IMMORTALS See *Amesha Spentas.*

🙐 **HOSTS** A term analogous to the heavenly host, used as a kind of generic term for angels. Other similar names include host of heaven, the armies of the sky, and the hosts of the high ones. One of the strongest uses of the word occurs in the Old Testament Book of Isaiah (24:21), when the Lord declared his promise to punish all, immortal and mortal alike: "On that day the Lord will punish the host of heaven, in heaven, and the kings of the earth, on the earth. They will be gathered together as prisoners in a pit; they will be shut up in a prison, and after many days they will be punished. Then the moon will be confounded, and the sun ashamed; for the Lord of hosts will reign on Mount Zion and in Jerusalem and before his elders he will manifest his glory." It is normally declared in legend and tradition that the leader of the hosts is Michael.

🙐 **HURIS** A type of female angelic being found in Islamic lore. They reside in paradise and exist to offer pleasure to those who have merited eternal bliss while on earth. Each new person arriving in the Islamic heaven is given seventy-two huris who fulfill his every want or desire. The huris, meanwhile, is rewarded in this union by becoming a virgin after each night's enjoyment. The legends of the huris are distinctly nontraditional in comparison with other tales related about angels and angelic beings, the most radical difference being the sexual component, largely absent in other angelic accounts. The acknowledged head of the huris in some sources is the angel Kalka'il. The spirits were said to be dark eyed and stunningly lovely. (See also *Female Angels* and *Gender of Angels*.)

IADALBAOTH A being that appears in the lore of Gnosticism (an offshoot of Christianity that advanced its own notions on the Creation). According to the Gnostics, Iadalbaoth was the creator of humanity and also the progenitor of the so-called seven elohim, the Gnostic equivalent of the seven great angels. He occupies a high position in Gnostic cosmology, in some accounts ranked just below the Creator of all things. In other cases, however, Iadalbaoth is considered a being of darkness.

IBLIS See under *Fallen Angels;* see also *Jinn.*

IMAMIAH A onetime angel who was a member of the angelic order or choir of principalities. Now a most unpleasant fallen angel, he is a noteworthy denizen of hell, called upon by sorcerers to bring total destruction to their enemies. Imamiah was mentioned in the lore of the Qabalah.

IMMORTALS, HOLY See under *Amesha Spentas.*

INIAS Also Iniaes, one of the angels who were officially removed from the list of honored angels recognized by the Christian Church at a council in Rome in 745. The angels were taken off the lists by Church officials to counter what they feared was an altogether unwholesome obsession concerning the angels in the popular thinking of the time. Inias was joined in disgrace by Uriel, Sabaoc, Tubuel, Raguel, and Simiel. The legend is told, however, that Inias responded quite poorly to the actions of the council and became an enemy of the faith. His means of striking back is to disturb the sermons or profound speeches of churchmen by performing a loud and especially obnoxious episode of flatulence. (See also *Rome, Council of.*)

INNOCENTS An all but forgotten choir of angels who ranked as the tenth order of the twelve that were proposed by occultist scholar Francis Barrett in his 1801 tome *The Magus.* Barrett argued that the generally accepted nine choirs of angels—as established in virtually recognized form by the theologian Dionysius the Areopagite in the sixth century—omitted three other orders: innocents (tenth choir), martyrs (eleventh choir), and confessors (twelfth choir). The chief angel of this tenth choir is Hanael. Barrett's additional orders, however, have never been adopted or used in common usage, remaining an interesting (albeit obscure) footnote in angel lore. (See also *Choirs.*)

IOFIEL An angel, also called Jophiel and Zophiel, whose name means "the beauty of God." (For details, see *Jophiel.*)

IRIN QADDISIM See under *Watchers.*

ISAAC A patriarch of the Old Testament, son of the great patriarch Abraham and Sarah, who was promised to them by the Lord. The birth of Isaac was predicted by the Lord, although the announcement is generally credited to the renowned archangel Michael and came about despite the fact that Sarah and Abraham were far too old to bear offspring. Born as promised, Isaac served as a means for God to test Abraham's faith. Abraham was told to take his beloved son and sacrifice him. Both Abraham and Isaac obediently set out to perform the most serious of all possible offerings, but they were stopped from going through with it by an angel who proclaimed: "By myself I have sworn, says the Lord, because you have done this, and have not withheld your son, your only son, I will indeed bless you, and I will multiply your descendants as the stars of the heaven and as the sand which is on the seashore" (Genesis 22: 9–17). Isaac married Rebecca, the future mother of Esau and Jacob. Aside from these close associations with the heavenly host, Isaac is connected even more directly with angels in Jewish legend, which declares him to be an actual angel, the angel of light. This name was bestowed upon him because of the unusual light that seemed to emanate from him at his birth. According to tradition, Isaac was an angel who was sent and made incarnate by the will of God to provide Abraham with a son and to give the Hebrews a mighty patriarch. The tales not only bolster Isaac's achievements, but give an interesting explanation for the birth of a son to such elderly persons.

ISCHIM Also Ishim, a group of angels who are honored in Jewish legend. According to the accounts recorded in the famed collection *The Legends of the Jews* by Louis Ginzberg, the ischim resided in the fifth heaven, a fact attested to by their presence there at the time that Moses supposedly visited the heavens. The ischim are thought to be made of fire and ice, an attribute seemingly or partially inferred from the Book of Psalms (104:1–4):

> *Bless the Lord, O my soul!*
> *O Lord my God, thou art*
>   *very great!*
> *Thou art clothed with honor and*
>   *majesty,*
> *Who covered thyself with light as*
> *With a garment,*
> *Who hast stretched out the heavens*
>   *like a tent,*
> *who hast laid the beams of thy*
>   *chambers on the waters,*
> *who makest the clouds thy chariot,*
> *who ridest on the wings of the wind,*
> *who makest the winds thy*
>   *messengers,*
> *fire and flame thy ministers.*

In the traditions of the Zohar, the Jewish mystical work, the ischim are equated with the bene Elim, the sons of God, as described in the Book of Genesis (6:2). Like the bene Elim, the ischim exist with only one purpose: they chant unceasingly in praise of God. The place of the ischim in the hierarchy of heaven—that is, their rank among the angelic choirs—varies according to the list that is consulted among the many compilations made over the years. They are ranked variously tenth, second, or sixth, making them potentially the same as the later choirs (the cherubim, angels, powers, or even thrones).

🦚 **ISLAM** One of the three great monotheistic faiths, with its own traditions and teachings concerning the angels, although it shares many
tenets with both Judaism and Christianity. The Arabic name for angel
is *mal'ak* or *malak,* meaning "messenger," and angels in Islamic custom are a useful intermediary between God and humanity; they also
serve as a kind of guardian, a function found in most of the Semitic
faiths and spiritual orientations and rooted in the Babylonian idea of
guardian beings. The belief in angels is one of the fundamental prin-
ciples of the Islamic faith, as they provide the important function of
encouraging mankind in the inclination to do good. They are to
counter the temptations placed before humanity to do evil by the
devil. That the angels should be accepted is made clear in the Qur'an
(surah 2:177): "It is not righteousness that you turn your faces towards the East and the West, but righteous is the one who believes in
Allah and the Last Day, and the angels, and the Book and the
prophets. . . ."

Angels are not, in Islamic teaching, superior to man, although
they exist closer to God. Their inferiority to humanity comes from
the idea of Adam's spiritual perfection in terms of his unfallen nature
and because he is able directly to know God, a relationship that the
angels do not possess. Adam, representing all of human life, was a kind
of culmination or amalgamation of God's Creation, a superiority over
all things by the fact that Adam knew the names of everything in the
world, including the angels. Humans were thus to use their knowledge in the conquest of nature, but for the other central role of man,
the overcoming of the self, revelation would be necessary. Further, the
angels do not possess free will; they can never disobey God and will
always fulfill his tasks. As they exist entirely through his will, they derive all pleasure and purpose exclusively in serving their Creator; humans, in contrast, have freedom of will and choose to worship God.
For these reasons, God commanded the angels to bow down before
Adam, an act of submission that the angel Iblis refused to do out of
pride. Iblis thus became the source of evil, synonymous with Satan;
Islamic scholars point out subtle but significant differences between
the appearance of evil as Iblis or Satan.

The ranks of the angels are apparently quite large but are organized into their own kind of hierarchy. The chief angels are the
archangels, of whom only four are named: Michael (Mika'il) and
Gabriel (Jibril or Jibra'il)—both listed in the Qur'an—and Azrael
(Izra'il), known as the angel of death, and Israfel (Israfil), the angel

who will blast the trumpet at the end of the world. The four archangels, especially Gabriel and Michael, fulfill special and important roles. Gabriel, for example, is called the angel of revelation, for he dictated to Muhammad the Qur'an. In Arabic and Persian lore, other traditions have been handed down about angels such as the jinn and the hafaza. (See also *Azrael; Death, Angel of; Gabriel; Guardian Angels; Hafaza; Jinn; Israfel; Michael; Moakibat; Muhammad, Angel of;* and *Qur'an.*)

ISRAEL In some Jewish lore Israel refers to an angel ranked among the high order of the hayyoth, the formidable angels circling or supporting the throne of God. Elsewhere, however, this angel is identified with a curious but understandable angelic being named Israel-Jacob, a union of the famous patriarch Jacob with the angelic. It is based in part upon the passage in the Old Testament Book of Genesis recording the struggle between Jacob and the unidentified "man" termed the dark angel. During the course of their titanic wrestling match, the angel declares to Jacob that his name henceforth shall be Israel. The direct association or naming of a patriarch as an angel is not unusual in Jewish lore, as such an honor was given to Jacob's father, Isaac, and even to Moses.

ISRAFEL Also Israfil, one of the great angels in Islamic lore, honored as the angel of the Last Judgment or angel of the Resurrection. At the end of the world, Israfel will descend to the earth, stand upon the holy rock in Jerusalem, and blow the awesome trumpet that will awaken the dead from their slumber and summon all who have ever lived to come forth and be judged. The trumpet in question is an enormous animal horn, with uncounted honeycombs or cells in which all of the dead sleep. Described as possessing four wings, he is said to be covered with hair and a host of mouths, his impressive appearance matched by his incredible height; he is so tall that he is able to reach from the earth to the very pillars of heaven. A beautiful angel and the master of music, Israfel sings the praises of God not just in Arabic, but in a thousand different tongues; the Lord is so touched by his singing that he uses the very breath of Israfel to inject life into hosts of angels, who themselves take part in the ceaseless singing of Allah's praises.

While not named specifically in the Qur'an, Israfel is nevertheless counted as one of the four angels who will be destroyed at the end of the world. He is also thought to have appeared and given assistance and counsel to Muhammad in the time of the Prophet's formation; the work of Israfel was later taken over by Gabriel, the angel who is honored as revealing to Muhammad the Qur'an. Israfel is also ranked with Michael and Gabriel as the angels sent by God from heaven to gather dirt from across the earth with which Adam was to be made. He thus shared in the failure of the angels in extracting it from the earth (the world refused to yield up its dirt because it knew that humanity would turn away from the Lord and it preferred to avoid the whole sorry event). Returning empty-handed to heaven, the three angels were replaced by Azrael, whose success earned him the post of the angel of death. With Michael and Gabriel, he is said to have been dispatched to warn Abraham of the impending destruction of Sodom and Gomorrah, although the three visitors to Abraham's camp are often thought to be God himself. Perhaps the most touching story about Israfel is the one that displays his deep compassion. According to this, Israfel looks down into hell six times a day and is so stricken with horror and grief at the plight of the damned souls that he begins to weep. His tears are so numerous and his weeping so intense that Allah must stop the flow lest the entire world is flooded. Edgar Allan Poe wrote in the poem "Israfel":

> In heaven a spirit doth dwell
> Whose heart-strings are a lute;
> None sing so wildly well
> As the angel Israfel,
> And the giddy stars (so legends tell)
> Ceasing their hymns, attend the spell
> Of his voice, all mute . . .

ITHURIEL An angel who is best known for his colorful activities in John Milton's *Paradise Lost*. In this part of the tale, Gabriel learns that Satan is loose in the Garden of Eden and so dispatches the cherub Ithuriel, with the cherub Zephon, to find the leader of the fallen angels. They find him disguised as a toad, squatting next to the sleeping Eve:

> Assaying by his devilish art to reach
> The organs of her fancy, and with them forge,
> Illusions as he list, phantasms and dreams

Touching Satan with his spear, Ithuriel causes the great deceiver to return to his actual form:

So started up in his own shape the fiend
Back stepped those two fair angels half amazed,
So sudden to behold the grisly king . . .

The cherubs Ithuriel and Zephon hunt for Satan, who is loose in the world, in *Paradise Lost;* by Gustave Doré.

Unfortunately, while Satan was disturbed and unmasked to reveal his appalling shape, his whispered temptations had their deadly effect. The hunt for Satan by Ithuriel and Zephon was the subject of a beautiful illustration in the 1794 edition of *Paradise Lost.* As with other Miltonian angels, such as Abdiel and Zophiel, there is question as to whether Ithuriel existed prior to his adventures in literature or was an invention of Milton. Jewish scholars note that Ithuriel is mentioned in lore dating at least to the late Middle Ages or the sixteenth century.

IZRAEL An angel of Islamic folklore, one of the four angels of the end of the world, with the angels Michael, Israfel, and Gabriel. Izrael is thus to be spared—with his angelic associations—the terrible effects of the first blast of the trumpet on the Day of Judgment that is to be sounded by Israfel. The angels will be free of the effects of the blasts until the final sounding of the trumpet, when all things and beings will be summoned to the Final Judgment.

JACOB A Hebrew patriarch of the Old Testament, son of Isaac and grandson of Abraham. Jacob is an important figure in the history of the Hebrews, for through his courage, as expressed in the account of the Book of Genesis, he earned a new name: from Jacob, meaning "hanger-on," he was rechristened Israel, receiving a vision of blessings and riches. He died in Egypt, but not before fathering twelve sons, from whom the twelve tribes of Israel took their names. The life of Jacob was deeply affected by angels, with two of the most angelic incidents in all of the Bible. The first was while Jacob was on a journey from Beer-sheba:

> *And he came to a certain place, and stayed there that night,*
> *because the sun had set. Taking one of the stones of the place, he*
> *put it under his head and lay down in that place to sleep. And*
> *he dreamed that there was a ladder set up on the earth, and the*
> *top of it reached to heaven; and behold, the angels of God were*
> *ascending and descending on it! And behold, the Lord stood*
> *above it and said, "I am the Lord, the God of Abraham your*
> *father and the God of Isaac; the land on which you lie I will*
> *give to you and to your descendants; and your descendants shall*
> *be like the dust of the earth, and you shall spread abroad to the*
> *west and to the east and to the north and to the south; and by*
> *you and your descendants shall all the families of the earth bless*
> *themselves. Behold, I am with you and will keep you wherever*
> *you go. . . ."*
>
> (GENESIS 28:11–15)

The story of Jacob's Ladder, emphasizing the hope to be offered by God and the close connection between things of this world and those of the next, has been depicted by numerous artists; perhaps the most lively is that of Gustave Doré. The second event is the wrestling match between Jacob and the unnamed but superhuman man who has been given the title over the years of the dark angel (see *Dark Angel* for details). The result of this struggle and Jacob's perseverance was his receiving the name of Israel.

Jacob dreams of the Ladder; by Gustave Doré.

In legend there is an additional connection between Jacob and the angels. This is the idea that Jacob was, in fact, an angel all along, entering into human affairs to aid the Chosen People. A similar tale is told about Isaac. In Jacob's case he is named Israel, an angel otherwise said to be member of the angelic order of the hayyoth. (See *Israel* for other details.)

JAEL One of the two cherubim, with Zarall, who were said to have been carved upon the Ark of the Covenant, although in some accounts there were said to be four angels instead of two. Jael, with his counterpart, was placed upon the so-called mercy seat of the Ark, their wings spread out, shadowing the mercy seat. (See also *Ark of the Covenant, Angels of the,* and *Zarall.*)

JEDUTHUN An angel and example of the infrequent but interesting transformation of a mortal into an angel through the labors of writers and the pervasiveness of legend (as with Enoch, Elijah, Jacob, and even Moses). Jeduthun was almost certainly the choirmaster of the Great Temple of Jerusalem, so honored that three Psalms from the Old Testament (39, 62, and 77) are dedicated "To the choirmaster: to Jeduthun" and "To the choirmaster: according to Jeduthun." Over time, however, Jeduthun was made the subject of a legend—with his fellow composers Heman and Asaph—in which he became an angel (or already was one), holding the high post in heaven of directing the choirs of angels during the evening hours in their endless praises of God. His colleagues Asaph and Heman occupy the post during other hours of the day. (See also *Asaph, Jehoel,* and *Singing, Angelic.*)

JEHOEL Also Jaoel and Yahoel, a powerful angelic prince who is variously honored in Jewish legend as the chief or leader of the angelic order of the seraphim and the master of the heavenly choirs that sing in eternal adoration of God. In the latter capacity it can be assumed that he is probably superior to the three other angelic choirmasters mentioned in lore, Asaph, Heman, and Jeduthun, who direct the angels in the endless chants at various times of the day.

In one account concerning Jehoel, recorded in the Jewish work called the Apocalypse of Abraham, he was sent by God to serve as a guide and companion to the great patriarch Abraham when he visited heaven, reaching paradise (it was said) on the back of a pigeon. Jehoel led him on a tour and then brought Abraham before the very throne of God. Surprisingly unintimidated, the patriarch peppered the Lord with questions concerning the nature of evil and why evil was allowed by God to flourish and bring such suffering to Creation. The Lord declined (as reported in the Apocalypse) to give a clear answer, but he permitted Abraham instead to receive from Jehoel a vision of the future of the world. (See also *Singing, Angelic.*)

JEREMIEL Also called Ramiel, an archangel whose name means "mercy of God." Identified with the archangel Ramiel as listed in the First Book of Enoch and 2 Esdras, Jeremiel has been named one of the archangels in the earliest lists ever assembled concerning the members of that most august angelic body. (For other details, see *Ramiel.*)

JESUS CHRIST In the teachings of Christianity the Messiah, the Son of God; Christ is also honored as king of the angels, both in recognition of his place as the Son of the Lord and through his many close associations with the members of the heavenly host during his time on earth. Catholic theologians will point out that angels served in the history recounted in the Old Testament not only as messengers of the Lord and guides in the life of the Jewish people, but also as preparers of the coming of the Messiah. In the period just before the actual arrival of Christ, one angel was quite active; Gabriel appeared to the priest Zachary to predict the birth of John the Baptist and then came to Mary with the Annunciation. The four Gospels and other writings of the New Testament are full of references and accounts concerning Christ and the angels.

The king of the angels; *Christ Crucified,* by Gustave Doré.

Angels celebrated the actual birth of Jesus in Bethlehem by appearing to shepherds in the field (see *Nativity, Angels of the*). An angel of the Lord then warned Joseph to take the holy family out of Palestine and into Egypt to keep Jesus safe from the evil plan of King Herod. An angel appeared again after Herod's death to inform Joseph that "those who sought the child's life are dead" (Matthew 2:20). Throughout his ministry Jesus seems to have angels ever ready to be at his side; the Church taught that the angels would naturally be more than desirous of serving him in any capacity and having the honor merely of looking upon his face. Thus they ministered to him in the desert, came to him in the dark hours before the start of his Passion—bringing him comfort in the garden of Gethsemane—and were witnesses to his Resurrection. Finally, there were two angels, dressed in white, who came to the side of the Apostles at the Ascension.

During his earthly ministry, Jesus spoke often of angels, imparting some information on their lives in heaven, their functions, and their total devotion to the Son of God. In Matthew (22:30), he implies that in heaven angels do not marry, nor are they given in marriage. He also speaks of their place as his invisible but ever-present guard, making clear as well that he could at a simple command bring down twelve legions of angels (Matthew 26:53). Angels also figured in the attempted temptation of Christ by the devil (Matthew 4:1–11) and were spoken of often by the Lord in relation to the Final Judgment and the end of the world, such as the promise that "[W]hen the Son of Man comes in his glory, and all the angels with him, then he will sit on his glorious throne" (Matthew 25:31) and that the "Son of man will send his angels, and they will gather out of his kingdom all causes of sin and all evildoers, and throw them into the furnace of fire; there men will weep and gnash their teeth" (Matthew 13:41–42). (See also *Ascension, Angels of* and *Gethsemane, Angel of.*)

JIBRIL Also Jibra'il and Jabril, a common spelling of the name of the archangel Gabriel as it appears in the literature of the Qur'an, the sacred scriptural text of Islam. (See *Gabriel* for details.)

JINN The Arabic name for the anglicized genies (sing. jinni), the supernatural spirits or beings found mostly in Islamic or Arabian mythology and the subject of intensive development in literature and folklore in Persia, Egypt, Syria, Arabia, Turkey, and across North Africa; one of the best-known sources on the lore of the jinn is the famed collection *The Thousand and One Nights.* According to mythology, the jinn were created some two thousand years before the making of Adam and were possessors of a lofty place in paradise, roughly equal to that of the angels, although they were probably considered beneath the angels. They are said to have been made of air and fire. After God made Adam, however, the jinn, under their proud and willful leader Iblis (or Eblis), refused to bow down before the mortal. For this grievous refusal, the jinn were cast out of heaven, becoming wicked and hideous demons. Iblis, who fell with them, became the equivalent of Satan. On earth they reputedly live in the Kaf Mountains, which supposedly circle the world.

While inferior to devils, the jinn are nevertheless strong and exceedingly cunning. They are composed of such varied beings as the ifrit and the ghul, with the ability to take virtually any form or shape, even seemingly inanimate objects such as trees or rocks. Ruthless and extremely vindictive, the jinn punish mercilessly all transgressions against them, those committed by both fellow demons and mortals. As with other infernal spirits, those who possess the magical means (and are obviously accomplished sorcerers) can summon a jinni and compel it to fulfill some task or provide desired, perhaps secret, knowledge. There is, though, a tradition that not all jinn are irredeemably fallen. Some, it is thought, are actually kindly disposed toward humanity, aiding them whenever help is needed—or when it is convenient to the jinni. A splendid example of such beneficence was given in *The Thousand and One Nights* when a jinni assisted Aladdin. There is also a custom in folklore that the more gullible jinni can be tricked by clever mortals who can coax them somehow into a bottle or box, then refuse to let them out until they promise to grant several wishes (the usual number is three); this pledge the jinni is honor bound to fulfill, albeit in a potentially diabolical fashion and with often gruesome or fiendish conditions. The jinn have appeared in a number of films, including the assorted versions of *The Thief of Baghdad* (the most memorable being the 1940 version with Sabu and Conrad Veidt) and the recent Walt Disney animated megahit *Aladdin*.

JOEL An archangel who had a leading part to play in the mythological account called the *Book of Adam and Eve*. In this tale, Joel has the task of leading Adam and Eve through the Garden of Eden. He instructs Adam to give a name to all of the creatures and objects of the world. This is a different version of events from the one recorded in the Old Testament Book of Genesis (2:19–20): "So out of the ground the Lord God formed every beast of the field and every bird of the air, and brought them to the man to see what he would call them; and whatever the man called every living creature, that was its name. The man gave names to all cattle, and the birds of the air, and to every beast of the field; but for the man there was not found a helper fit for him." In some sources Joel is considered the first of the names borne by the great angel Metatron—in the Third Book of Enoch, for example (there spelled Yaho'el).

JOHN THE BAPTIST The prophet and preacher of the New Testament who is called the forerunner of Jesus Christ and who had the task from God "to prepare the Way for the Lord." The birth of John was foretold by the angel Gabriel to his father, Zechariah (Zachary), a priest. Both Zechariah and his wife, Elizabeth, were in their old age, but the angel appeared suddenly and declared to him:

> *Do not be afraid, Zechariah, for your prayer is heard, and your*
> *wife Elizabeth will bear you a son, and you shall call his*
> *name John.*

*And you will have joy and gladness, and many will rejoice at his
     birth;
for he will be great before the Lord, and he shall drink no wine
     nor strong drink,
and he will be filled with the Holy Spirit,
even from his mother's womb.
And he will turn many of the sons of Israel to the Lord their
     God,
and he will go before him in the spirit and power of Elijah,
to turn the hearts of the fathers to the children,
and the disobedient to the wisdom of the just,
to make ready for the Lord a people prepared.*
                                            (Luke 1:13–17)

The arrival of John is said to have been itself predicted in the
Old Testament in such sources as the Book of Malachi (3:1): "Behold,
I send my messenger to prepare the way before me, and the Lord
whom you seek will suddenly come to his temple; the messenger of
the covenant in whom you delight, behold, he is coming, says the
Lord of hosts." Others, meanwhile, argue that John the Baptist should
be considered an actual angel, citing biblical references like the Book
of Exodus (23:20): "Behold, I send an angel before you, to guard you
on the way and to bring you to the place which I have prepared." The
logic for this can already be seen in the legends surrounding the great
prophet Elijah—who was supposed to come to announce to the
world the imminent arrival of the Messiah—namely that he was
taken into heaven and transformed into the angel Sandalphon and
the gradual adoption of the Greek god Hermes (the god of messengers) as a member of the angelic community. Interestingly, Greek
artists long depicted St. John with wings, making clear to the observer
that the Baptist was fulfilling his mission of bringing the news of
Christ's coming.

JONATHAN In full, Jonathan Smith, the exceedingly compassionate
but humorous (even whimsical) angel played by actor Michael Landon in the television program *Highway to Heaven*. Landon (d. 1991)
created an angelic character who wanders the world trying to aid humanity in a quiet and unobtrusive manner, always encouraging mortals to help themselves. He is not without resources, however, when

troubles come. In one episode, for example, he teaches a lesson to an indifferent driver who parks in a handicapped space. When he is laughed off, he exacts a suitable revenge: coming out of the store, the driver finds the car sitting, without a scratch, upside down. Jonathan can only look heavenward apologetically and explain that he could not help himself. (See also *Films.*)

JOPHIEL An angel also called Iofiel and Zophiel, whose name means "the beauty of God." Jophiel is a formidable angelic personality, said in Jewish lore to be a special friend of the archangel Metatron. He is listed among the seven archangels by the early medieval theologian and angelologist Dionysius the Areopagite, occupying the sixth place. Additionally he is ranked as one of the chiefs or princes of the angelic choir of the cherubim, with such heavenly notables as Gabriel, Uriel, Raphael, and, before his Fall, Satan. Jophiel is credited in Christian lore with two other significant tasks. First, in Eden he was the appointed guardian of the tree of life (a role also given to Raphael); second, and most memorably, he is credited with being the fell angel who drove Adam and Eve out of the Garden of Eden after they had eaten the fruit of the forbidden tree, an event mentioned in the Book of Genesis (3:24): ". . . and at the east of the garden of Eden he [the Lord] placed the cherubim, and a flaming sword which turned every way, to guard the way to the tree of life." (See also *Eden, Garden of.*)

JUBILEES, BOOK OF An apocryphal Jewish work (meaning that it was not accepted into the canon—or list—of those works included in the Old Testament) that is also called the "Little Genesis" because it offers essentially a retelling of the Books of Genesis and Exodus. Written probably in the late second century B.C., the Book of Jubilees purports to be the account of Moses, given to him on Mount Sinai by the angel of the presence. Its name is derived from the jubilees, a period of time equal to forty-nine years, and the work contains an account of a jubilee of jubilees, forty-nine periods of forty-nine years each. Immensely popular in some Jewish circles, the Book of Jubilees is especially rich in its angel lore, with mention of such diverse angels as those of the cold and heat, winter, spring, autumn, and fall, and hail and darkness. While not counted among the accepted sacred texts, the writing is nevertheless a fascinating example of the abiding place of angels in lore and apocryphal literature.

JUDAISM One of the great monotheistic religions of the world and, with Christianity and Islam, one of the central sources for lore and teachings about the angels. Judaism is perhaps the most important of the three in angelological terms, for its traditions about the angels served as the basis for so much that was later adopted by the both the Muslims and especially the Christians. Additionally, through its many forms of internal development and expression (the Hebrew Bible, Talmud, Essenes, Apocrypha, and especially the Qabalah), Judaism stands as a vast treasure house of beautiful accounts, stories, and legends about angels.

Despite this rich legacy, Judaism has always been clear in its teaching that angels are purely the messengers of God and should not in any way be worshiped or made objects of adoration (a tenet enforced with equal vigor by the Christian faith). This precept rests in the central declaration of the Jews: "Hear O Israel, the Lord our God, the Lord is One." There is only one God, who needs no assistance or aid from any creature. While this would seemingly make belief in angels both unnecessary and perhaps even blasphemous, the presence of angels is attested by the Old Testament and is considered valuable for humanity in that the angelic beings are the agents of God, a way for him to communicate his love to the world and to give assistance and direction to his Chosen People. The Old Testament notes the role of angels in the history of the Jewish people, from the lives of Abraham, Jacob, and Moses to the prophets of Ezekiel, Elijah, and Daniel. One of the most interesting but often overlooked angel stories is that of Gideon, in the Book of Judges, who greeted the arrival of God's messenger with surprising aplomb. He refused to accept God's command that he lead his people against the Midianites until the angel had proven to his satisfaction that he was, in fact, hearing the word of the Lord. Three miracles were needed, including the neat trick of causing flame to burst forth from a rock and consume a sacrifice of meat and bread. Once convinced, Gideon went on to smash the Midianites.

Beyond the accepted book of the Bible, there exists in Jewish literature a body of apocryphal and pseudepigraphical writings, composed over a wide period stretching from the late third century B.C. to the early second century A.D. A dark and difficult time for the Jews, including the conquest of Palestine by the Romans, the destruction of the Great Temple of Jerusalem in 70 A.D., and the Diaspora (the spreading of the Jewish people out of their homeland), these years produced writings that emphasized the place of angels as supports and assistants to the Lord, existing in a complicated heavenly hierarchy. Such was the excessive concern with angels in many of these works that rabbis feared near idolatry toward the angels; they thus proscribed the books. These survived, however, largely through their use by early heretical Christian sects such as the Gnostics. (See *Enoch, Books of,* and *Jubilees, Book of*).

In the wake of the Diaspora and the apocryphal writings, the rabbis sought to provide a religious underpinning for their people by encoding the Jewish law, a task that ultimately produced the Talmud, the collected rabbinic writings comprising the Mishnah and the Gemara. Within the Talmud, angels are the subject of some discussion, not surprising given their presence in so much apocryphal literature and in Jewish legends. The rabbis who compiled the Talmud, however, sought to restore the angels to a proper place, deemphasizing their powers and activities separate from a direct connection to the Lord while making them a kind of personification of God's will. The angels were still combative, opinionated, and even stubborn, as in one Talmud story detailing the opposition of the angels of truth and peace to the creation of humanity. As the Lord ousted the angel of truth from heaven, the Talmud makes unquestionable the total superiority of God and the Creator's greater concern for humanity.

Another important source of Jewish traditions concerning angels is found in the mystical movement of the Qabalah and in the Zohar, the great work of mysticism published in the thirteenth century. The Qabalah featured many facets related to angels and devils. Finally, two other notable angel traditions were the Merkabah, a mystical sect that flourished among the Jews in the early centuries of the Christian era, and folklore, especially during the Middle Ages. Influenced by the Qabalah and the Zohar, Jewish legends and tales included a host of angel stories. The place of angels in Jewish history is thus considerable, remaining so even into the modern era. Contemporary Jewish thought has considered the angel, as attested by the writings of Isaac Bashevis Singer, Walter Benjamin, Franz Kafka, Adin Steinsaltz, and Martin Buber.

JUDGMENT, ANGELS OF THE LAST The angels who are to appear at the Last Judgment, the final day, when all who have ever lived will be brought before the throne of God. The idea of the Last Judgment is especially prominent in Islamic and Christian lore. In the latter, the angel Israfel shall play a blast upon his mighty trumpet to awaken the slumbering dead. Some angels will be spared the effects of the first blasts, but after the third or fourth even they shall be destroyed by the Lord and the end of time will have descended upon all of creation. In the Christian tradition, the Second Coming of Christ will be announced not by Israfel, but by Gabriel, who will likewise sound an irresistible note upon his trumpet. Also prominent in the expected Day of Judgment is St. Michael the Archangel, captain of the hosts of the Lord, who will presumably have just led the heavenly hosts in their final triumph over Satan and the legions of darkness.

 KADISHIM Another spelling for the angels called the qaddisin (or holy ones), who are the close companions of the angels known as the irin, the watchers. (For other details, see *Watchers.*)

KADMIEL An angel who is listed in the Jewish work called the Book of the Angel Raziel. Kadmiel is one of the seventy angels who are to be invoked by expectant mothers to assist in making the entire process of childbirth safe and successful for both mother and child.

KAKABEL See *Kokbiel.*

KALKA'IL The angel in Islamic lore who has authority over the highly unusual angelic spirits known as the huris. He is thought to exist or reside in the fifth heaven of the Islamic vision of paradise. (See also *Huris.*)

KALMIYA An angel prince who has authority, with six other princes, of guarding the gate or the so-called veil of the seventh heaven. Among the other angel guardians were Gabriel and Sandalphon.

KASB'EL Once a high angel in the hierarchy of heaven originally named Beqa (or Biqa), which meant "good person." His name, however, was changed to Kasb'el—also Kazbiel and Kesb'el, meaning "he who lies to God"—after his fall into sin. Kasb'el is called the "chief of the oath" because of his efforts to learn the secret or hidden name of

God and thereby wield its power to create an oath to cause all to tremble in fear before it.

KEMUEL Another spelling for the great angel Camael. (See *Camael* for other details.)

KERUBIEL Also Cherubiel or Kerubial YHWH, the "valiant prince" who is chief of the choir of the cherubim. A colorful description of this most impressive angelic prince was given in the Third Book of Enoch, that useful source for often imaginative details on angels. His body was said to be full of burning coals and was as tall and as wide as the seven heavens. His mouth was like a torch, his tongue like a burning fire, and his whole body was covered with eyes and with wings. Lightning was said to shoot from his face, while coals were flashed from his body and flames blazed from his hands. (See also *Cherubim*.)

KEZEF One of the angels of destruction who was the subject of several Jewish legends. One in particular identifies him with or in the role of an angel of death, who was forced by the Old Testament figure of Aaron to reside or be imprisoned for a time in the holy tabernacle, the portable shrine first established by Moses for the Jews during their long wanderings in the wilderness. In the tabernacle was to be found the "holy of holies," the Ark of the Covenant. The incarceration of Kezef did not last long, but for its duration all death ceased. The tale is recounted in *The Legends of the Jews* by Louis Ginzberg.

KIPOD, NASRAGIEL, AND NAIRYO SANGHA Three stern angels who stand as wardens at the upper gates of hell. Another angel also mentioned in this role is Kinor. Nasragiel (or Nagrasagiel) is said in legend to have acted as a guide to Moses when that patriarch visited the underworld. The description of Nasragiel has him possessing a great lion head.

KOKBIEL Also Kajabel and Kochbiel, an angel whose name means "the star of God" and who is variously considered a good or an evil angelic prince. In the First Book of Enoch, for example, he is among the fallen angels, while the work called Book of the Angel Raziel describes him as an honored angel. As he is said to have special powers over the stars, Kokbiel is an expert on astrology.

🌀 **KOLAZONTA** An angel of destruction whose name means "the chastiser." Kolazonta is identified with the fiery angel (an angel of vengeance), who was overcome by Aaron in the desert when the angel threatened to bring a murderous plague upon the Jewish people who were journeying across the wilderness. The multitude was saved when Aaron, carrying a censer, ran through the crowd, thereby purifying all in the camp. In this tale Kolazonta is considered the personification of plagues or pestilence, an event recorded in the Fourth Book of Maccabees (7:11).

L **ABBIEL** Used in Jewish legend as the original appellation for the archangel Raphael. According to the tales—as recounted in the famed collection *The Legends of the Jews* by Louis Ginzberg—the archangel (or angel) Labbiel was singular among certain groups of angels (namely the angels of peace and the angels of truth) in that he did not speak out and oppose the creation of humanity. Thus Labbiel was spared when the angry Lord wiped out the angelic bodies with fire. In honor of his fidelity Labbiel was renamed Raphael ("God has healed"). (See *Raphael* for other details.)

LAHABIEL A companion angel to the great archangel Raphael, Lahabiel was also an angel called upon to aid mortals against the dangers of evil. His name appeared on various charms and amulets.

LAHASH An apparently misguided angel who, with a fellow angel, Zakum, made the unfortunate decision to intercept a prayer concerning death offered by Moses to God. Lahash and Zakum were assisted in this difficult task by "184 myriad spirits"—a term often used to denote a great force, perhaps equaling over a million, which gives some impression as to the power of the Lawgiver's prayers. Not surprisingly, their efforts went for naught, and the two angels were brought before the Lord to receive punishment for their presumption and improper behavior. In one legend Lahash and Zakum were punished with sixty blows of a fiery lash, a flogging similar to the one given the great angel Metatron; another version has Lahash whipped seventy times by the angel Samael and ousted from heaven, while Zakum's fate remains unknown. (See also *Moses.*)

LAILAH Also Layla, an angel in Jewish legend who is said to be a holy being in some accounts and a wicked angel in others. Called the angel of the night and the prince of conception, Lailah was named from the Hebrew word *lailah,* meaning "night," taken from the passage in the Old Testament Book of Job (3:3): "After this Job opened his mouth and cursed the day of his birth. And Job said: 'Let the day perish wherein I was born, and the night which said, "A man-child is conceived." ' " In the sense of being the prince of conception, Lailah is responsible for overseeing all of the conceptions that take place on earth. When a child is conceived, it is taken immediately before God, who infuses into it a soul already in existence. In making the choice, God decides what the entire future of this person will be—gender, intelligence, attributes, and final destiny in matters of wealth and opportunity. The soul chosen is often quite unhappy about this development, much preferring to remain in the joyous peace of heaven. There is no resisting the Lord, however, and Lailah ensures that the soul is fully infused, watching to see that the soul does not make a run for freedom. As birth approaches, Lailah gives the soul a complete vision of its coming life. Just before birth, though, the angel touches the upper lip (or perhaps the nose) of the child to make the body forget everything he or she has seen. In folklore this touch is used to explain the dimple just beneath the nose. There is a tradition that Lailah is equatable to the exceptionally wicked demoness Lilith, who is also considered a spirit of conception and a fell creature of the night. However, there seems to be more weight to the concept of Lailah as an entirely beneficent angel.

The supposed written language of the angels; from Robert Ambelain's *La Kabbale Pratique.*

LANGUAGE, ANGELIC See box on pages 164–165.

LARES The name used in ancient Rome for the household gods (sing. lar) or spirits. Divided into two groups, the *lares domestici* and *lares publici,* these spirits were said to have begun as deities of nature. The *lares domestici* were the spirits of the deceased members of the family, who were honored and expected to protect all surviving other members. They were under the leadership of the *lar familiaris,* the spirit of the founder of the particular house or family. By tradition, all foods that might be dropped or spilled during a meal were gathered up carefully and burned as a fitting sacrifice to the lares in the morning, given with prayers and proper rites in a small shrine maintained in every self-respecting household and known as the lararium. This altar was one of the most important possessions of a family and was treated with much care and reverence anytime the family moved to a new house. Sacrifices comprised honey, cakes, wine, and incense. On a far wider scale were the *lares publici,* the guardian spirits of open areas, such as crossroads, roads, and parts of the entire Roman state and its later empire. The lares can be considered a kind of precursor to the guardian angel of later Christian lore, although the Christian Church was always clear on discouraging excessive veneration of angels or any rites that might appear to be worship.

LAST JUDGMENT, ANGELS OF THE See *Judgment, Angels of the Last.*

LAWIDH An angel found in Islamic lore, appearing specifically in the legends related to the Muslim holy figure Abu Yazid, one of the leading adherents of the mystical Islamic movement of Sufism. Yazid was said to have visited heaven—an honor bestowed throughout history on various holy men such as Abraham, Moses, Enoch, and later Jewish rabbis—and while there was greeted by the angel Lawidh. This angel offered him a mighty kingdom, a realm refused by Yazid, who perceived that Lawidh had been testing his faith and utter devotion to the Lord.

LIFE, ANGEL OF The angel, dressed in white and "crowned with amaranth as with flame" who appears, with the angel of death, in the poem "The Two Angels" by Longfellow.

LIGHT, ANGEL OF The title borne by several angels over the centuries and in assorted religious traditions. In Judaism and Jewish legend Isaac is called the angel of light because of the unusual, even

LANGUAGES OF
THE ANGELS

As strange as it might seem, scholars have devoted much attention to the question of what language is spoken by the angels. Unfortunately the results have served only to reinforce the cultural biases of the researchers. For example, Jewish angelologists up to the Middle Ages were firmly convinced that angels spoke only Hebrew. It was, after all, the tongue of the Jewish people (excepting Aramaic, of course) and the language of most of the figures in the Old Testament. Christian theologians until the time of St. Thomas Aquinas (d. 1274) were of the view that angels spoke only in Latin. The reader is doubtless not surprised to learn that in Islamic lore, angels spoke Arabic exclusively. Some angels, such as Gabriel, received dispensation from this linguistic exclusivity. Gabriel was able to speak Syriac and Chaldaean, aside from Hebrew.

St. Thomas Aquinas rejected all of these notions.

Instead the philosopher suggested that angels communicate both with man and each other through a process he termed "illumination." A spiritual form of expression that moderns might term telepathy, this wordless speaking conveys the entire essence of their message without need of language or dialect. Such an explanation makes sense of the fact that angels are understood by everyone who "speaks" with them, be it a saint, a shepherd, or a person of our own time. The Swedish visionary Emanuel Swedenborg wrote: "Angels can express in only one word what humanity cannot do in a thousand; and besides this, there are comprised in one word of angelic language countless things, which cannot be expressed in the words of human language at all; for in every one of the word spoken by angels there are arcana of wisdom in continuous connection, beyond what the human sciences can ever discern."

supernatural light that seemed to emanate from him at the time of his birth. Isaac has, as a consequence of this brightness and the unusual circumstances of his birth, been considered in some lore as an actual angel who was granted incarnation (for details, see *Isaac*). Jesus has been called by some an angel of light, but in Christian traditions Gabriel is the acknowledged and current holder of the title.

A radically different claimant to the position is Satan, who can be termed an angel of light for two different reasons. First, in the understanding (some would say entirely erroneous) that Lucifer ("bearer of light") is synonymous with Satan (the devil), it would follow that the evil one was once the greatest angel of light. Second, there is a direct reference to the title in the New Testament, 2 Corinthians (11:14), when St. Paul writes: "For such men are false apostles, deceitful workmen, disguising themselves as apostles of Christ. And no wonder, for even Satan disguises himself as an angel of light." From this passage it may also be possible to infer that "angel of light" is a kind of generic term for all good angels, in sharp contrast with the

A rather literary angel; from *The Annunciation,* by Mathias Grunewald, in the Isenheim Altar, Musee Unterlinden, Colmar
(COURTESY ART RESOURCE).

angels of darkness. Still other variations on the title have been borne by such angels as Uriel and Raphael; the connection is made because of the appellation regent of the sun, held by both. The same may be applied to one other angel, Shamshiel, a powerful prince and guardian angel, whose name translates as "light of day."

LIGHTNING, ANGEL OF An angel who has special authority over lightning or who is so named because of his attributes or skills. By custom, the angel of lightning is Barakiel (also Barachiel or Barkiel), although another proposed candidate is the great archangel Uriel.

LIGHTS A broad or generic term for angels. (See also *Light, Angel of.*)

LITERATURE See box on pages 167– 169.

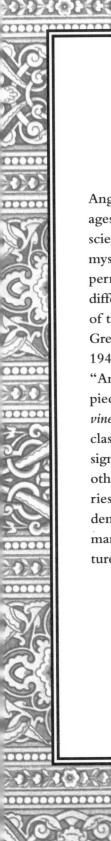

LITERATURE

Angels have been an inspiration to writers across the ages, from the prayerful praises of the Psalmists to the science fiction masters of the modern age. As beings of mystery and the supranatural (as compared with the supernatural), angels have proven remarkably adaptable to differing depictions, ranging from the awesome beings of the Book of Revelation to the humble angel of "The Greatest Gift" (the source for Clarence Oddbody in the 1946 film *It's a Wonderful Life*) to the extremely peculiar "Angel of the Odd." Unquestionably, the two greatest pieces of angel literature remain Dante Alighieri's *Divine Comedy* and John Milton's *Paradise Lost*. Both are classics in the genre and are, as well, some of the most significant works in the history of literature; but many other eminent writers have also contributed short stories and novels about angels, angel-like beings, and also demons and devils. Following are some of the more remarkable contributions to the body of angelic literature:

Isaac Asimov, "The Last Trump," 1955.
Saul Bellow, *Humboldt's Gift,* 1976.
Bruce Boston, "Curse of the Angel's Wife,"
   1993.

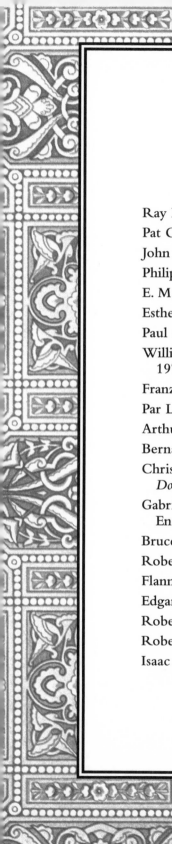

Ray Bradbury, "The Fire Balloons," 1951.

Pat Cadigan, "Angel," 1987.

John Cheever, "The Angel of the Bridge," 1961.

Philip K. Dick, "Upon the Dull Earth," 1954.

E. M. Forster, "Mr. Andrews," 1928.

Esther M. Friesner, "All Vows," 1992.

Paul Gallico, "The Small Miracle," 1950.

William Hoffman, "The Question of Rain," 1978.

Franz Kafka, "The City Coat of Arms," 1946.

Par Lagerkvist, "The Marriage Feast," 1954.

Arthur Machen, "The Bowmen," 1914.

Bernard Malamud, "Angel Levine," 1955.

Christopher Marlowe, *The Tragical History of Doctor Faustus,* 1604.

Gabriel García Márquez, "A Very Old Man with Enormous Wings," 1971.

Bruce McAllister, "Angels," 1990.

Robert Nathan, *The Bishop's Wife,* 1928.

Flannery O'Connor, "Revelation," 1964.

Edgar Allan Poe, "The Angel of the Odd," n.d.

Robert Sampson, "A Plethora of Angels," 1989.

Robert Silverberg, "Basileus," 1983.

Isaac Bashevis Singer, "Satan in Goray," 1955.

————. *Short Friday,* 1964.

Wilbur Daniel Steele, "The Man Who Saw through Heaven," 1925.

John Steinbeck, "Saint Katy and the Virgin," 1938.

Robert Louis Stevenson, "Markheim," n.d.

Leo Tolstoy, "The Three Hermits," n.d.

Mark Twain, "The Story of the Good Little Boy," n.d.

Philip Van Doren Stern, "The Greatest Gift," 1943.

Eudora Welty, "A Still Moment," 1942.

Jane Yolen, "Angelica," 1979.

Marguerite Young, *Angel in the Forest,* 1945.

Roger Zelazny, "The Man Who Loved the Faioli," 1967.

Many of these titles can be found in the excellent collection *Angels and Awakenings* (1980), edited by M. Cameron Grey. There are also angelic references in the works of Franz Kafka, Anatole France, Pier Pasolini, Thomas Mann, George Trakl, Robert Burton, and even Salman Rushdie in his *Satanic Verses.* (See also *Dante; Milton, John;* and *Poetry.*)

🙿 **LORD, ANGEL OF THE** A general name used especially in the Bible to denote an angelic messenger; it is also thought at times to mean God and, in several rare instances, the devil, in the sense of the enemy of good or as a kind of accusing angel and not as Satan in his later understanding. The Old Testament is full of references to the angel of the Lord, with such angelic emissaries playing often very substantial roles in the events recorded, such as the plight of Hagar; Abraham's sacrifice of his son, Isaac; Balaam's ass; and the destruction of an Assyrian host. From time to time scholars also accept that angel of the Lord denoted the Lord himself, such as the famous visitation to Abraham by the three "men." This conception does not apparently apply to the angelic events of the New Testament where the angel of the Lord struck down King Herod (12:23) and freed St. Peter from prison (in one of the most interesting angelic interventions in all of Scripture). In all of these cases, however, it should not be forgotten that the angel—even if not the Lord himself—serves entirely at the consent and charge of the Lord, fulfilling a task that God wishes to have completed. (See also *God, Angel of.*)

🙿 **LORD OF HOSTS** One of the high honorific names for God that makes clear the Lord's mastery over the hosts of heaven, the armies of angels at his complete disposal. Other terms for God as the lord of hosts include Sabaoth (Hebrew for "hosts") and Akatriel, although both these names are used also for angelic beings. It is acknowledged that the chief or leader of the hosts is the archangel Michael. (See also *Hosts.*)

🙿 **LORDS** An alternative name for several of the orders or choirs of angels. Among those angelic groups for which it is sometimes substituted in translations are dominations (or dominions), virtues, and even principalities, such as in some versions of the Second Book of Enoch when the patriarch Enoch visits the seventh heaven.

🙿 **LUCIFER** One of the names used in common parlance for Satan or the chief of the fallen angels. This usage is actually entirely inaccurate; the name does not denote Satan or any other vile being of the darkness but was used in ancient astronomy for Venus, the bright morning star. How this peculiar state of affairs came about can be traced to a passage in the Old Testament Book of Isaiah (14:12): "How you are fallen from heaven, O Day Star [or Lucifer, meaning "light bearer"], son of Dawn! How you are cut down to the ground, you who laid the nations low!" The "Day Star" to which the author refers is not some wicked unrepentant angel, but Nebuchadnezzar, king of Babylon, who had declared that he would ascend to the heavens and there place himself on equal footing with the Lord; instead he was doomed, according to Isaiah, to fall and be laid low. The name, however, and the idea of a light-bearing angel falling from the heavens were apparently too much for later writers to pass up. Thus St. Jerome and other Fathers of the Church took to using Lucifer as another name for Satan. In the custom that thereafter developed, Lucifer was the supposed name of a great angel in heaven before his famous Fall from grace and renaming as Satan. This most beautiful of angels, and one especially beloved by God, suffered from an overwhelming pride; he refused to bow down before mankind and was thus ejected from the heavenly host.

Not surprisingly, Lucifer has been the subject of many writers and artists. Milton, in his *Paradise Lost* (Book X), makes Lucifer the demon of sinful pride. Edmund Spenser, in his poem "An Hymne of Heavenly Love," terms him the brightest angel, even the "Child of Light." (See also *Satan*.)

MADAN An angel mentioned in *The Hierarchy of the Blessed Angels,* the 1635 treatise on angels by Thomas Heywood. According to that quite imaginative account, Madan is the patron or guardian of the planet Mercury. (See also *Planets, Angels of the.*)

MAHANAIM The Hebrew name, meaning "two armies," used by the Old Testament figure Jacob (in Genesis 32) to describe the vast double host of angels who met him during his journeys. Upon seeing them, Jacob is said to have exclaimed, "This is God's army!" naming the place occupied by the hosts Mahanaim. In the legends of the Jews, the numbers of each grand angelic army was placed at six hundred thousand. (See also *Hosts.*)

MALACHY Also Malachi, one of the many members of the heavenly host who have earned the name angel of the Lord, although in this angel's case it is especially apt: his name means "angel of God" in the sense of being "my messenger." The last book of the Old Testament is that of Malachi, although there is nothing in the work or tradition to support any possibility that the author was the angel.

MALA'IKAH The Arabic word for angels (sing. malak) and hence the name used for them in the traditions, teaching, and lore of Islam. Mala'ikah is often interpreted as meaning "messenger" and is said to be derived from the word *alk* (*ma'lak* or *malak*), meaning "to send." This thus describes the primary function of the angel in the Islamic world, that of a vital intermediary between Allah and humanity. Some say, however, that the name is actually taken from *malaka,* or "he controlled," denoting the control or power exercised by the angels over the elements and the physical world. Both possible meanings are still consistent with the Muslim conception of angels as spiritual beings sent by God to intervene or bring the message of the Lord into the lives of humans.

MALAK The Arabic word meaning "angel" (pl. mala'ikah). (For details, see under *Islam* and *Mala'ikah.*)

MALAKIM One of the ancient (Hebrew) names for the angelic order or choir known as the virtues. Also called the tarshishim, the malakim (as virtues) are generally placed as the fifth choir—of the nine—in the second triad of the angelic hierarchy. Nicknamed the shining ones, although malakim means "kings" or "rulers," the choir is traditionally said to be ruled by the angelic princes Raphael, Gabriel, Uriel, Tarshish, Bariel, and Michael; Satan, before his mighty Fall from heaven, was also counted as one of their chiefs. In some Jewish lists of the angelic orders, the malakim are separated from the tarshishim, being numbered differently as well from the fifth place appointed by the influential angelologist and theologian Dionysius the Areopagite. In these other lists the angels are numbered first, fourth, and eighth. (See under *Virtues* for other details; see also *Choirs.*)

MALIK In Islamic lore, a righteous but nevertheless truly frightful angel who has authority over all of the damned souls in hell and who guards and watches over the infernal land of suffering (the name means "master" or "king"). Malik is assisted in his unpleasant duties by nineteen other angels, perhaps to be equated with the much-feared angels of destruction in angelic lore. Malik and his able companions torment the damned souls and respond to their pleas of mercy by observing (as written in the Qur'an, surah 43:77–78): "You shall stay. Certainly we bring the Truth to you, but most of you are averse to the Truth." Malik is also known to make cruel jokes from the cries and begging of the condemned. For the damned, however, some relief can be found from the brutalities of Malik by reciting one important formula from Islamic teaching: "Allah, the Compassionate and the Merciful." Special and most savage treatment is saved for the infidels, who have heard the truth but refused to accept the words of the Prophet. Muslims sent to hell are, as Malik well knows, to be freed at some point in the future through the intervention of Muhammad.

MAMMON See under *Fallen Angels.*

MAN CLOTHED IN LINEN An angel appearing in the Old Testament, in particular the Book of Ezekiel, which features the account of the prophet of the exiles, who predicts the wrath of the Lord toward the Jewish people:

> *Therefore I will deal in wrath; my eye will not spare, nor will I have pity; and though they cry in my ears with a loud voice, I will not hear them.*
>
> *Then he cried in my ears with a loud voice, saying, "Draw near, you executioners of the city, each with his destroying weapon in his hand." And lo, six men came from the direction of the upper gate, which faces north, every man with his weapon for slaughter in his hand, and with them was a man clothed in linen, with a writing case at his side. . . . And the Lord said to him, "Go through the city, through Jerusalem, and put a mark upon the foreheads of the men who sigh and groan over all the abominations that are committed in it." And to the others he said in my hearing, "Pass through the city after him, and smite; your eye shall not spare, and you shall show no pity; slay old men outright, young men and maidens, little children and women, but touch no one upon whom is the mark." (8:18; 9:1–6)*

The identity of the "Man Clothed in Linen" has been the subject of much speculation, although most agree that he was most likely an angel. Among the proposed angels are Gabriel, Michael (who is mentioned in a similar role in the Book of Daniel 12), or the so-called Angel of Peace. As the man functions as a kind of heavenly scribe, he may also be identified with the patriarch Enoch or one of several other scribes supposedly taken to heaven.

MAN OF MACEDONIA A person, most often described as an angel, who appeared to St. Paul in a dream and beseeched that famed evangelist to cross into Europe to preach, as recorded in the Acts of the Apostles: "And a vision appeared to Paul in the night: a man of Macedonia was standing beseeching him and saying, 'Come over to Macedonia and help us.' And when he had seen the vision, immediately we sought to go into Macedonia, concluding that God had us to preach the gospel to them."

MANNA By tradition, the food of the angels and the blessed in heaven; it is best known as the food sent to the Israelites as they fled from Egypt and wandered in the desert under the leadership of Moses. Meaning in Aramaic "What is this?" manna was described in the Book of Exodus as "like coriander seed, white, and the taste of it was like wafers made with honey." This is the generally accepted meal of the angelic hosts, although there is naturally some question why angels, being entirely spiritual creatures, might have need for substantial food. (See under *Food* for more details.)

The prophet Elijah is brought manna by an angel; by Gustave Doré.

MANY-EYED ONES The impressive title or nickname given to the angels belonging to the choir or order of the thrones (called in the Hebrew the ophanim or the galgallim), also known as the "wheels." There is, however, a tradition that the "many-eyed ones" may be said to represent the cherubim, although this is probably the result of the frequent jumbling over the years of angelic descriptions and attributes. The name is derived from a number of writings, two of the most interesting being the Second Book of Enoch, that compendium on angelic lore, and the Old Testament Book of Ezekiel. In Enoch there is reference to the "many-eyed thrones" residing in the seventh heaven. Ezekiel, meanwhile, describes in vivid detail the angels he beheld in the land of the Chaldaeans, by the river Chebar; the thrones are called the wheels: "The four wheels had rims and they had spokes; and their rims were full of eyes round about." (See *Virtues.*)

🙟 **MARIOKH** Also Mariuk, one of the two angels, with Ariukh (or Oriokh), supposedly named to serve as a guardian over the family of the great patriarch Enoch to preserve them from the impending flood (Noah's well-known deluge) so that his line might endure and his writings might last forever; these writings are said to be the useful—if not somewhat unreliable—source on angelic lore known as the Books of Enoch. In Jewish lore, as recorded in the famous collection *The Legends of the Jews* by Louis Ginzberg, Mariokh was the angel who protected Enoch while he wrote his works. (See also *Enoch, Books of.*)

🙟 **MARY, VIRGIN** The mother of Christ, honored in the teachings of the Catholic Church as the queen of heaven and the queen of angels. The blessed Virgin Mary had numerous close associations with angels, from the Annunciation to the Assumption. In the Annunciation Mary was visited by the archangel Gabriel, who announced to her the coming of Jesus. When she gave birth in the stable in Bethlehem, the event was so glorious that angels appeared to shepherds in the surrounding hills. And according to tradition, when she was taken to heaven (the Assumption), the angels accompanied her.

Growing in importance throughout the Middle Ages, the Virgin Mary has been the subject of some of history's greatest paintings. These paintings have included some magnificent examples of angels, from the awe-inspiring Gabriel of the Annunciation to the adorable cherubs and putti of the kind found in some paintings of the Madonna and Child.

The Virgin Mary is also intimately connected with the so-called Holy House of Loreto, the small shrine now preserved in a sumptuous basilica in Italy and long said to have the relics of the house in which Jesus was conceived at the Annunciation. More of a room, the relic was revered as early as the fourth century as the site where Mary was visited by an angel. A basilica was built over it in the Holy Land and was the center of vibrant pilgrim activity. Toward the end of the Crusades, in 1291, the house reportedly miraculously disappeared from the Holy Land (which had been abandoned by the Crusaders), suddenly arriving in northern Italy. It moved again three years later, supposedly after two brothers in whose field it startlingly arrived began squabbling about how much money they could make from the shrine, and was discovered at a spot near Ancona in Italy, on the Adriatic. Popular lore long declared that its transportation from site to site had been the work of angels who have ever kept it safe from harm. The holy house remains one of the most important of all Marian shrines, receiving visits from many popes, including John Paul II. (See also *Annunciation, Angel of the; Nativity, Angels of the;* and *Queen of the Angels.*)

MASHIT An angel appearing in Jewish lore, he is counted as one of the dread beings who bring misery or inflict punishment upon souls in hell. In some sources he is ranked as a demon or dark spirit, serving with the angels (or demons) Af and Hemah as a brutal torturer in Gehenna (or Gehinnon, the Hebrew hell). According to the tale recorded in *The Legends of the Jews* by Louis Ginzberg, Mashit has the additional and most unpleasant duty of presiding over the deaths of children so declared to pass away before their time. (See also *Hemah.*)

MASKIM The name used in the Babylonian religion for the seven evil deities who reside in their hell. According to later custom, the terrible being Mephistopheles, a fallen angel, was one of their number. (See also *Babylon.*)

MASTEMA The so-called Accusing Angel, an evil angel who nevertheless is the servant of God, acting as the great tempter of humanity. A recurring figure in Jewish legend, Mastema is equatable with Satan (and less correctly Lucifer) in later lore, ever working to tempt mortals as a means of testing their faith in the Lord. According to one tale, the devils or spirits of evil who assist Mastema were created through the wicked souls of the cruel giants who roamed the earth, the children of the fallen angels who had mated with mortal women. The Flood, however, wiped out nearly all of them and would have deprived Mastema of his servants had he not successfully petitioned God to spare some of them in order to have spirits with which to test men's faith. The Lord thus allowed one-tenth of the devils to survive, with Mastema as their chief. Once permitted to live, Mastema was quite active, especially in opposition to Moses. The evil angel supposedly secretly convinced Pharaoh not to consider permitting the Israelites to leave Egypt and then gave assistance to the Egyptian sorcerers, who performed some of the same feats of magic as Moses, such as turning a stick into a snake. Many of these actions have also been attributed to the angel of Egypt.

🕸 **MASTINIM** The Hebrew name for the angels who serve under the powerful angelic being (or devil) Samael.

🕸 **MELKYAL** Also Melkejal, Malchidiel, and Machidiel, an angel whose name means the "fullness of God" and who is said to rise and rule at the beginning of the year for a total of ninety-one days. According to the First Book of Enoch, Melkyal gives the sign of his rule by the way the trees bear fruit, the leaves grow on a tree, the harvest is good, and the winter trees wither and die. Melkyal, under assorted names, also appeared in occult magical rites, including one said during medieval times to be an absolutely certain way of securing the love of a maiden.

🕸 **MEPHISTOPHELES** See under *Fallen Angels*.

🕸 **MERKABAH ANGELS** The collective name for those angels appearing in the lore and traditions of the mystical Jewish sect of the Merkabah. The Merkabah (or Merkava)—meaning "Chariot"— flourished in Judaism from the time of the first century A.D. and continued in various centers throughout the early Middle Ages. Adherents of the sect believed in the necessity and desirability of using esoteric and mystical means to ascend through the great seven heavens or mansions, called hekhalot (or hechaloth), to the glorious throne of God, which rests upon an incomparable chariot—the Merkabah.

It was the objective of members of the Merkabah sect, deemed fit and deserving by superiors, to fast, pray, and recite arcane and powerful formulae as a means of rising through the heavens. The initiates, called the Yorde Merkava ("Travelers to the Supernatural World"), would be aided along the way by angels, but progress is ever challenged by evil spirits and demons and, most dangerous of all, the terrible and merciless angelic guardians of the gateway to each of the heavens. To gain entry, the initiate was supposed to recite the proper formula (known as a seal) to the gate guard angel—the possessor or keeper of the seal. If successful, entry was permitted; failure had the most frightful consequences, as the remorseless angel would eject the impertinent claimant, doing severe damage physically or mentally, or simply cause the initiate to be burned to death in a fiery eruption of heavenly wrath. For the successful traveler, the seventh heaven would be reached and the veil of power surrounding the Merkabah would itself be breached.

The seal-keeping angels are sometimes equated with the seven merkaboth, a group of angelic beings who stand as the corresponding figures of the seven heavens. They can perhaps also be identified as the virtual embodiment of the heavens themselves. Aside from these angels, the Merkabah accepted that there were groups of angels always surrounding the throne of God. These were said to include the seraphim, the galgallim, and especially the hayyoth. (See also *Heaven*.)

MESSENGERS One of the most important of all duties of angels, so much so that the very Hebrew word *mal'akh* and Greek word *angelos,* denoting these beings, both mean "messenger." The angel stands as one of the central intermediaries or representatives of the Lord to humanity. Existing entirely at the will and in the service of God, the angel is frequently dispatched to earth to deliver some important revelation or declaration, usually having much impact upon the lives of the recipients. Aside from the other tasks given to them in relating to earthly affairs, angels are mentioned frequently in the Bible in the ministering role of messengers. They brought word of the impending doom of Sodom and Gomorrah, informed Mary of the incarnation of Christ, announced his coming to Joseph, suggested to Joseph that he should flee to Egypt with Mary and Jesus, and joyously proclaimed the birth and later the resurrection of the Lord. While angels have many other duties in tradition, both in heaven and on earth, their role as messengers is still one central to their ex-

An angel bringing a message from God to a mortal; by Albrecht Dürer.

istence, serving to remind an often forgetful world that God loves all of his Creation and is concerned for its well-being.

🏵 **MESUKIEL** See under *Sefiroth*.

🏵 **METATRON** One of the greatest of all angels, honored as the angel of the face, the angel of the presence, chief of the ministering angels, the chief recording angel, chancellor of heaven, the angel by whom the world is maintained, and a being so mighty that he possesses seventy-two other names. Few angels have been the source of such a wide-ranging body of legends and tales, but precious few of the celestial hierarchy are credited with such majesty and power. Also called Metatetron, Merraton, and Metaraon, he was supposedly once a humble mortal being, the antediluvian patriarch Enoch. According to widely reported lore, Enoch earned such merit in the eyes of the Lord for his goodness and abilities as a scribe that he was taken to heaven, an event noted in the Book of Genesis (5:24): "Enoch walked with God; and he was not, for God took him." If the rather fanciful Books of Enoch are to believed, Enoch was transported to heaven and given a comprehensive tour of Creation. He was then chosen by the Lord for the incomparable honor of being transformed into an angel, the angel Metatron. After overcoming the objections of some of the other angels, Enoch was blessed by God with 1,365,000 blessings and the transformation was begun. He was enlarged and increased in size until he was nearly equal to the entire earth in length and breadth; he then received 36 pairs of wings (for 72 wings in all) and was given 365,000 eyes. Each eye was full of the glory of the Lord and each wing the size of the world. The heralds of heaven then went forth across the blessed realm and announced that Metatron was to be seated at the entrance of the seventh (or highest) heaven upon a magnificent throne and all who approached the throne of God should first approach him, for he was henceforth the prince of wisdom and the prince of understanding. To make the metamorphosis complete, the Lord turned Metatron into a burning, living flame, his sinews like the hottest of fire, his eyes like torches, and his flesh the very essence of heat. After this glorious rebirth, the angels were apparently suitably impressed, but one angel supposedly was terrified of Metatron, groveling before him and announcing that there were now two Masters in heaven. This did not sit well with the Lord, who ordered a slight humiliation for Metatron—the angelic prince Anafiel YHWH flogged him sixty times with lashes of fire, a reminder that while he might be truly awe-inspiring, he was still only one angel of the heavenly host. As for why exactly Metatron was chosen for this honor, the Jewish mystical work the Zohar states that he was born with the divine spark of spiritual perfection that had originally been bestowed upon Adam but which he had lost owing to his sin. Enoch, however, was a mere mortal, so the Lord could not permit such perfection to remain within a member of fallen humanity. Transported to heaven, Enoch became Metatron in order to give proper expression to his perfection. At the same time, he became the foremost intermediary between God and humanity, the link between the divine and the human, possessing experience both of the earthly and the heavenly. In this sense he is also a special guardian of humanity and is the chief of the so-called Guardian Angels of the Nations.

As might be deduced from the Enochian tales, Metatron is one of the tallest angels in all of heaven, matched only by Anafiel and possibly Sandalphon, his brother, and, according to other tales, the one-time prophet Elijah. His primary task among the heavenly court is to maintain the eternal archives of the Lord, recording each and every event that transpires. As the archives would theoretically date back to the beginning of time, one can only wonder about their size.

While understandably busy with his many offices and duties, Metatron has still found the time to involve himself in a host of legends. He thus appears in numerous diverse events, as the angel who prevented Abraham from sacrificing his son, Isaac; wrestled with Jacob (see *Dark Angel*); and led the Israelites under Moses out of the wilderness. One of his most dramatic, not to mention unlikely, achievements involved two evil Egyptian sorcerers who used their advanced knowledge of magic to ascend to heaven. Such was their strength that neither Michael nor Gabriel could expel them. Metatron, however, broke their spells and cast out the impudent Egyptians. For this reason, Metatron is considered by some to be superior to most of the angels, including Michael, Gabriel, and Uriel.

MICHAEL Also St. Michael the Archangel and, in Arabic, Mika'il, perhaps the greatest of all the angels, whose name likely means "Who is like God?" He is captain of the hosts of the Lord and the most beloved of all residents of the heavenly host (with the possible exception of the archangel Gabriel). The figure of Michael probably originated in Chaldaea as a protective god or spirit. Accepted by the Jews, he emerged as so major an angel in Jewish lore that he was honored as the patron angel of Israel. In this particular role he was the only guardian angel of the nations (out of seventy) who did not fall from grace, his bias entirely understood since it favored God's Chosen People.

Michael appears twice in the Old Testament and is noted, with Gabriel (and Raphael in the Book of Tobit), as one of the few angels actually mentioned in the Bible: in Daniel (10:13), he is called "Michael, one of the chief princes," and later (12:1) is a "great prince." Aside from these specific references, he is declared the ruling prince of the archangels, chief of the choir of virtues, the prince of the presence, and an angel of mercy and repentance. He is also credited with being the angel who spoke to Moses in the burning bush (an honor often bestowed upon Zagzagel); the messenger who stayed the hand of Abraham before he sacrificed his son; and the angel responsible for massacring the Assyrian army of Sennacherib, a deed normally attributed to an otherwise unnamed angel of destruction but perhaps accomplished by Uriel, Gabriel, or others. He is accepted in lore as well as being the special patron of Adam. Supposedly he was the first angel in all of the heavens to bow down before humanity. Michael then kept an eye on the first family, remaining vigilant even after the fall of Adam and Eve and their expulsion from the Garden of Eden. In the apocryphal Book of Adam and Eve, Michael taught Adam how to farm. The archangel later brought Adam to heaven in a fiery chariot, giving him a tour of the blessed realm. After Adam's death, Michael helped convince the Lord to permit Adam's soul to be brought to heaven and cleansed of its great sin. Jewish legend also states Michael to be one of the three "men" who visited Abraham and one of the five angels, with Uriel, Metatron, Raphael, and Gabriel, who buried Moses. Apparently Michael had to fight with Satan for the body of the Lawgiver, an event mentioned in the New Testament Letter of St. Jude. Finally, in the Dead Sea Scrolls is the story "The War of the Sons of Light and the Sons of Darkness," in which Michael is described as the prince of light, leading the forces of good against the darkness of evil.

Michael was embraced enthusiastically by Christianity and honored as the leader of the angels whose very name was used as a war chant by the holy angels during the war in heaven. As commander of the heavenly host, he led the good angels in their successful conflict against Satan and the fallen angels. He is named in the Book of Revelation, fighting against Satan, and at the end of the world will command the hosts of the Lord in the final conflict.

The Catholic Church honors Michael with four main titles or offices. He is the Christian angel of death, carrying the souls of all the deceased to heaven, where they are weighed in his perfectly balanced scales (hence Michael is often depicted holding scales). At the hour of death, Michael descends and gives each soul the chance to redeem itself before passing, thus consternating the devil and his minions. Michael is the special patron of the Chosen People in the Old Testament and is the guardian of the Church; it was thus not unusual for the angel to be revered by the military orders of knights during the Middle Ages. Last, he is the supreme enemy of Satan and the fallen angels.

Michael has been the object of considerable examination on the part of theologians, especially regarding the apparent inconsistency of having an archangel—a member of the eighth and second-lowest choir of angels—lead the hosts of the

St. Michael the Archangel, in battle with Satan and the fallen angels; by Albrecht Dürer.

Lord. Some, such as St. Thomas Aquinas, declare him to be the chief of the order of archangels. His high post is presumably explained by the fact that archangels are in the forefront of the fight in the world against evil, so Michael, as their chief, assumes the command of the angels by virtue of his experience. Others, most notably the Greek fathers such as St. Basil the Great, wrote that Michael was superior to all the angels; others appointed him the ruling prince of the seraphim, which would place him in the highest position in heaven.

Michael has been venerated by the Church from an early time. His elevated position is made clear by his title of saint, by the number of churches dedicated to him, and by his many appearances in history. He supposedly visited Emperor Constantine the Great (d. 337) at Constantinople, intervened in assorted battles, and appeared, sword in hand, over the mausoleum of Hadrian, in apparent answer to the prayers of Pope St. Gregory I the Great (r. 590–604) that a plague in Rome should cease. In honor of the occasion, the pope took to calling the mausoleum the Castel Sant'Angelo (Castle of the Holy Angel), the name by which it is still known.

The last visit certified one major aspect involving Michael, namely his role as an angel of healing. This title was bestowed at Phrygia, in Asia Minor, which also propagated the cult of angels and became a leading center for their veneration. Michael is reputed to have caused a healing spring to flow in the first century at Colossae, and his churches were frequently visited by the sick and lame. The angel is invoked additionally as the patron of sailors in Normandy (the famous monastery of Mont-Saint-Michel on the north coast of France is named after him) and is especially remembered in France as the spirit who gave St. Joan of Arc the courage to save her country from the English during the Hundred Years' War (1337–1455). Perhaps his most singular honor was given to him in 1950 when Pope Pius XII (r. 1939–1958) named him patron of policemen. Michael is also said to have announced to the Virgin Mary her impending death, declaring himself to be "Great and Wonderful." (See also *Feast Days* and *Michaelmas*.)

Among the Muslims, Michael is one of the four archangels (with Azrael, Israfel, and Gabriel), and one of the two angels, with Gabriel, named in the Qur'an. He resides in the seventh heaven and is popularly believed to have wings of emerald green.

A favorite angelic subject in art, matched only by Gabriel, Michael is most often depicted as a proud, handsome angel in white or magnificent armor and wielding a sword, shield, or lance. In some paintings he is shown with a banner or holding scales. Quite often he is seen, like St. George or some Madonnas, in conflict with a dragon or standing upon a vanquished devil. Of him was declared in Milton's *Paradise Lost* (Book VI):

> *Go, Michael, of celestial armies prince,*
> *And thou, in military prowess next,*

> *Gabriel; lead forth to battle these my sons*
> *Invincible; lead forth my armed saints*
> *By thousands and by millions ranged for fight.*

MICHAELMAS The holiday, celebrated September 29, honoring the archangel St. Michael, although in the Catholic Church the day was revised to honor the three angels Michael, Gabriel, and Raphael. This change brought to an end the individual feast days for all three angels (Raphael on October 24 and Gabriel on March 24). The Feast of Michaelmas developed its own traditions and customs, especially in England and Ireland. In Ireland a special Michaelmas pie was fixed, with a ring hidden in it; the person—presumably a young one—who first finds it is said to be destined to marry early. In England it was accepted custom to prepare a roast goose.

MIDAEL An angel mentioned in the occult works *The Magus* by Francis Barrett (1801) and the *Greater Key of Solomon* by S. L. Mac-Gregor Mathers (1889). Midael is described as a member—even an officer—in the army of heaven. He is also the supposed "angel of the Lord," noted in two of the Psalms (34 and 35): "The angel of the Lord encamps around those who fear him, and delivers them" and "Let them be like chaff before the wind, with the angel of the Lord driving them on! Let their way be dark and slippery, with the angel of the Lord pursuing them!"

MIK'AIL The Arabic name for the great archangel Michael. (For details on the Islamic lore of this angel, see under *Michael*.)

MILTON, JOHN English poet (1608–1674), best known for his masterpiece, *Paradise Lost,* which is honored as one of the foremost works in the English language and one of the greatest of all writings relating to angels. Milton was born in London, studied at Cambridge University, and then occupied a variety of positions, including Latin secretary to the council of state, which was in charge of the English government under Oliver Cromwell. Starting in 1644 his eyesight began to fail, and by 1652 he was completely blind, fulfilling his duties by dictating to an assistant, Andrew Marvell. Long writing poetry, Milton was the composer of such early works as *Comus* (1637) and *Lycidas* (1638). It was not until his retirement, however, that he devoted all of his energies to his larger poetic works, including *Samson Agonistes* (1671). His two finest works were *Paradise Lost* (1667) and *Paradise Regained* (1671), dictated to his daughters.

Written in twelve books, *Paradise Lost* presents the tale of Adam's fall from grace and the expulsion of Adam and Eve from Paradise. Central to the tale are the activities of Satan and his fallen angels and the efforts of the good angels to thwart humanity's temptation and sin. The characterizations are superb, especially of the angelic beings such as Satan, Raphael, Gabriel, and Michael, and the imagery of heaven, hell, and the earthly Paradise are still some of the most magnificent ever penned. The story ends with the exile of the first family, but it offers up hope of an eventual restoration. This is provided in *Paradise Regained,* in which the possible redemption hinted at in *Paradise Lost* is fulfilled by Christ. The poet died in London.

MINISTERING ANGELS The name given to a special group or body of angels, called in the Hebrew *malache hashareth,* who appear frequently in Jewish lore and legend. For example, the ministering angels are said to have been sent to Adam and Eve when they still resided in the Garden of Eden. These angels gave to Adam all of their assistance, including cooking his meat and preparing his wine. The descendants of Adam—the children of Noah—also were sent ministering angels who were supposedly under the authority of the archangel Michael. The angels were charged with teaching Noah's descendants the skill of language. It is unclear exactly how many ministering angels exist, although one tradition declares them to be the most numerous of all the species or orders of angels and hence the least important in the celestial hierarchy. In the legends surrounding the Talmud, ministering angels are created every day, born once a day with the task of singing a great hymn of praise to God before being absorbed back into the divine essence. It is possible to equate the ministering angels with the guardian angels.

MITHRA See *Yazatas.*

MOAKIBAT Properly al-Moakibat, another name used in Islamic lore for the set of angels—known also as the hafaza—who accompany and protect each living person. These angels also perform the extremely important task of recording each and every act performed by the person, whether good or evil. These recording angels, as they are known, then read their books at the time of judgment, an event mentioned in the Qur'an (surah 82:10–14): "And surely there are keepers over you, Honorable recorders, They know what you do. Surely the righteous are in bliss, And the wicked are truly in Burning Fire."

MONS, ANGELS OF One of the most famous episodes of angelic intervention, namely the supposedly widely reported descent of an angelic army in August 1914, which came to the aid of the British forces against the Germans in Mons, Belgium. The angelic host's assistance could not have come at a more propitious moment, as the British (with their French allies) were being driven back by the relentless German advance. Accounts of what happened varied considerably according to eyewitness reports of those involved, but it seems that a kind of phantom army appeared on several occasions, helping to stave off disaster for retreating English troops.

One account, said to have been corroborated by German prisoners, described a force of phantoms, armed with bows and arrows and led by a towering figure on a shining white horse, who spurred on an English force during its assault on German trenches. Another story spoke of three angelic beings seen by the British, hovering in the air over German lines, a source of deep inspiration to the Allies, especially as some hardbitten soldiers saw them as well, adding details about the brightness of their faces and their wings. Aside from these beings, soldiers later claimed to have seen St. Michael the Archangel, the Blessed Virgin Mary, and even Joan of Arc.

Once the stories began to spread about the phantom soldiers of Mons, more soldiers came forward with their own tales. As for the figure on the white horse, many swore that it was Saint George, supported by the ghostly soldiers of the English army that had fought and won the great Battle of Agincourt in 1415 against the French. It was thus immediately assumed that this apparition was the cause of the hysterical reporting among the troops, and the remaining stories grew out of this event.

Skeptics naturally rejected any claims of spiritual intervention by St. George, angels, or anyone else. They were bolstered in their resistance by a curious work of the English writer Arthur Machen, "The Bowmen." This short story, presenting the purely fictitious march of St. George and a phantom English army from Agincourt in the dark days of 1914, was published in September 1914 in the *Lon-*

don Evening News. Machen insisted he had heard nothing of the battlefront accounts, claiming that the story had obviously served as the genesis of the hysteria. Soldiers stood firm in their statements, and as Machen himself wrote in the short story: "But the man who knew what nuts tasted like when they called themselves steak knew also that St. George had brought his Agincourt bowmen to help the English."

MOON, ANGEL OF THE The title borne by several angels, each of whom is credited with possessing authority and guardianship over that celestial body. The angel most consistently declared angel of the moon is Ofaniel (Ophaniel), who was described as such by Longfellow in a later edition of his *The Golden Legend,* although in the work Ofaniel is spelled Onafiel. In an earlier version Longfellow had named instead the archangel Gabriel, one of a host of offices, titles, and powers attributed to that angel of the Annunciation. Qafsiel is also honored as an angel with some dominion over the moon. Another commonly named angel is Yahriel. (See also *Planets, Angels of the.*)

MORONI The angel who, according to the teachings of the Mormon Church (the Church of Jesus Christ of Latter-day Saints), appeared on September 22, 1827, to Joseph Smith (d. 1844), founder of Mormonism. The angel—or perhaps the resurrected spirit—is said to have claimed to Smith that he (the angel) had once been the last of the prophets, the final leader of the nephites. He is also believed by the Mormons to have given to Smith on Hill Cumorah, near Palmyra, New York, a set of gold plates containing details on the prophets in ancient America. From these Smith was able to compose the Book of Mormon. Once this had been completed, Moroni retrieved the gold plates. The plates were supposedly covered with arcane hieroglyphics, similar to ancient Egyptian. Smith was apparently able to translate the words.

MOSES The Lawgiver, the leader of the Hebrew nation who, according to biblical accounts, led his people out of bondage in Egypt and mediated the covenant established on Mt. Sinai; aside from his famed efforts to free the Hebrews in Egypt, Moses is best known for delivering the Ten Commandments. He is also one of the leading figures in Jewish legend and was supposedly both assisted by angels and given a certain power over them by the Lord. In the Book of Exodus is told of Moses' call from God through the burning bush and his long struggle to free the Israelites from their supposed bondage under the Egyptians. Beyond the Scriptures, however, the life of Moses is interwoven with legends and tales. For example, the burning bush is often described as the appearance of an actual angel, named as Michael or, more often, as Zagzagel. He was then supposedly assisted in his labors against the Egyptians by various angels who helped him perform the feats of the plagues and the magic tricks before Pharaoh, such as turning the staff into a snake. Interestingly, however, he was thought to have been opposed in this venture by the angel of Egypt (Duma, Rahab, Uzza, or Mastema), who showed a great favor for the nation over which he had charge. (See angels of nations under *Guardian Angels.*)

Moses additionally was thought to have been taken to heaven and hell on guided tours while he was still alive. In hell, the flames of suffering were withdrawn from the area where he was walking to keep him from burning his beard. Surprisingly, his trip to heaven was less cordial. Several angels did not like his special place with the Lord and felt that he should not be shown around the blessed realm. God, however, disagreed, arming the Lawgiver with his secret name. Moses then uttered it and reduced the angels to quivering, kneeling servants. While in heaven, he met the so-called Tall Angel. Moses' prayers had special weight, so much so that some angels supposedly grew jealous. Zakun and Lahash, in fact, tried to steal a prayer sent from Moses to the Lord. They were caught and subjected to punishment. The Lawgiver long struggled against death, resisting it for as long as possible. Finally, when at last his time had come, the Lord himself descended from heaven to take his soul away; but just to be sure, God took with him several angels, including Gabriel and Michael. Upon the patriarch's demise, the angel Semalion (or Samael) flew throughout the heaven and proclaimed, "The Lawgiver is dead!" Moses was buried with tears and love by several archangels, variously named as Michael, Gabriel, Raphael, Metatron, and Uriel. Michael had to fight with Satan for control of Moses' mortal remains. (See also *Ark of the Covenant, Angels of the.*)

MOVIES For details on cinematic angels, see under *Films.*

🕸 **MUHAMMAD** See *Islam;* see also *Muhammad, Angel of* and *Qur'an.*

🕸 **MUHAMMAD, ANGEL OF** The angel reportedly beheld by the prophet Muhammad when he was taken to heaven. He described this angel as the most enormous of all beings, possessing 70,000 heads, each possessing 70,000 faces; each face had 70,000 mouths, each mouth 70,000 tongues, and each tongue spoke 70,000 languages. Every word spoken was devoted to singing the endless praises of God. Another angel eligible for the title is the beloved archangel Gabriel, who is honored in Islamic lore as the angel who brought to the Prophet the Qur'an.

🕸 **MULCIBER** In mythology, the name used by the Romans for the Greek god Vulcan. This god's name is derived from "softener" in recognition of his ability to soften metals. As an angel, Mulciber appeared in John Milton's *Paradise Lost* (Book I) as one of the fallen of the angelic hierarchy, but his position in heaven had been as a mighty architect. Once fallen, he put his considerable skills to fiendish use, constructing the very capitol of hell, Pandemonium. As Milton wrote:

> *The hasty multitude*
> *Admiring entered, and the work some praise*
> *And some the architect: his hand was known*
> *In heaven by many a towered structure high,*
> *Where sceptered angels held their residence,*
> *And sat as princes, whom the supreme king*
> *Exalted to such power, and gave to rule,*
> *Each in his hierarchy, the orders bright.*
> *Nor was his name unheard or unadored*
> *In ancient Greece; and in Ausonian land*
> *Men called him Mulciber; and how he fell*
> *From heaven, they fabled, thrown by angry Jove*
> *Sheer o'er the crystal battlements; from morn*
> *To noon he fell, from noon to dewy eve.*
> *A summer's day; and with the setting sun*
> *Dropped from the zenith like a falling star.*

🕸 **MUNKAR AND NAKIR** Two angels appearing in Islamic lore. Described in some traditions as demons, Munkar (also Monker) and

Nakir are sent throughout the world to visit the souls of the recently deceased while they are still in the freshly buried corpses. The two will seize the body and examine the soul as to its worthiness to be admitted into paradise. The believers will naturally respond to their queries concerning Muhammad by declaring that Muhammad is the prophet and the messenger of God. Deemed worthy, they will be permitted to enjoy a peaceful rest in anticipation of their entry into paradise following the Day of Judgment. The unbelievers—the infidels—will not respond properly and will be tortured in their graves by the two angels until their final damnation at the end of the world. Munkar and Nakir are described in tradition as being black in color with piercing blue eyes. (See also *Ruman.*)

MUSIC See box on pages 192–193.

Angels making music; from *Christ Surrounded by Musical Angels,* by Hans Memling, Royal Museum of Fine Arts, Antwerp (COURTESY ART RESOURCE).

MUSIC

One of the most overlooked facets of the lives of angels, music forms a vital part of the duties and activities of all the members of the heavenly host. On a cosmic scale, the angels take part in the so-called Music of the Spheres, the harmonious sound that emanates from the throne of God, is echoed by all parts of Creation, and is joined by the music and singing of the nine choirs. This profound image was presented in literary form by the renowned fantasy author J. R. R. Tolkien in his work *The Silmarillion,* in which Eru, the One, leads his angel-like creations, the Valar, in an incomparable piece of music that is finally marred by the proud and stubborn independence of the Valar, Melkor, who becomes Morgoth, the father of evil.

There is a so-called Angel of Music, the resident of heaven who is patron over all aspects of things musical. According to the Muslims, the angel of music is Israfel, best known as the angel who will blast the trumpet at the end of the world. Another angel named to the post is Uriel, who may have authority over the choirs of angels who sing eternally in praise of God. (See *Singing, Angelic.*)

Much as angels would seem to have phenomenal language skills, by virtue of the will of God, so too do they possess remarkable abilities in the playing of musical instruments. Their supposedly favorite instrument is the harp, but artists have portrayed them using every-

thing from trumpets and horns to violins and drums. While virtually any instrument can be played by angels, in art, at least, they choose the more delicate and lovely music makers, eschewing such ungainly pieces as the tuba or glockenspiel. (This is not to say that an angel hoping to assist some mortal could not, if it so chose, play an instrument close to the human's heart, be it a harp, a saxophone, a bagpipe, or even a kazoo.)

Angels have also been the objects of music themselves. For example, they figure prominently in Christmas carols and are the subjects of classical and modern composers. Angels were mentioned in Gregorian chants and the sacred music of the Church, especially in the pieces for the Christmas season and the *Missa de Angelis.* Among the classical composers writing angel-related works are Liszt (*Dante* Symphony and the *Mephisto* Waltz), Prokofiev (Third Symphony), Mahler (Second and Third Symphonies), Wagner (*Der Engel*), Schumann (*Faust*), and Verdi (*Giovanna d'Arco*). Even modern composers and musicians have pondered about angels. Elvis Presley, for example, lamented in one song: "You walk like an angel; / You talk like an angel; / But my, oh my; / You're like the Devil in disguise!" On the other hand, a band called the Heights, speaking for everyone, asked in a song: "How do you talk to an angel?"

NA'ARIRIEL **YHWH** An angel appearing in the Third Book of Enoch and ranked as one of the mighty princes of heaven. It is said that when the angel prince Atrugiel beholds him, he removes his crown and falls prostrate; likewise, when Na'aririel sees Sasnigiel, he removes his crown and falls prostrate.

NABU See *Nebo.*

NAGRASAGIEL See *Nasragiel.*

NAIRYO SANGHA An angel who, with the angels Kipod and Nasragiel, stands as one of the guardian princes of the upper gates of hell or Gehenna (Gehinnon). In Persian lore this angelic being is honored as a trusted servant of the great Persian deity Ahura Mazda.

NAKIR A fearsome angel, described in Islamic lore as black in color and with piercing blue eyes, who labors with his fellow angel Munkar to test the recently deceased as to their worthiness to enter paradise after the Day of Judgment. (For details, see under *Munkar and Nakir.*)

NASARGIEL See *Nasragiel.*

NASRAGIEL Also Nagrasagiel and Nasargiel, an angel who, with Kipod and Nairyo Sangha, serves as a guardian prince of the upper gate of hell or Gehenna (Gehinnon). Nasragiel is often described as possessing a fearsome head of a lion. He is also mentioned in Jewish lore as having acted as a guide to the underworld when the great Lawgiver, Moses, paid a visit; Moses supposedly made a similar visit to heaven. The visit of Moses to hell has been the subject of considerable legend, such as the tale that to permit him a comfortable walk, the unquenchable and merciless flames were withdrawn from around the Lawgiver to a distance of some 500 parasangs (an ancient measurement equal to 1,750 miles), giving some indication as to how hot and severe the fires must be if such a distance was necessary to prevent discomfort. On the tour, Moses was given the firsthand opportunity of seeing the unspeakable suffering inflicted upon sinners. One of the most memorable punishments was meted out to those husbands who looked with lust in their hearts upon their neighbors' wives (one of the Ten Commandments, of course, forbids this): they are hung forever by their eyelids.

NATHANIEL Also Nathanael, Xathanael, and Zathael, an angel whose name means "gift of God" and who has a rather varied portfolio. He is best known as an angel of fire. In this capacity he saved seven Israelites from the flames when they were sentenced to death by the Israeli king Jair, who was a follower of the pagan deity Baal. Nathaniel appeared, quenched the fire, and then burned the servants of Jair; he later gave the same conflagrational end to the king. (For other details, see under *Fire, Angel of,* for the account recorded in the work of Pseudo-Philo.) In other legends Nathaniel is honored as the sixth angel to be created by God and as the guardian or patron angel of the sixth hour. Still other tales name him as one of the three angels who have a special patronage over all things hidden, mysterious, or arcane.

NATIONS, ANGELS OF THE For the patron angels of nations, see under *Guardian Angels.*

NATIVITY, ANGELS OF THE The angels who were sent down from heaven to announce and celebrate the birth of Christ in the town of Bethlehem, an event recorded in the Gospel of St. Luke:

> *And in that region there were shepherds out in the field, keeping watch over their flocks by night. And an angel of the Lord appeared to them, and the glory of the Lord shone around them, and they were filled with fear.*

And the angel said to them, "Be not afraid; for behold, I bring you good news of a great joy which will come to all the people; for to you is born this day in the city of David a Savior, who is Christ the Lord. And this will be a sign for you: you will find a babe wrapped in swaddling clothes and lying in a manger." And suddenly there was with the angel a multitude of the heavenly host praising God and saying,

"Glory to God in the highest, and on earth peace among men with whom he is pleased!" (2:8–14)

The angels were then said to have gone back into heaven. It is unclear how many angels there might have been, but the host was certainly sufficient to impress upon the shepherds that something momentous had taken place. The angels of the Nativity have since proven one of the most enduring images from the entire occasion of the birth of Jesus, receiving enthusiastic representation by artists, including some of the greatest painters in history, who included them in any work depicting the nativity.

NAYA'IL Another name for the angel Lawidh, who served as the guide to the Islamic (Sufi) holy man Abu Yazid when he visited heaven. According to legend, the angel offered to Abu an incredible realm for him to rule alone. This offer was rejected by the Sufi leader because he perceived it to be a test of his devotion to the Lord. (See also *Lawidh* for other details.)

NEBO Also Nabu and Nabo, an angelic being found in the traditions of the Babylonians and among the Chaldaeans a god of wisdom and learning; he is considered by scholars to be predecessor or foreshadowing of the angel found in later Judaeo-Christian customs. Nebo is one of the so-called sukallin, the spirit messengers of the Sumerian and Babylonian deities, the clear forerunners of the angels, especially as they were to appear in Biblical custom. Nebo is especially so in this sense, for just as the Bible's Old Testament is replete with the angels of the Lord (or angels of God), so does this being serve as a messenger and servant to the god Marduk, possessing the name "minister of Marduk." He served in other capacities, such as the representative of the gods in the affairs of mortals and as the keeper of the Book of Fate, the mighty tome containing the destinies of all living things. In this, again, Nebo is the precursor of the recording angels who appear so regularly in Islamic and Jewish lore. As an offshoot of this role, Nebo was considered in some Jewish legends as the source of later stories related about the Old Testament patriarch and heavenly scribe Enoch, who was supposedly taken to heaven and transformed into the towering angel Metatron.

NEFILIM See *Nephilim*.

NEPHILIM Also the nefilim, the name given in Jewish or Hebrew legend for the offspring sired by the union of mortal women with the fallen angels, although at times it is also understood to denote the fallen angels themselves and their semidivine children. The nephilim, having angelic or divine blood coursing through their veins, are said to have been giants, described in the Old Testament Book of Genesis as "the mighty men that were of old, the men of renown." The imaginative First Book of Enoch notes that the giants were three hundred cubits in height (a cubit traditionally measured between seventeen and twenty-two inches in length). They possessed ravenous appetites, consuming so much food that the people finally refused to feed them; in response, the nephilim took to eating the people, a move that not surprisingly caused irreparable damage in relations between them. The giants then reportedly sinned against all of Creation, hastening the Lord's decision to flood the earth. Prior to the famed deluge, the nephilim reportedly helped to build the Tower of Babel, which does much to explain its height. According to custom, the tower was of such prodigious size that it took a year to climb all the way to the top and permitted King Nimrod and his insufferably arrogant court to shoot arrows into heaven itself; the arrows fell back to the earth dripping with the blood of angels. This outrage caused the Lord and his wounded angelic choirs to descend to the world and cause confusion among Nimrod's people. If one accepts the tale, it may be assumed that Nimrod himself was probably the son of the nephilim (see also *Confusion, Angels of*). The nephilim were finally wiped out in the Flood that made Noah so famous. There is, however, a curious tradition that at least one of the nephilim was able to survive. Named Og, this giant cleverly hid himself upon the roof of Noah's ark (it seems strange that no one noticed before it was too late that a being three hundred cubits tall was sitting there). Taking pity upon him—and probably reluctant to anger him—Noah supposedly fed him one thousand cattle every day, a feat of some skill, as the ark was already crowded. The nephilim are also known by many other names, such as the gibborim and the zamzummim.

🐚 **NEW TESTAMENT** The collection of twenty-seven books constituting the traditional second division of the Bible, with the Old Testament. The New Testament tells of the life of Jesus Christ, his Passion, Crucifixion, and Resurrection, and the subsequent spread of the Christian faith. It includes the work of the Apostles, especially Saints Peter and Paul (as told in the Acts of the Apostles); the often profound letters of Paul, Jude, James, Peter, and John; and the famed enigmatic work of prophecy, the Book of Revelation. Throughout the New Testament there is considerable mention of angels; indeed, the angels appear in the first chapter of the Gospel according to Matthew (1:20) and have a major part to play in the mysterious events described in Revelation. Much about the angels is rooted in the angelophanies of the Old Testament, and the two angels named in the earlier works, Gabriel and Michael, make another appearance. Gabriel announces the coming birth of John the Baptist and especially that of Christ, and

St. Peter is rescued from prison by an angel, the only angelic event in the New Testament; from the Duomo, Palermo (COURTESY ART RESOURCE).

his appearance to Mary is called the Annunciation. Michael appears in Revelation. Other, albeit nameless, angels figure in the Gospel accounts: they proclaim the birth of Christ (see *Nativity, Angels of the*); warn Joseph about the hunt for the child Jesus by King Herod and tell him to flee to Egypt; tell Joseph to return to Palestine after Herod's death; minister to Jesus in the desert after the attempted temptation of the Lord by Satan; give comfort to Christ in the garden of Gethsemane (see *Gethsemane, Angel of*); were present at the tomb after the Resurrection and at the Ascension; and rescued St. Peter from prison, an event presented in glorious terms by the Renaissance master Raphael in a Vatican painting. The Letters of St. Paul also offer important facets of angel lore, such as his Letter to the Ephesians, in which he actually names what are believed to be angelic choirs such as the powers and principalities. There are also the hosts of angels in the Book of Revelation. (See also *Bible* and *Revelation, Book of.*)

NINE ANGELS The collective name given to the ruling princes of the nine accepted orders of the angels, the nine choirs of the celestial hierarchy. The exact names of the nine angels vary according to the many lists of the reigning angels and of the assorted choirs. (For details on the heads of the choirs, see under *Princes, Angelic.*) The apocryphal Gospel of Bartholomew, written in the third century and full of interesting, if not peculiar, angel lore, mentions a group of nine angels who, according to the demon Beliar (who is bound by 660 angels and fiery chains and compelled to answer the questions of Bartholomew), "run together through the heavenly and earthly regions. . . . Together they fly through the regions of heaven, of earth, and the underworld." The nine angels are listed as Chalkatura, Mermeoth, Onomatath, Duth, Nephonos, Hoethra, Melioth, Charuth, and Graphathas.

NISROCH Also Nisroc originally, a deity worshiped among the Assyrians who was later ranked by Milton among the angels and in the lore of demons as one of the fallen spirits. He was also possibly once one of the chiefs of the angelic choir of principalities. As was written in the Old Testament book 2 Kings (19:37): "Then Sennacherib king of Assyria departed, and went home, and dwelt in Nineveh. And as he was worshipping in the house of Nisroch his god, Adramelech and Sharezer, his sons slew him with the sword and escaped into the land of Ararat." In art, Nisroch was depicted in classic Assyrian style as a being with the body of a man and the head of a fearsome eagle, with wings. Nisroch would resurface as an angel in John Milton's *Paradise Lost* (Book VI) during the debate in heaven:

> . . . *and in the assembly next upstood*
> *Nisroch, of principalities the prime;*
> *As one he stood escaped from cruel fight,*
> *Sore toiled, his riven arms to havoc hewn,*
> *And cloudy in aspect thus answering spake.*
> *"Deliver from new lords, leader to free*
> *Enjoyment of our right as gods; yet hard*
> *For gods, and too unequal work we find*
> *Against unequal arms to fight in pain,*
> *Against unpained, impassive; from which evil*
> *Ruin must needs ensue; for what avails*
> *Valor or strength, though matchless, quelled with pain*
> *Which all subdues, and makes remiss the hands*
> *Of mightiest. Sense of pleasure we may well*
> *Spare out of life perhaps, and not repine,*
> *But live content, which is the calmest life:*
> *But pain is perfect misery, the worst*
> *Of evils, and excessive, overturns*
> *All patience. He who therefore can invent*
> *With what more forcible we may offend*
> *Our yet unwounded enemies, or arm*
> *Ourselves with like defense, to me deserves*
> *No less than for deliverance what we owe."*

Nisroch is also found in demonic legend as a member of the dark brethren of hell. His position there is rather unique. He serves as the chef of hell, preparing the fell repasts enjoyed by the ruling princes of the underworld. Nisroch's specialty is to include generous helpings of the fruit of the forbidden tree in all of his dishes.

NOGAHEL An angel mentioned in the occult work *Three Books of Occult Philosophy* by the famous mystic and occultist Cornelius Heinrich Agrippa von Nettesheim (d. 1535). According to Agrippa, Nogahel belongs to the truly fortunate angels who stand ever before the throne of God and behold the very face of the Lord.

NURIEL A prominent angel in Jewish lore, Nuriel is honored as being one of the tallest of all beings in heaven, declared to be three hundred parasangs tall (a measurement used among the Persians and accepted as being around three and a half miles). Nuriel is also supported by fifty myriads of angels said to have been formed out of fire and water. Associated with these angels is Nuriel's post as the angel responsible for hailstorms. A resident of the second heaven, he supposedly met Moses when the great Lawgiver journeyed to heaven.

O CH An angel much honored in occult lore. In one tradition Och is considered a protecting or patron angel of alchemy, granting knowledge and wisdom to individuals who are able successfully to invoke his aid. He is also called upon by supplicants seeking other benefits from him, such as an extended life span. To assist him, Och is accompanied by a group of angels or spirits numbering 35,536 legions (according to the scholar E. A. Wallis Budge in his *Amulets and Talismans*). While other beings and angels bear the same title (such as Uriel), Och is ranked in some lists as the angel of the sun. (See also *Sun, Angels of the.*)

ODD, ANGEL OF THE The very peculiar angel appearing in the memorable Edgar Allan Poe tale "The Angel of the Odd." In this story a man is visited by perhaps the most bizarre angel in the history of literature, a member of the heavenly hierarchy whose endless task is to convince the disbelieving or skeptical that incredible, even unbelievable, events do take place. He appears to one particular skeptic and puts him through a series of increasingly improbable "accidents." The narrator writes:

> His body was a wine-pipe, or a rum-puncheon, or something of
> that character, and had a truly Falstaffian air. In its nether
> extremity were inserted two kegs, which seemed to answer all the
> purpose of legs. For arms there dangled from the upper portion of
> the carcass two tolerably long bottles, with the necks outward for
> hands. All the head that I saw the monster possessed of was like

*a Hessian canteen which resembled a large snuff-box with a hole
in the middle of the lid. This canteen (with a funnel on its top,
like a cavalier cap slouched over the eyes) was set on edge upon
the puncheon, with the hole toward myself; and through this
hole, which seemed puckered up like the mouth of a very precise
old maid, the creature was emitting certain rumbling and
grumbling noises which he evidently intended for intelligible
talk.*

The Angel of the Odd speaks in an often incomprehensible
Dutch accent: " 'I zay,' said he, 'you mos pe dronk as de pig, vor zit
dare and not zee me zit ere; and I zay, doo, you most pe pigger vool as
de goose, vor to dispelief vat iz print in de print. 'Tis de troof—dat it
iz—eberry vord ob it.' " (See also *Literature*.)

OFANIEL Also Ophaniel and Opanniel, the generally recognized
chief or ruling prince of the angelic order or choir of the thrones,
called in Hebrew the ofanim after their leader. As the ofanim are also
termed the wheels and the "many-eyed ones," Ofaniel is known as
the keeper of the wheels and even the angel of the wheels of the
moon, the wheels of heaven. He is described in the Third Book of
Enoch in glorious terms: "He has sixteen faces, four on each side, and
100 wings on each side. He has 8,766 eyes, corresponding to the
number of hours in a year, 2,191 on each side. In each pair of eyes in
each of his faces lightnings flash; from every eye torches blaze, and no
one can look on them, for anyone who looks at them is at once consumed. The height of his body is a journey of 2,500 years; no eye can
see it." While revered in some aspects of Jewish lore as the head of the
thrones, Ofaniel is only one of several angels proposed as heads of
that angelic choir; other candidates are Raphael and Orifiel, although
in the complicated lore of angels, these angels, including Ofaniel (in
the form of Ophaniel) are termed the heads of the order of ophanim,
the Hebrew equivalent of the cherubim. (See *Ofanim* and *Thrones;* see
also *Cherubim*.)

OFANIM The Hebrew name for a choir or order of angels that is
considered synonymous with the later choir of the thrones. Also
known as the galgallim (the wheels), ofanim (also ophanim) means
"the wheels," a reference to the traditional description of these angels
as the wheels of God, serving as the wheels of the heavenly chariot.

In the Old Testament Book of Ezekiel they were said to be wheels within wheels, their rims full of eyes, the latter description thus providing their other common name, "many-eyed ones." By custom their chief is the angel Ofaniel, although other proposed ruling princes include Raphael and Orifiel. In the often tangled lore of angels, the name ofanim is switched with the ophanim (the name used for the cherubim). Thus it is hardly surprising that the ofanim (or ophanim) have been placed in various positions in the lists of the angelic choirs over the years. In the accepted compilation of nine choirs, they have occupied the second, fifth, and ninth places. (For other details, see under *Thrones.*)

OG In Jewish legend, a member of the nephilim, the giants who were born out of the union of women with the fallen angels. Og is said to be a descendant of the infamous fallen angel Semyaza. He is mentioned in the Old Testament in the Book of Numbers (21:33–35) as the king of Bashan, who went out with an army to crush Moses at Edrei. The Lord, however, delivered him into the hands of the Lawgiver, and thus Moses "slew him, and his sons, and all his people, until there was not one survivor left to him. . . ." This is consistent with the legend that Moses was able to slay the huge Og by attacking his ankle. There is yet another legend, however, that proclaims that only Og, of all the nephilim, was able to survive the Great Flood by hiding on the roof of Noah's ark. The kindhearted Noah kept him alive by feeding him one thousand cattle every day until the waters subsided.

OLD TESTAMENT The collection of sacred books that form the commonly accepted first half of the Bible, with the New Testament. The Old Testament presents the story of Creation and the religious history of the Jewish people; it utilizes a variety of literary forms, including parables, allegories, poetry, proverbs, prose, and hymns. It is divided into three main sections by the Jews: the Law, the Prophets, and the Writings. The Old Testament is also one of the foremost sources anywhere for stories and details on the angels, combining with the New Testament to serve as the foundation for much of subsequent angelology.

The angels of the Old Testament are found in many of its books, such as Genesis (with its fearsome cherubim, the dark angel, and Jacob's Ladder) and the Book of Daniel, with the archangels Gabriel and Michael. They are an amazing collection of divine messengers, agents of vengeance, confusion, and destruction sent by the Lord and patrons and protectors of God's Chosen People. Angels are known by many names—angel of the Lord, sons of God, princes, cherubim, seraphim, chariots of God, watchers, morning stars, and holy ones—and assume many shapes, from the men who came to Abraham, Jacob, and others to the stunning beings described in the Book of Ezekiel. Above all, the angels of the Old Testament are memorable and significant intermediaries between God and humanity, expressing in concrete terms the divine concern for the Chosen People and one way in which the Lord shaped their history and their destiny. (See also *Bible*.)

An angel appearing to the Israelites in the Old Testament; by Albrecht Dürer.

ONAFIEL An angel given the title angel of the moon—although other angels with this post are said to be Gabriel, Zachariel, and Yahriel—by the poet Longfellow in *The Golden Legend*. While the poet initially (in earlier editions) names Gabriel the angel of the moon, in subsequent versions he uses the name Onafiel or even Ofaniel, the latter derived by transposing the *n* and the *f* in Onafiel. It is generally agreed that Onafiel was the total invention of Longfellow, based on the real and famous angel Ofaniel.

ONAYEPHETON An angel or a spirit who was mentioned in the famous work on sorcery by S. L. MacGregor Mathers, *The Greater Key of Solomon*. According to this source, Onayepheton can be summoned by a competent sorcerer and compelled or convinced to assist them. He is also believed to be an angel used by God to raise the dead to life anytime the Lord chooses to do so.

ORDERS, ANGELIC One of the terms used for the hierarchy of angels as it has been proposed over the years by numerous experts, theologians, and writers. Other names used for the angelic orders include the angelic choirs (perhaps the most famous) and angelic lists. According to accepted custom, based on Pseudo-Dionysius, there are nine orders of angels organized into three triads: first triad —seraphim, cherubim, and thrones; second triad—dominations, virtues, and powers; third triad—principalities, archangels, and angels. There are, however, many other lists, such as those of Pope St. Gregory the Great, Dante, Isidore of Seville, and a number of Jewish traditions. In these lists the order of angels changes, often considerably, both in the arrangement of the actual orders and in the names used for them. In one Jewish tradition, for example, as found in the mystical work of the Zohar, the list is quite different: malachim, erelim, seraphim, hayyoth, ophanim, hashmallim, elim, elohim, bene Elohim, and ishim. These often correspond to the orders of angels found in other lists, although some, such as the hayyoth, are rather unique. Each order also has its own precise functions, attributes, and duties as well as its own ruling prince or chief. (For other details, see under *Choirs.*)

ORIFIEL An angel with a varied portfolio depending upon the list or traditional source of information about him. Also called Orifel, Orfiel, and Oriphiel, he is often termed the ruling or governing angel of the planet Saturn, termed this in the custom of the mystical Qabalah; the poet Longfellow, in *The Golden Legend,* describes this angel as Orfiel, although in later editions of the work he names Anachiel as the angel of Saturn. Orifiel is also ranked among the archangels in the lists compiled by Pope St. Gregory the Great (r. 590–604), with such other notables as Uriel, Raphael, and Michael; Orifiel, however, does not appear in any other major lists of the accepted archangels, placing some question on the matter of whether he truly belongs among the select angels of heaven. In yet another source, he is ranked among the angels belonging to the order or choir of thrones.

ORIGINS OF ANGELS See under *Creation of Angels.*

ORIOKH An alternate name for the angel Ariokh, the companion of the angel Mariokh. The two were commanded by God, as recorded in the Second Book of Enoch, to give their protection to the great patriarch Enoch while he was writing his famous works (see *Enoch, Books of*). The angels also had the task of guarding the descendants and family of Enoch, thereby ensuring their survival during and after the Great Flood. (See *Mariokh.*)

ORION An angel appearing in the epic poem *Der Messias (The Messiah)* by the German poet Friedrich Gottlieb Klopstock (1724–1803). According to this work, Orion is the guardian or protecting angel of St. Peter. Occultist Eliphas Levi, among others, posited a connection or correlation between the angel Orion and the famed archangel Michael; one of the most obvious ones is in the constellation Orion (called the hunter) and the military or warrior attributes possessed by Michael.

ORMAZD Another name for Ahura Mazda, the supreme deity of the Zoroastrian religion, which dominated the Near East and the Persian empire for many centuries. (For details, see under *Ahura Mazda.*)

OTHEOS An angel or spirit, mentioned in a number of occult works, invoked by sorcerers as a help in finding treasures, perhaps lost, buried, or hidden.

OUZA See *Uzzah.*

PACHRIEL Another name for the high angel Baraq'iel, who is one of the seven reigning princes in charge of the seven heavens. Pachriel (Baraqi'el) has authority over the second heaven and is attended by "496,000 myriads of ministering angels," as noted in the Third Book of Enoch.

PAHADRON An angelic being appearing in Jewish legend as a feared angel of terror, as noted in the popular work *Jewish Magic and Superstition* by Joshua Trachtenberg (1939).

PALATINATES An alternative name given to the angelic choir of powers or perhaps some other order. According to the renowned grimoire (or book of magic) called the *Greater Key of Solomon,* the angels belonging to the palatinates can be summoned by a trained sorcerer using spells and invocations conveniently provided in that work. Once summoned, the palatinates are said to be able to bestow invisibility upon the sorcerer.

PARADISE See *Eden, Garden of,* and *Heaven.*

PARADISE LOST For details on this famed work, see under *Milton, John.*

PARASIM A group of angels, perhaps to be considered a complete order or choir, that has the singular task of singing the praises of God.

They are said to be under the authority of the high angelic prince Tagas (Radueriel is also ranked as a possible chief).

PASCHAR An angel who is listed among the so-called seven throne angels. They perform any possible mission at the command of God or his powerful servants. Paschar is also considered a guard or watcher of the curtain or gate surrounding the seventh heaven, the veil that in some Jewish traditions surrounds the very throne of God. (See also *Merkabah Angels.*)

PATRIARCHS The name given to a number of the most prominent and significant of the Old Testament figures; it is also used in the Christian tradition for high-ranking Church officials, especially the heads of the most powerful dioceses. The term *patriarch* is derived from the idea of the head or founder of a family or tribe. In this sense, then, the patriarchs are the founders or progenitors not just of the Chosen People of Israel, but of the human race itself. These patriarchs are generally the antediluvian fathers, meaning that they lived before the Great Flood of Noah's time, through which their seed was able to survive by the will and protection of the Lord. The famed patriarchs of the Old Testament are listed specifically as Abraham, Isaac, and Jacob. Other patriarchs are Jacob's son Joseph, with Joseph's brothers, as well as King David, who is ranked among the patriarchs in the New Testament Book of the Acts of the Apostles (2:29). The place of the patriarchs in the history of Scriptures is quite considerable, and these mighty leaders were deeply revered by the Hebrews. The main accounts of the patriarchs are found in the Book of Genesis, specifically chapters 12 to 50, a section of the book termed the Hebrew patriarchal history. Their presence there is also noted by scholars as significant in that it shifts emphasis in the Book of Genesis from a history of all of humanity to an account of the people of Israel.

While often deeply flawed, the patriarchs demonstrated very complex characters and certain attributes that made them essential to the future greatness of their people. Abraham, for example, had so profound a faith in the Lord that he was actually willing to sacrifice his son; Jacob was exceedingly shrewd and determined, so much so that he was able to wrestle an angel for an entire night (see *Dark Angel* for details); Joseph was utterly chaste. With this background, then, extending to the historical, cultural, and spiritual importance of the patriarchs to their people, it is hardly surprising that they should often be closely associated with angels. Abraham met angels repeatedly; Jacob, as noted, wrestled one; and Isaac was even considered to have been the incarnation of an angel as a means of explaining the supernatural brightness that seemed to emanate from him at his birth.

Beyond the meetings of the patriarchs with angels, there are two other interesting facets of this angelic connection. First is that each of the patriarchs possessed a kind of special guide, guardian, or protecting angel, sometimes known as a preceptor angel. This custom was prevalent among the lore of the Qabalah, the great mystical Jewish tradition, and it was believed that not just patriarchs, but virtually all of the Old Testament figures of note, possessed angelic guides:

Patriarchs: Abraham (Zadkiel), Isaac (Raphael), Joseph (Gabriel), Jacob (Peliel), and Davis (Cerviel).

Others: Adam (Raziel), Noah (Zaphkiel), Samson (Camael), and Solomon (Michael).

The second tradition declares that the patriarchs were themselves given the incomparable honor of being taken to heaven after their earthly lives had come to an end and transformed into angels. Perhaps the most famous of these episodes was that of Enoch, the patriarch who is honored as the father of the staggeringly long-lived Methuselah of the Book of Genesis. In some circles it was declared that all of the patriarchs were turned into angels, although others argue that such a custom is not supported by any other legends or lore in Jewish traditions. (See also individual patriarchs.)

PATRON ANGELS For details on these angels, see box on pages 212–214; see also under *Guardian Angels* and *Patriarchs.*

PEACE, ANGEL OF An angel who was supposedly devoted utterly to the cause of peace and serenity, so much so that his passion ultimately led to his destruction. There is also a long-standing custom that the angel of peace is actually a member of a group probably numbering seven, one of the holy numbers. That there is more than one angel of peace is attested perhaps by the passage in the Old Testament Book of Isaiah (33:7), in which it is declared, "Behold, the valiant ones cry without; the envoys of peace weep bitterly"; the envoys of peace were interpreted variously as angelic beings. They weep because of the lack of peace in the world. In support of the tradition that there is only one angel of peace (or at least that there is one angel of several with the title) is the interesting passage in the First Book of Enoch (40), in which that great patriarch writes of his visit to heaven and the tour given of the first heaven conducted by the angel of peace:

> I saw a hundred thousand times a hundred thousand, ten million times ten million, an innumerable and uncountable [multitude] who stand before the glory of the Lord of the Spirits. I saw them standing—on the four wings of the Lord of the Spirits—and saw four other faces among those who do not slumber, and I came to know their names, which the angel who came with me revealed to me; and he [also] showed me all the hidden things. [Then] I heard the voices of those four faces while they were saying praises before the Lord of Glory. The first voice was blessing the name of the Lord of the Spirits. The second voice I heard blessing the Elect One and elect ones who are clinging onto the Lord of the Spirits. And the voice I heard interceding and praying on behalf of those who dwell upon the earth and supplicating in the name of the Lord of the Spirits. And the fourth voice I heard expelling the demons and forbidding them from coming to the Lord of the Spirits in order to accuse those who dwell upon the earth. And after that, I asked the angel of peace, who was going with me and showed me everything that was hidden, "Who are these four faces which I have seen and whose voices I have heard and written down?" And he said to me, "The first one is the merciful and forbearing Michael; the second one, who is set over all disease and every wound of the children of the people, is Raphael; the third, who is set over all exercise of strength, is Gabriel; and the fourth, who is set over all actions of repentance unto the hope of those who would inherit eternal life, is Phanuel by name."

Perhaps the most famous story told of the angel of peace is the one found in Jewish traditions. According to this legend, the angel was quite opposed to the proposed creation of humanity by the Lord. His opposition was based on his awareness that human beings would be the source of much sadness and violence and would cause war and a disruption of the tranquillity existing in the world. He was joined in

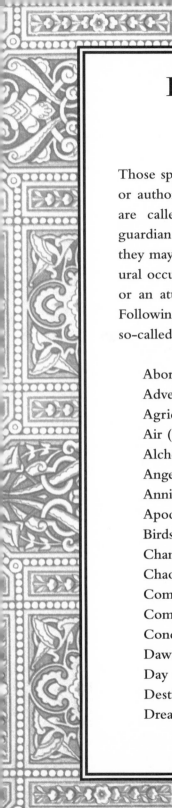

PATRON ANGELS

Those special angels who have a particular devotion to or authority over certain people, places, or professions are called patron angels. They are similar to the guardian angels, but unlike their guardian brethren, they may in many cases have actual mastery over a natural occurrence (such as earthquakes, dreams, or snow) or an attribute (such as strength, anger, or abortion). Following are some of the patron angels, aside from the so-called Ethnarchs, the angels of the nations:

Abortion (Kasdaye)
Adversity (Mastema)
Agriculture (Risnuch)
Air (Chasan)
Alchemy (Och)
Anger (Af)
Annihilation (Harbonah)
Apocalypse (Orifiel)
Birds (Arael)
Chance (Barakiel)
Chaos (Michael or Satan)
Comets (Ziqiel)
Compassion (Raphael)
Conception (Lailah)
Dawn (Lucifer)
Day (Shamshiel)
Destiny (Oriel)
Dreams (Duma)

Dust (Suphlatus)

Earthquakes (Rashiel)

Embryo (Sandalphon)

Fear (Yroul)

Fertility (Samandiriel)

Fire (Nathaniel or Gabriel)

Forests (Zuphlas)

Free Will (Tabris)

Friendship (Mihr)

Glory (Sandalphon)

Grace (Ananchel)

Hail (Bardiel)

Healing (Raphael)

Health (Mumiel)

Hope (Phanuel)

Hurricanes (Zaapiel)

Insomnia (Michael)

Justice (Tzadkiel)

Knowledge (Raphael)

Light (Isaac, Gabriel, and Satan)

Lightning (Baraqiel)

Love (Raphael, Theliel)

Memory (Zadkiel)

Mountains (Rampel)

Music (Israfel or Uriel)

Night (Leliel)

Obedience (Sraosha)

Oblivion (Purah)

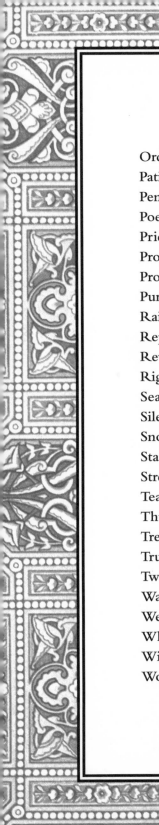

Order (Sadriel)

Patience (Achaiah)

Penance (Phanuel)

Poetry (Uriel or Israfel)

Pride (Rahab)

Progress (Raphael)

Prostitution (Eisheth Zenumin)

Purity (Tahariel)

Rain (Matariel)

Repentance (Michael, Uriel, or Raphael)

Revelation (Gabriel)

Righteousness (Michael)

Sea (Rahab)

Silence (Shateiel or Duma)

Snow (Salgiel or Michael)

Stars (Kokabiel)

Strength (Zeruel)

Tears (Sandalphon or Israfel)

Thunder (Uriel or Ra'amiel)

Treasures (Parasiel)

Truth (Amitiel, Michael, or Gabriel)

Twilight (Aftiel)

War (Michael or Gabriel)

Weakness (Amaliel)

Whirlwind (Zaamiel)

Wind (Ruhiel)

Womb (Armisael)

his steadfast resistance by the angel of truth and the myriad legions of minor angels who existed under their command. Incensed at such temerity and impudence, the Lord took the severe step of incinerating both angels and all of their angelic minions.

PELIEL An angel found in Jewish lore who is acknowledged as one of the chiefs or ruling princes of the angelic order or choir of the virtues. He is also counted among the ten holy sefiroth (see *Sefiroth* for other details) and is the so-called angelic guide or patron of the Old Testament figure Jacob, the patriarch who wrestled with the dark angel. (See also *Patriarchs.*)

PENANCE, ANGEL OF The title given to the angel Phanuel.

PENEMU Also Pinem'e, a onetime holy angel who fell from grace. He is especially vilified in the literature of Enoch, specifically the First Book of Enoch (69), because he taught humanity many terrible things, such as the secrets of wisdom and, worst of all, the use of ink and paper in writing. As a result of this ability, many humans "have erred from eternity to eternity, until this very day. For indeed human beings are not created for such purposes to take up their beliefs with pen and ink"; this may be a rather stern denunciation of writing and the field of journalism. Interestingly, Penemu is also credited with the ability to cure stupidity.

PENIEL The name, meaning "face of God," that was used by the Old Testament figure Jacob for the place he visited across the ford of Jabbok, where he spent an entire night wrestling the being called in lore the dark angel. According to the Book of Genesis, "Jacob called the name of the place Peniel, saying, 'For I have seen God face to face, and yet my life is preserved' " (32:30). Another tradition found in many occult writings considers Peniel to be an actual angel, the very dark angel who was the wrestling companion of Jacob (although this title is also given, with perhaps more authority, to such angels as Michael, Uriel, and even Metatron).

PERI A type of fallen angel or celestial spirit mentioned in the lore of Islam and Persia. According to Persian custom, they were exceedingly attractive, but this only masked their evil nature, being fallen spirits. There is a custom that the peri were the children of the evil angels, a tradition that would make them the equivalent of the nephilim. Unlike those beings of angelic origin, however, the peri were said to be eligible for redemption from their unfortunate progeny and their wicked tendencies. This is because the prophet Muhammad turned his attentions to them and labored to convert them from their sinful lives. In some legends they will remain unable to enter paradise until the sins of their parents, the fallen angels, are finally forgiven by a suitable penance.

PERSIA, ANGEL OF A title given to the angel Dubbiel as the special patron or protector of Persia. He is said to have managed to overthrow the archangel Gabriel as the high potentate of the Lord in the celestial hierarchy, thereby permitting Dubbiel to promote the greatness of Persia at the expense of Israel. Such a favored status, however, did not long endure, for Gabriel was restored to prominence and ended the suffering of the Chosen People. As the patron of Persia, Dubbiel was apparently unable to prevent the eventual conquest of the Persian empire under Alexander the Great in 331 B.C. It is possible that there is an additional reference to the angel of Persia in the Old Testament Book of Daniel (10:13), where mention is made of Michael, the archangel and "one of the chief princes," entering into a struggle with the "prince of the kingdom of Persia," perhaps to be identified with the angel of Persia. (See also *Dubbiel* and *Guardian Angels.*)

PESTILENCE, ANGEL OF Also the angel of plague, a certain highly feared and destructive angelic servant sent by God to bring wholesale death and ruin through the spreading of a kind of plague or disease as punishment for some great sin or as a symbol of divine wrath. The angels of pestilence were perhaps responsible for bringing some of the woes inflicted upon Egypt recorded in the Book of Exodus, such as the terrible plague that devastated the cattle, horses, asses, camels, and the herds and flocks of the Egyptians yet miraculously spared the same livestock of the Israelites. (See also *Death, Angel of.*) Such an undertaking, however, pales in comparison with the incredible massacre perpetrated by the angels in the time of King David and recorded in the First Book of Chronicles.

According to this account, David decided to take a census of the Jewish people. As this was, for whatever reason (possibly pride), extremely displeasing to the Lord, David was chastised for his sin. The

Lord gave to David a choice of three punishments: three years of famine, three months of cruel domination by David's foes, or three days of an absolutely dreadful pestilence delivered by the angel of the Lord. David somewhat ambivalently responded that he would rather fall into the hands of the Lord than those of his enemies. As it was written:

> So the Lord sent a pestilence upon Israel; and there fell seventy thousand men of Israel. And God sent the angel to Jerusalem to destroy it; but when he was about to destroy it, the Lord saw, and he repented of the evil; and he said to the destroying angel, "It is enough; now stay your hand." . . . And David lifted his eyes and saw the angel of the Lord standing between earth and heaven, and in his hand a drawn sword stretched out over Jerusalem. Then David and the elders, clothed in sackcloth, fell upon their faces. And David said to God, "Was it not I who gave command to number the people? It is I who have sinned and done very wickedly. But these sheep, what have they done? Let thy hand, I pray thee, O Lord my God, be against me and against my father's house; but let not the plague be upon thy people." . . . Then the Lord commanded the angel; and he put his sword back into its sheath.

David had placated the Lord by offering a suitable sacrifice on a threshing floor, although his sacrifice came rather late to the seventy thousand Israelites who had already died. (See also *Destruction, Angels of.*)

PHALEC A prominent angel in the occult who is chief or ruling prince of the angelic order or choir of angels. He is also said to have a special area of authority over the planet Mars, a guardianship that explains the rather bellicose nature he is said to possess.

PHANUEL One of the four so-called Angels of the Presence (or the Face), angels who have the cherished position of actually beholding the very face of God or spending time in his direct presence. Phanuel is often listed among the four chief angels of the Presence as a substitute to the great archangel Uriel, standing with his fellows, Michael, Raphael, and Gabriel. Phanuel appears in the First Book of Enoch (40) with the other three major angels of the Presence and is described in a role quite similar to the one normally held by Uriel: ". . . and the fourth, who is set over all actions of repentance unto the hope of those who would inherit eternal life, is Phanuel by name"; in the same source, he is "heard expelling the demons [or Satans] and forbidding them from coming to the Lord of the Spirits in order to accuse those who dwell upon the earth." Not surprisingly, Phanuel is also called the angel of penance and has been identified with the angel of the *Shepherd of Hermas.* This treatise on Christian doctrine was written by the second-century author Hermas and tells of a series of visions granted to Hermas by an angel in the form of a shepherd, by which the content of the work was bestowed upon the writer. (See *Shepherd of Hermas, The.*) If, as is often stated by scholars, Phanuel may be declared synonymous with Uriel, then that mighty angel's attributes, achievements, and legends may be said to be Phanuel's as well. (See *Uriel* for other details.)

PHOENIX (1) Also Phenex, an angel who is fallen but who, according to the occult work *The Lemegeton* by Arthur Edward Waite, has high hopes of returning after 1,200 years to the light of goodness. According to one source, *The Encyclopedia of Occultism* by Lewis Spence, Phoenix was formerly a member of the angelic order or choir of thrones. In the meantime he is said to be a respected poet in the nefarious regions, with authority over many legions of presumably damned spirits.

PHOENIX (2) A type of bird found in Greek mythology that was said to inhabit the Arabian or Egyptian desert, living to the age of six hundred years. At the end of that time it settled into a nest made of spices, sang a hauntingly beautiful song, and, flapping its wings, managed to set itself on fire and reduce itself to ashes; soon after, it literally rose out of the ashes and began a resplendent new cycle of life. The phoenix has become one of the most common symbols for resurrection and eternal life and was especially used by alchemists who sought for the *elixir vitae,* the secret to immortality. The phoenix enters into the history of the angel in only one place, the Second Book of Enoch, in which they are counted as a group of high angels, residing in the fourth or even the sixth heaven with such remarkable angelic bodies as the chalkydri, cherubim, and seraphim. Termed "solar elements," they take part in the endless singing of praises to God:

The light-giver is coming,
to give radiance to the whole world;
and the morning watch appears,
which is the sun's rays.
And the sun comes out over the face of the earth,
and retrieves his radiance,
to give light to all the face of the earth.

When appearing in the sixth heaven, the phoenixes are said to number seven and stand with the seven cherubim and seven unidentified six-winged beings. All together they sing in perfect harmony and with one voice a song reportedly defying a proper description. Scholars are generally in agreement that this is the only known direct association of the phoenix with angels.

PILLARED ANGEL A rather awe-inspiring angel who appears in the New Testament Book of Revelation (10). As was written by St. John: "Then I saw another mighty angel coming down from heaven, wrapped in a cloud, with a rainbow over his head, and his face was like the sun, and his legs like pillars of fire. He had a little scroll open in his hand. And he set his right foot on the sea, and his left foot on the land, and called out with a loud voice, like a lion roaring; when he called out, the seven thunders sounded. . . . And the angel whom I saw standing on sea and land lifted up his right to heaven and swore by him who lives for ever and ever,

The pillared angel of the Book of Revelation; by Albrecht Dürer.

who created heaven and what is in it, and the sea and what is in it, that there should be no more delay, but that in the days of the trumpet call to be sounded by the seventh angel, the mystery of God, as he announced to his servants the prophets, should be no more delay, but that in the days of the trumpet call to be sounded by the seventh angel, the mystery of God, as he announced to his servants the prophets, should be fulfilled." The pillared angel was presented in a woodcut by Albrecht Dürer that remains one of his greatest and most evocative works. (See illustration.)

PILOT ANGEL The name used by Dante in the *Purgatorio* of his *Divine Comedy* for an angel who transports souls. He ferries the deceased from the mouth of the Tiber to their unpleasant, albeit temporary, abode in Purgatory. The pilot is heard to shout:

The pilot angel, from the *Divine Comedy*; by Gustave Doré.

Down! Down! Bend low
Thy knees! Behold God's
*   angel! Fold thy hands!*
Now shalt thou see true
*   ministers indeed!*
Lo! how all human means he
*   sets at naught;*
So that nor oar he needs, nor
*   other sail*
Except his wings, between such
*   distant shores.*
Lo! how straight up to heaven
*   he holds them rear'd,*
Winnowing the air with those
*   eternal plumes,*
That not like mortal hairs fall
*   off or change.*

In *Purgatorio* the pilot angel meets Dante and his guide, Virgil, as they begin their tour of Purgatory. Dante describes him in vivid detail:

As more and more toward us came, more bright
Appear'd the bird of God, nor could the eye
Endure his splendor near: I mine bent down.
He drove ashore in a small bark so swift
And light, that in its course no wave it drank.
The heavenly steersman at the prow was seen,

Visibly written "Blessed" in his looks.
Within, a hundred spirits and more there sat.

(See also *Bird of God.*)

PINEM'E See *Penemu.*

PISTIS SOPHIA One of the aeons, the superior angelic beings of the lore of the Gnostics, a heretical sect of Christianity. Also called simply Sophia (meaning "wisdom"), she supposedly helped bring into being the material world, ironically by her fall from heaven. She pondered certain questions that the aeons were forbidden from considering and so was ejected from her state of grace. Plummeting into the darkness, she collapsed into despair; but, remembering the light of heaven, she emanated and brought forth the being who came, in Gnostic thinking, to be Jesus. He then appealed to the other aeons to come to the aid of Pistis Sophia. They helped rid her of the negative, imperfect thoughts that had plagued her. Unfortunately the negative energy was later put to use to create the imperfect and flawed material world in which are trapped untold millions of souls who struggle fruitlessly to achieve salvation, an unobtainable goal because they are not chosen and made members of the elect (read "saved") souls. In the rather peculiar thinking of the Gnostics, Pistis Sophia encouraged the redemption of humanity by sending the serpent into the Garden of Eden to tempt Adam and Eve, thereby setting in motion the events that led to the defeat of Demiurge, the cruel lesser god who controls the world and prevents the ascension of the souls to the Supreme God, who is perfection. (See also *Aeons.*)

PLAGUE, ANGEL OF THE Another name for the so-called Angel of Pestilence. (For details, see *Pestilence, Angel of.*)

PLANETS The celestial orbs that inhabit the sky and are often revered in astrological lore as commanding the lives and destinies of humankind. This understanding of the planets normally encompasses not only the known planets (to the degree of scientific knowledge at the time—which means that not all of the planets were known), but the sun and the moon as well. One of the most common and interesting ways in which the planets were said to influence directly the lives of humans was through the planetary ages. By this concept, each plant has a specific area of effect on a person at differing times in that person's life. Thus the Moon governs the first four years of life; Mercury from the ages of five to fourteen; Venus from fifteen to twenty-two; the Sun from twenty-three to forty-two; Mars from forty-three to fifty-seven; Jupiter from fifty-eight to sixty-nine; and Saturn (always depicted in legend and art as an old man) from seventy to ninety-nine. As few people are expected to live much past ninety-nine, it can be assumed that in such rare cases the planetary influence of Saturn will be extended for the appropriate amount of time (or perhaps, having lived for so long, the person is on his or her own). Beyond this idea, there are other traditions pertaining to the planets, such as the one that says the planets determine whether a person born under its influence will be lucky or unlucky; Saturn is considered unlucky, while Jupiter is decidedly lucky. Given this body of lore, it is hardly surprising that there should also be legends and traditions connecting the angels with the planets, just as there are associations of angels with the houses of the zodiac, the months of the year, and the days of the week. By this custom there are certain governing or ruling angelic figures who care for the planets and ensure their smooth continuation in their heavenly orbit. As seems ever the case with angel lore, there is not one but several accepted lists of angels who rule the planets. Two of the most famous are by Francis Barrett in *The Magus* (1801) and by the poet Henry Wadsworth Longfellow in *The Golden Legend*. (For details, see *Planets, Angels of the.*)

Aside from these planetary rulers, there are also reported to be angelic messengers and so-called intelligences who help govern the traditionally recognized seven planets: Mercury, Venus, Mars, Jupiter, and Saturn, along with the Sun and the Moon. While most of these spirits and messengers are fairly unknown, there are to be found in some lists a number of famous and even beloved angels and archangels. Among them are Gabriel (a spirit of the Sun and the Moon), Raphael (a spirit of Mercury), Uriel (a spirit of Mercury and an intelligence of the Moon), and Samael (a spirit of Mars and Saturn).

PLANETS, ANGELS OF THE A group of angels who possess certain powers over the planets they administer as a kind of governor or ruling prince. By custom the angelic rulers of the planets are headed collectively by the angel Rahatiel. The list of the planets was connected intimately with astrology and was formulated based upon the concept of the seven planets: Mercury, Venus, Mars, Saturn, and Jupiter, along with the Sun and the Moon (the last two normally counted in astrological lore as part of the famed seven planets). Beyond these, however, the actual list of the angels varies considerably depending upon the source used for the names and attributes. Perhaps two of the most famous are in the well-known occult work *The Magus* (1801) by Francis Barrett and in *The Golden Legend* by poet Henry Wadsworth Longfellow. Barrett lists the ruling angels as follows: Mercury (Michael or Raphael); Venus (Haniel or Anael); Mars (Camael); Saturn (Orifiel or Zaphiel); Jupiter (Zadkiel or Zachariel); the Sun (Michael or Raphael); and the Moon (Gabriel). Longfellow, relying less upon angelic tradition and more upon his considerable imagination, created his own list: Mercury (Michael); Venus (Anael); Mars (Uriel); Saturn (Orifel); Jupiter (Zobiachel); the Sun (Raphael); and the Moon (Gabriel). Of the angels of Longfellow's list, Zobiachel is considered by scholars to be a complete creation of the poet, not the only newly christened angel to appear in *The Golden Legend*. Longfellow also later changed (in other editions of *The Golden Legend*) the name of the governing angel of Saturn, from Orifel (or Orfiel) to Anachiel.

🌸 **POETRY** See box on page 224.

🌸 **POPULATION** See box on pages 226–227.

🌸 **POTENTATES** A name used by poet John Milton in *Paradise Lost* for the angelic order or choir of powers. In Book V he writes:

> *Far was advanced on winged speed, an host*
> *Innumerable as the stars of night,*
> *Or stars of morning, dewdrops, which the sun*
> *Impearls on every leaf and every flower.*
> *Regions they passed, the mighty regencies*
> *Of seraphim and potentates and thrones*

Elsewhere in the same book, Milton speaks of "thrones, dominations, princedoms, virtues, powers." (For other details, see under *Powers*.)

🌸 **POWERS** (Choir) One of the nine accepted choirs of angels according to the celestial organization developed by the sixth-century the-

POETRY

One of the most beautiful ways of expressing the wonder and beauty of angels has been through poetry. The two most famous epic poems treating this subject are Dante's *Divine Comedy* and John Milton's *Paradise Lost.* These two masterpieces, however, are not alone. They have been joined by works from such mighty poets as Goethe, Blake, Rilke, and Longfellow. William Blake, who communicated with members of the heavenly host, wrote extensively of angels, such as in *The Marriage of Heaven and Hell* and *Book of Urizen.* Longfellow elegantly described angels in *The Golden Legend* and especially *Sandalphon,* which immortalized that noble angel. Other notable poetic angel works include Robert Browning's *The Guardian Angel;* Henry Vaughan's *Providence;* Goethe's *Faust,* most notably his "Prologue in Heaven"; Francis Thompson's *Little Jesus;* Jean Reboul's *The Angel and the Child;* and Emily Dickinson's *Opus 78.* Other notable poems include Leigh Hunt's *Abou Ben Adhem;* Percy MacKaye's *Uriel;* Friedrich Klopstock's *Der Messias;* Geoffrey Landis's *If Angels Ate Apples;* and Bruce Boston's *Curse of the Angel's Wife.* The angelic patron of poetry and poets is Radweriel, the chief archivist of heaven.

ologian Dionysius the Areopagite; also called potentates, authorities,
dynamis, and forces, the powers are placed in the second triad of the
nine choirs (with the dominations and virtues) and are numbered
sixth overall. The powers were supposedly the very first of the angels
created by God, although this disagrees with the teaching that all angels came into existence at the same moment. Regardless, they are
described by Dionysius as having the task of defeating the efforts of
the demons in overthrowing the world and are declared the awesome
defenders of the cosmos against all evil and the maintainers of all cosmic order and equilibrium. They are the guardians of the heavenly
paths, policing the routes to and from heaven to the earth, which
means that they concern themselves as well with all humanity. The
great harmonizers, they assist each soul to overcome the temptations
placed before it to do evil and to lean instead toward the proper action, which is to love and worship God, a duty perhaps expressed by
St. Paul in his Letter to the Romans (13:1): "Let every person be subject to the governing authorities," another name used for the powers.
Their colors are green and gold, and their symbol is the flaming
sword. Their chiefs are named as Camael, Gabriel, Raphael, Verchiel,
and even Satan, albeit before his Fall; the most common named ruling
prince, though, is Camael.

The powers have been the subject of some speculation by angelologists because of the curious statement by St. Paul in his Letter
to the Ephesians (6:12): "For we are not contending against flesh and
blood, but against the principalities, against the powers, against the
world rulers of this present darkness, against the spiritual hosts of
wickedness in the heavenly places." Based on this, some have proposed that the powers may have fallen entirely as a choir (with, perhaps, the principalities), but most others feel that this is a reference to
the members of the choir who joined Satan in his rebellion against
God. The powers certainly were given a job that brought them into
constant proximity with the much-flawed humanity, and it is possible
that many succumbed to the words of the evil one. Demonologists
will point out that a surprisingly large percentage of onetime angels
came from the ranks of this choir, including such high-placed dukes
of hell as Crocell (commander of forty-eight legions of devils) and
Beleth (with control over eighty-five legions). Interestingly, Crocell
supposedly once told King Solomon that he had aspirations of making peace with God and returning to the powers. The defection of
their comrades served only to make the remaining powers all the

POPULATION

Among the most frequently asked questions concerning angels is that inquiring as to how many members there are in the heavenly host. It is hardly surprising that Scripture is rather ambiguous in this area, but assorted references would seem to indicate that the angelic population is a large one. The Book of Revelation, for example, proclaims: "Then I looked, and I heard around the throne . . . the voice of many angels numbering myriads of myriads and thousands of thousands" (5:11). In the Letter to the Hebrews (12:22) are mentioned "innumerable angels in festal gathering," while in Genesis (28:12) there is the account of Jacob's dream of the Ladder, on which "the angels of God were ascending and descending on it!" A further idea of the possible size of the hosts of the Lord is given in the Books of Enoch. In the Third Book of Enoch, each prince of heaven is assisted by 496,000 myriads of ministering angels (a myriad in archaic terminology denotes either a vast number or perhaps ten thousand), and elsewhere in the Enochian writing is mention of thousands and millions of angels.

There are thus at the very least millions of angels, a number apparently supported by two customs in Jewish lore: first, there are said to be eleven thousand guardian angels for each person's soul, and every blade of grass has its own angel giving it encouragement to grow and reach its own grassy potential.

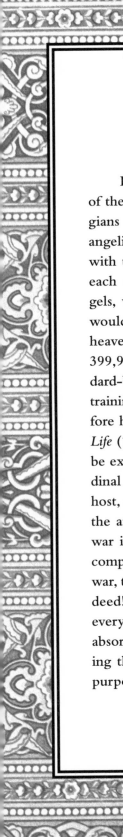

Despite this relatively limited specificity in terms of the angelic population, undaunted rabbis and theologians have attempted to put an exact number on the angelic choirs. An aspect of the medieval fascination with the angels, this speculation included the idea that each of the nine choirs possesses 6,666 legions of angels, with every legion claiming 6,666 members. This would give each choir 44,435,556 angels; the entire heavenly host would boast an enormous body of 399,920,004 angels—give or take a few princes, standard-bearers, and potential angels on probation or in training, if one wants to include Clarence Oddbody before he won his wings in the classic film *It's a Wonderful Life* (1946). From this population, however, can perhaps be excluded the fallen angels, said by one medieval cardinal to claim fully one-third of the entire heavenly host, or 133,306,668 wicked souls. It is unclear whether the aforementioned population was before or after the war in heaven. If it was before, then the current hosts comprise only 266,613,336 angels. If it was after the war, then the total size of the heavenly body is large indeed! Adding to the confusion is the idea that with every breath the Lord creates more angels, but he also absorbs angels into his divine essence each night, bringing them back to life in the morning with the express purpose of singing his eternal praises.

more faithful and determined to defend Creation against the predations of evil, even the wickedness of those who had shared with them in the light of the blessed realm. (See also *Choirs*.)

POWERS OF THE ANGELS See box on page 229.

POWERS, ANGEL OF THE The name given to certain angels belonging to the angelic choir or order of powers. The chief angels of this order are listed as Gabriel, Camael, and even Satan (albeit before his famed Fall). Other angels receiving this title have been Verchiel, Samael, and especially Zacharel, who is also the governing angel of the planet Jupiter. Yet another angel mentioned under this title was the famed archangel Michael, as noted in the apocryphal work the Testament of Abraham. (See also *Powers*.)

PRAISE, ANGELS OF A group or even order or choir of angels that, as the name might suggest, has the perpetual duty of singing the divine praises of the Lord. According to the famed work *The Legends of the Jews* by Louis Ginzberg, the angels of praise were supposedly created by God on the second day of Creation, along with the angel hosts and the ministering angels. It is generally accepted that the angels of praise can be considered synonymous with the angelic choir of thrones. (See also *Thrones*.)

PRAVAIL See *Vrevoil*.

PRAYER, ANGEL OF An angel appearing in various traditions with special authority over prayer, such as the privilege of bringing before the throne of God the prayers of certain exceedingly worthy mortals, in particular the saints and holy men and women. The angels can also be said to have competence over the endless recitation of prayers to the Lord that is undertaken by the angels, in conjunction with the perpetual singing of the praises of God. The exact number of the angels of prayer is somewhat unclear, being placed at five, six, or seven. Seven is perhaps the most likely number, as there is a tradition that the seven archangels (as listed by Pseudo-Dionysius: Michael, Gabriel, Raphael, Uriel, Chamuel, Jophiel, and Zadkiel; as per St. Gregory the Great: Michael, Gabriel, Raphael, Uriel, Simiel, Orifiel, and Zachariel) have a heightened ability to bring prayers to the attention

POWERS OF
THE ANGELS

Although the angel is only one spiritual being among the entire heavenly host, and merely one creature in all of Creation, it has no limitations of any kind upon its powers and abilities for the simple reason that its entire existence and the capacity to fulfill all tasks given to it are derived from God. One should not think, however, that because their powers come from a source outside themselves angels are weak or feeble. On the contrary, because their strength comes directly from God it is beyond compare and has no equal anywhere in the universe. Such a conception of angelic power helps to stress the close relationship between angels and God and the degree to which they are different from humanity.

of God. Other angels sometimes included in the listing of the angels
of prayer are Metatron and Sandalphon.

PRESENCE, ANGELS OF THE A special kind of angel, also called the
angels of the face, who receives the incomparable honor of standing in
the presence of or before the very face of the Lord. Often nameless,
the angels of the presence are regularly grouped in accounts with such
other angelic bodies as the angels of sanctification, angels of glory, angels of the spirit of fire, and the angels of the spirits of the winds. In
the Book of Jubilees, for example, it is written that on the first day God
created the heavens and the earth and all the spirits, including the angels of the presence. They are mentioned again in the unorthodox
apocryphal work Testaments of the Twelve Patriarchs, which purports
to be the final, deathbed statements of the twelve sons of Jacob. In the
testament credited to Judah (25:3), the fourth son of Jacob and Leah,
it is declared that Judah had received the blessing of the angel of the
presence. In both of these accounts the angels are not named, but in
other traditions they are listed as being twelve in number. Among
them are to be found such angelic notables as Michael, Uriel, Metatron, Phanuel, and Sandalphon; others are Akatriel, Zagzagel, Yefefiah,
Astanphaeus, Jehoel, Saraqael, and Suriel. While it would be illogical to
accept that such potentates as Michael, Uriel, and especially Metatron
could have been involved, the Zohar (the Jewish mystical work) declares that the angels of the presence revealed to humanity certain secrets that were best left unknown, and in punishment for breaking his
commandment, the Lord forced them to depart from their treasured
place at his side. It is of course possible that the term in this sense may
refer to a group of angels different from the named body or perhaps
some of the myriad angels who are always said to accompany the great
angels—in some accounts a host of 496,000 myriads of ministering
angels. (See also *Face, Angels of the;* see also *Metatron.*)

PRIDE, ANGEL OF A name frequently given to Satan (or incorrectly
Lucifer). It is derived from his hubris, his pride, which caused, according to Christian teaching, his Fall from the light and his expulsion
from heaven. The title is also sometimes given to Rahab. (See *Satan;*
see also *Fallen Angels* and *Lucifer.*)

PRIMUM MOBILE In the ancient (and of course ultimately dis-
proved) conception of the universe in which the heavens revolved

around the earth, the *primum mobile* was the outermost sphere, the place where all of the stars were carried in their daily progress across the sky. Derived from the Latin for "the first moving thing," the *primum mobile* was said to revolve around the earth, carrying all of the other heavenly spheres with it and journeying from east to west each twenty-four hours. In some teaching, such as that of the famous astronomer Ptolemy, the *primum mobile* was a kind of boundary marker for material creation; beyond it is found the Empyrean, the very realm of God and the angels. John Milton, in his *Paradise Lost,* described it as "that first mov'd." While no longer used in astronomy, the *primum mobile* continues to have applications in astrology.

PRINCES, ANGELIC The name given to certain powerful and highly placed angels who are honored with the title of prince or ruling princes of heaven. The angelic princes are found especially in Jewish lore, with princes governing not only the seven heavens, but the angelic orders or choirs. In the Third Book of Enoch, for example, there is a list of the princes of the seven heavens, named as Michael, Gabriel, Satqiel, Sahaqiel, Baradiel, Baraqiel, and Sidriel. They are said to be attended by 496,000 myriads of ministering angels. In this lore of Enoch there are also hosts of other angelic princes, all part of the angelic hierarchy. There are thus Galgalliel, the prince in charge of the sun; Opanniel, prince of the moon; Rahatiel, prince of the constellations of the stars; Tagas, prince in charge of the

St. Michael, one of the foremost of the angelic princes; from the treasury of San Marco, Venice (COURTESY ART RESOURCE).

great singing choirs of heaven; Barattiel, the prince who holds all of Arabot (heaven) on the tops of his fingers; Anapiel, whose brightness overshadows all of the heavens; Soterasiel, who controls admission before the throne of God; and Soqedhozi, who weighs the merits of humans in a scale when they die and come before the throne of God for judgment. Only a few of the multitude of princes are found in the Enochian writings, giving an ample demonstration of the greatness of the angelic hierarchy in some traditions.

There are additionally the princes of the angelic choirs as they have evolved over the centuries in Jewish and Christian lore. According to tradition, each choir has its own chiefs or so-called ruling princes. While some of the names are easily recognized, others are quite obscure and known only to dedicated angelologists. Further, the lists are complicated by the fact that each choir has several chiefs, the presence of the various princes a testament to the many different customs related to the angelic. Following are some of the princes of the individual choirs:

Seraphim:	Michael, Metatron, Uriel, Seraphiel, and Satan (before his mighty Fall from heaven)
Cherubim:	Gabriel, Raphael, Uriel, Zophiel, and Satan (before his Fall)
Thrones:	Zaphkiel, Raziel, Orifiel, and Jophiel
Dominations:	Zadkiel, Zacharel, and Muriel
Virtues:	Gabriel, Michael, Uzziel, Tarshish, Sabriel, and Peliel
Powers:	Camael, Gabriel, Verchiel, and Satan (before his Fall)
Principalities:	Amael, Nisroch, and Haniel
Archangels:	Metatron, Raphael, Michael, Gabriel, Barachiel, Jehudiel, and Satan (before his Fall)
Angels:	Gabriel, Chayyliel, Phaleg, and Adnachiel

As is clear from this list, certain angels appear in more than one choir, such as Michael, Metatron, Raphael, Uriel, and Gabriel. Their presence can be attributed to the fact that in the celestial hierarchy some angels are more important and princely—and more popular—than others. Still another group comprises angels who bear the title of prince in relation to some specific duty or activity (such as prince of light, prince of fire, and prince of peace).

PRINCIPALITIES (Choir) One of the nine accepted choirs of angels as organized by the sixth-century theologian Dionysius the Areopagite and adopted largely by the Christian Church. The principalities are placed first in the third triad of angels (with the archangels and angels) and are ranked seventh overall. Also called princedoms and princes, these angels are the first of the choirs most concerned with the earth and are traditionally declared to have the roles of caretakers over every nation, province, county, district, city, town, village, and house, working with the guardian angels, who also are assigned to every spot and person; while this seems to be bureaucratic doubling of angelic activity, it can be argued that guardian angels function as the personal angelic protectors, while the principalities are the administrative or technical writers. They are supposedly empowered with greater strength by God than the guardian angels and thus receive permission more frequently to have a direct involvement in the affairs of humanity, using the incalculable strength of heaven to move the hearts and minds of those mortals with whom they have direct contact or even to perform inexplicable miracles or events that are not even noticed by humans, left unexplained, or dismissed as unusual natural phenomena. Two other areas of concern for the principalities are religion and, according to Dionysius, politics. The former they encourage to spread by prayer and spiritual encouragement; the latter they seek to regulate for the good of humanity by guiding the thoughts and especially the ethics of what Dionysius termed the "leaders of people" all over the world. Some would say that the angels have perhaps not been devoting their full concentration in either area the last decades. Their symbols are the scepter, the cross, and the sword, and their chiefs are listed as Haniel, Cerviel, and Amael. Nisroch, a onetime angel and now the master chef of hell, may have been a chief of this order. (See also *Choirs.*)

PROPHETS Those individuals who are blessed with the ability to predict future events. The most famous of the prophets throughout history are those who appear in the Old Testament, although today the best-known visionaries are such figures as Nostradamus, Edgar Cayce, and other modern seers such as Jeanne Dixon. The visions of the prophets of the Old Testament are often said to have been granted by the will of God, and their lives were frequently touched by angelic messengers. For example, Elijah was fed manna by an angel and was transported to heaven in a fiery chariot. Daniel was spared from certain death by lions by an angel of the Lord and had his dreams interpreted by the archangels Michael and Gabriel. While not a biblical prophet, Edgar Cayce (1877–1945), the American visionary, had much to say about angels, seeing them and receiving some of his remarkable visions through their efforts. William Blake (1757–1827), English visionary, poet, and artist, was firmly convinced that he saw and communicated with angels.

Angels also have served as prophets in their own right. The archangel Gabriel assisted Daniel, as noted, and brought word of both the birth of St. John the Baptist and the conception of the Virgin Mary leading to the birth of Christ. St. John also received from angels his often terrible images, which formed the basis of his Book of Revelation. Angels also predicted the destruction of Sodom and Gomorrah.

PSEUDEPIGRAPHA The name given to those works that are considered noncanonical (meaning that they are not accepted as sacred literature and included in the books of the Bible), were deliberately written in a style that emulated actual biblical literature, and were named after or attributed to some great personage in order to establish for them some kind of heightened authority or credibility. There is a large body of these pseudepigraphical writings, with details about angels included in many of them. Among the most notable angel sources are the Books of Enoch, the Books of Baruch, and the Gospel of St. Bartholomew.

PSEUDO-DIONYSIUS See under *Dionysius the Areopagite.*

PUNISHMENT, ANGEL OF The title borne by several different angels denoting their special powers and authority in handing out the divine punishment of God. Among the possible members of this association—although there is no indication that such angels should be thought of as forming their own choir or order—are Amaliel, Ariel, Kushiel, Puriel, Makatiel, Hemah, Mashit, Af, Kezef, and Hasmed. The last five of this list were supposedly encountered by Moses during his legendary tour of heaven. Like the angels of destruction, angels of vengeance, and angels of wrath, these angelic beings are not to be taken lightly and are truly feared.

🦪 **PURIEL** Also Puruel and Pusiel, an angel who appears in the apocryphal work of the Testament of Abraham, the second-century A.D. apocalyptic tale of Abraham's journey to heaven. Puriel is described as utterly pitiless, with the task of examining the soul of each person brought to heaven for examination after death.

🦪 **PUTTI** The small, adorable angels (sing. putto) found in both painting and sculpture during the Renaissance and Baroque periods. The putti were probably adopted originally from Greek and Roman art, with their depictions of stylized figures of Eros, the god of love, who later became personified by Cupid with his arrows of love. The putto, however, represented angels in the highly devotional works of fifteenth-century Italian artists, especially in their renderings of the popular theme of the Madonna with Child. The putti specifically depicted cherubim, usually surrounding the Virgin Mary and the baby Jesus, decorating some painting of a Bible scene or holy person, or adorning architectural features such as pillars, columns, or ceilings. The presentation of the cherubim as a harmless, chubby little angel unfortunately did much to diminish the original conception of the cherubim as one of the most profound and formidable angelic beings in all of the celestial hierarchy. (See also *Art, Angels in; Cherub;* and *Cherubim.*)

Chariot Race with Putti, Vatican Museums, Vatican City State (COURTESY ART RESOURCE).

QABALAH Also Kabbala, Cabalah, and Cabala, the great mystical tradition of Judaism. Qabalah was in existence from around the late second century B.C., seeking to express the mystical tendencies of the Jewish people. The Qabalists, or students of the Qabalah (meaning "tradition"), sought to enter into communication with God and to answer the most difficult and esoteric questions about the Lord and his Creation. It became one of the most complex and detailed systems of thought and practice ever developed, forming an influential aspect on Judaic life. Scholars point to its origins in neo-Platonism, Gnosticism, and occult teachings from the East, and many of its precepts and methods were charged by some rabbis as being both heretical and dangerously pantheistic.

The Qabalah flourished in the first century A.D. in the mystical movement called the Merkabah (see *Merkabah Angels* for other details). It was subsequently given vigorous examination, with Qabalists compiling such works as the Sefer Yetzira, the Bahir, and the Sefer ha-Temuna. The chief writing in all of the Qabalah, however, is the Zohar (Book of Radiance), created by Moses de Leon, a Spanish mystic, in the thirteenth century. In the wake of the expulsion of the Jews from Spain in 1492 and the continued brutal oppression of the Jewish people elsewhere in Europe, the center of Qabalistic studies shifted from Spain and elsewhere to Safed, Galilee, in the Holy Land. There, in the sixteenth century, lived Rabbi Isaac Luria, considered the greatest of all Qabalists. The Qabalah remained a major element in Judaism, producing in the twentieth century the renowned scholar Gershom Scholem.

As the Qabalah is concerned with the nature of God and the cosmos, students of the field wrote extensively on angels and demons. While Talmudic rabbis discouraged such speculation, the Qabalists formulated such angel-related systems as the merkabah and the sefiroth and wrote about individual angels such as Metatron, Phanuel, Raphael, Gabriel, Michael, Sandalphon, and Samael. There was also a detailed study of demons, and advanced Qabalists sought to summon and control both angels and devils by mastering incantations and forging amulets. Such undertakings were naturally extremely risky, bringing the possibility of injury, madness, or death.

QADDISIN The hebrew name meaning "holy ones," given to the two extremely powerful beings who stand with the watchers (the grigori) on either side of the very throne of God and serve, again with the watchers, as the final court of law in all of heaven. While their names are not given specifically, they are each said to possess seventy names, corresponding to the seventy languages then spoken throughout the world (based on the idea of seventy nations, each with its own angelic patron; see *Guardian Angels* for other details). Their title is derived from the Book of Daniel in the Old Testament: "I saw in the visions of my head as I lay in bed, and behold, a watcher, a holy one, came down from heaven. . . . The sentence is by the decree of the watchers, the decision by the word of the holy ones, to the end that the living may know that the Most High rules the kingdom of men, and gives it to whom he will, and sets over it the lowliest of men" (Daniel 4:13,17). There is some question as to whether the watchers and holy ones should form their own order of angels. Nevertheless, they are called in the Third Book of Enoch "high, honored, terrible, beloved, wonderful, noble, and greater than all the celestials and among all the ministers there is none equal to them, for each of them singly is a match for all the others together" (28).

Their powers are certainly needed and deserved, for the two sets of angels are ever in the presence in God almighty, giving their counsel and acting as the court officials of heaven, debating each and every case that is brought before the throne; they declare the final and irrevocable decision of God with the proclamation "The sentence is by the decree of the Watchers, the decision by the word of the Holy Ones." By custom they are said to be positioned each on one side of the throne, their companions, the watchers, standing equally divided next to them. Always they face the Lord, reflecting the unapproachable splendor of his light and perfection. (See also *Watchers* for other details.)

QAFSIEL Also called Qaphsiel, an angel often identified with Atrugiel and who is given in tradition a certain authority over the moon. He was also invoked by the Hebrews as a means of repelling an enemy. The custom dictated that the name of Qafsiel be written in the blood of a bird on a parchment, which was then tied to the leg of a dove. The bird was then released; if it flew away, the angel was informing the supplicant that his enemies, too, were in flight, but if it remained or was reluctant to set off, it was taken as a sign that the enemy was still a threat.

Virgin Mary surrounded by Angels, by Benozzo Gozzoli, S. Francesco, Montefalco (COURTESY ART RESOURCE).

QEMUEL Another name used for the angel Camael. (See *Camael* for details.)

QUEEN OF THE ANGELS One of the honorific titles given to the Virgin Mary in recognition of her place as "Queen of Heaven" in the Catholic faith and the very special intercessor of all who seek her aid and protection. Her official Latin title is *Regina Angelorum* or *Regina Angelium.* Her queenship was pronounced in 1954 by Pope Pius XII and is celebrated on August 22. Aside from the angels, she is queen of saints, patriarchs, prophets, apostles, peace, heaven and earth, and confessors. (For other details, see under *Mary, Virgin.*)

QUI ANGELORUM SOCIUS EST A Latin phrase meaning "who is in the company of the angels." It is often used to describe someone especially good or holy, although it can also denote someone who has passed on, a delicate way of expressing the death of a friend or loved one. In the more mundane use of language, sentiments of a person's demise, with some (even oblique) reference to angels, can be expressed as "He [or she] has joined the choir angelic," or (most flippant) "He [or she] is being fitted for harp and wings." There are, no doubt, many other possible angel phrases.

🐚 **QUR'AN** Also the Koran, the sacred text of Islam, said to have been revealed to the prophet Muhammad by the angel Gabriel and to contain the true Word of God. Derived from the Arabic for "to read" or "to recite," the Qur'an was given to Muhammad by Gabriel in ecstatic trances over the space of many years (perhaps twenty-three) and was subsequently written down on whatever was handy at the moment—palm leaves, stones, paper, and even parts of the human body. The teachings of the Prophet spread, however, and many learned them by heart. After Muhammad's death in 632 at Medina, those who followed him decided to gather together all of the teachings, called chapters or suras (sing. surah), into the work known as the Qur'an. Islamic scholars will point out, however, that the work's structure and organization were undertaken by the Prophet himself and not by any of his successors. Nevertheless, the first completed volume was copied out by a friend and companion of Muhammad, Zayd ibn Thabit, for Caliph 'Umar; under Caliph 'Uthman, a final, authoritative text was promulgated.

The Qur'an has a large number of references to angels, making clear their important place in the second surah (2:177): "It is not righteousness that you turn your faces towards the East and the West, but righteousness is the one who believes in Allah, and the Last Day, and the angels and the Book." The book also mentions specifically two important angels, Gabriel and Michael, Jibril and Mikal (although Islamic lore boasts four named angels, Michael, Gabriel, Israfel, and Azrael). Gabriel—who is also thought to be the Holy Spirit—is termed the "Faithful Spirit," while Michael and Gabriel are mentioned together in the second surah (2:98): "Whoever is an enemy to Allah and His angels and His messengers and Gabriel and Michael, then surely Allah is an enemy to disbelievers." (See also *Muhammad, Angel of.*)

R A'AMIEL The angel who is in charge of thunder. He is one of several angels with the task of monitoring or controlling the natural elements. He works closely with the angel Matariel, the patron angel of rain.

RA'ASIEL The angel who is in charge of all earthquakes.

RABDOS A onetime angel who possessed the ability to stop the very stars in their celestial path. He apparently fell from grace, for he is now ranked among the fallen angels. His specialty among the legions of the netherworld is to strangle his victims.

RADWERIEL Also Radueriel, the archivist (a job also attributed to Metatron) of the heavenly host who is ranked among the high angelic personages in the divine court. He is said in the Third Book of Enoch, that helpful source on angels, to be a prince, more highly honored than all the other princes, and to be in charge of the archives of the Lord. He maintains all of the scrolls and records of heaven, bringing forth for the Lord's consideration all relevant documents and accounting that might be needed in the resolutions of each case brought before the throne of God. He has the special honor of handing directly to the Lord the records needed. It is thus assumed that Radweriel works very closely with the other angels of the heavenly court, the watchers and the holy ones, the grigori and the qaddisin.

Radweriel also possesses the unique ability that every time he opens his mouth and makes an utterance, an angel is created or springs into being; these newly formed angels immediately join the choirs of singing angels, whose task it is to sing in eternal, unceasing praise of God. This power is genuinely unusual, for it is given to him directly by God, the only source from whom new angels can be created, and is not possessed by any other angel in the celestial hierarchy. He is also honored as the angel of poetry. (See also *Recording Angels.*)

RAGUEL An angel whose name means "friend of God" and who has the difficult task of maintaining discipline among the angels in heaven, described in the First Book of Enoch as the angel who takes vengeance for the world and for luminaries. He is also in charge of the second heaven and is listed in traditions related to the famed patriarch Enoch as having been responsible for translating Enoch to heaven; this event is referred to in the Old Testament Book of Genesis, although there is nothing in that account concerning Raguel (the other angel regularly thought possibly to have been the transporting agent is Anafiel). Raguel is also well-known in angelological circles for his membership in the select group of angels who were stricken from the official ranks of the heavenly host as recognized by the Christian Church at a council in Rome in 745 under Pope Zachary. Raguel joined Uriel, Inias, Tubuael, Adimus, Simiel, and Sabaoth. (See *Rome, Council of.*)

RAHAB The so-called Angel of Violence (or Violent Angel), also called the angel of the sea and an angel who suffered from an unbelievable pride. According to legends surrounding Rahab, he was around at the very Creation of the world, with powers over the seas. The Lord, in order to make the land fit for habitation by humanity, commanded Rahab to drink enough of the water to form the ground. The angel, however, was quite content with his territory of the waters and told the Lord to leave him alone. God was understandably incensed at such disobedience and supposedly stomped Rahab to death. In the Book of Isaiah (51:9) is written perhaps an allusion to this event:

> *Awake, awake, put on strength.*
> *O arm of the Lord;*
> *awake, as in days of old,*
> *the generations of long ago.*
> *Was it not thou that didst cut Rahab*

in pieces,
That didst pierce the dragon?

Rahab, however, still caused trouble, for his rotting body gave off such an unbearable stench that the Lord shoved it into the depths of the seas; thus the onetime realm of this angel became his watery grave. It is possible that Rahab came back to life—or was merely the subject of other legends—for he figures in the Jewish tales about the departure of the Israelites from Egypt under Moses. As the Hebrews were crossing the Red Sea, Rahab tried to stop them. Once again the Lord was appalled at his pride, destroying the angel with special vigor. Rahab thus gave his name to Egypt in an evil sense, an enslaving power that was rebuffed at the Red Sea (an allusion to the parting of the Red Sea and the drowning of the Egyptian cavalry that tried to pursue the Hebrews); in the Book of Job, Rahab was mentioned: "By his power he stilled the sea; by his understanding he smote Rahab." He is at times identified with the fallen angels (or devils) Leviathan and Behemoth, two dreadful beings of the sea. Rahab is also considered responsible for rescuing from the waters the Book of Angel Raziel, which had been given to Adam by Raziel and then stolen by envious angels who threw it into the ocean to keep Adam from reading its secrets. In this one matter, it seems, Rahab was entirely obedient to the Lord.

RAHATIEL An angel mentioned in the Third Book of Enoch as the prince of the constellations. He thus has authority over the stars in the heavens, making the constellations pass across the sky each night. He is assisted in his labors by a group of seventy-two angels, "great and honored."

RAHMIEL Also Rahamiel, the so-called Angel of Mercy, who helps to promote compassion and mercy among all peoples. One of the other names for this angel is Rhamiel.

RAIN, ANGEL OF A title given to several angels, including Matariel, who is credited with the post in the Third Book of Enoch.

RAMIEL Also Ramael and Remiel, an angel whose main claim to fame is assisting Baruch in the Apocalypse of Baruch (2 Baruch) with the interpretation of his visions; in the work, Ramiel gives an announcement of the impending arrival of the Messiah. The angel also appears in the First Book of Enoch, described in the same work as both a good and a bad angel. In angel lore Ramiel is often perceived in the same post as a number of other angels, including Uriel, Michael, and even Gabriel; one act—the massacre of the 185,000-man army of Sennacherib, the Assyrian king (r. 705–681 B.C.)—is attributed to Ramiel, although credit is given regularly to an otherwise unnamed angel of destruction. Ramiel as an evil angel appears in John Milton's *Paradise Lost,* sharing in the severe beating received by the fallen angels Arioc and Ariel on the first day's fighting in heaven at the hands of the formidable seraph Abdiel:

> *Nor stood unmindful Abdiel to annoy*
> *The atheist crew, but with redoubled blow*
> *Ariel and Arioch, and the violence*
> *Of Ramiel scorched and blasted overthrew.*

RAPHAEL One of the seven archangels and one of the best loved of all angels, with such other notables as Michael and Gabriel. Raphael is honored as the regent of the sun, the angel of healing, the angel of science, the angel of knowledge, head of the guardian angels, and chief of the angelic order of virtues, although he is also a member of the seraphim, the dominations, and the cherubim. Raphael, whose name means "God has healed," is best known for his appearance in the Book of Tobit, a biblical work that is accepted as canonical by the Catholic Church but is set

The archangel Raphael appearing to Tobias, in the Book of Tobit; by Gustave Doré.

aside as apocryphal by the Jewish and Protestant faiths. In this writing, Raphael gives much-needed assistance to Tobias, especially in freeing him from the plague of the demon Asmodeus. Even though he has traveled with Raphael from Media to Nineveh, Tobias does not know that he is an angel until the very end of the book, at which time Raphael declares: "I am Raphael, one of the seven holy angels who present the prayers of the saints and enter into the presence of the glory of the Holy One" (12:15). It is additionally reported in the Book of Tobit that Raphael was able to give Tobias the means of expelling the demon—by burning the heart and liver of a fish and making them smoke so that the smell was unbearable. "And when the demon smelled the odor he fled to the remotest parts of Egypt, and the angel bound him" (8:3), a demonstration of Raphael's power.

Aside from his extensive labors in Tobit, Raphael has appeared in other writings and has been the star of numerous legends. In the First Book of Enoch he is declared one of the seven archangels, with special responsibility over the spirit of humanity. In this sense he is most concerned with helping humanity advance on the road of spiritual progress and thus is shown in art with a walking stick much like a pilgrim or a shepherd staff. He supposedly healed Abraham of the pain he felt after being circumcised at a rather old age, was perhaps one of the three angels who visited Abraham (perhaps with Michael and Gabriel), was the special patron of Isaac, restored the injured hip of Jacob after his famous wrestling match with the dark angel, gave Noah secret knowledge so that he was able to build the ark and thus survive the Flood, and assisted Solomon in the building of the Great Temple. This last legend states that Solomon prayed to the Lord for help. In response, God dispatched Raphael with a special ring with which Solomon was able to command legions of demons who were forced to act as the construction crew for the temple.

Raphael is said to possess the happiest disposition of any of the angels, having as well the best sense of humor. This may well be a result of his close relationship with the sun; he is, after all, regent of the orb and was called by the poet Longfellow the angel of the sun. He delights in bringing health, happiness, and joy everywhere he goes and encourages the guardian angels in their work. Two other tasks of his are to act as guardian of the tree of life in the Garden of Eden and to serve as a guide to the underworld. As a result of this last role, he has been quite incorrectly identified as a demon. In *Paradise Lost* (Book V) by John Milton, Raphael is called "the sociable spirit, that deigned to travel with Tobias." He has a long and merry chat with Adam and Eve, warning them of sin.

RASH Also Rashnu and Rashin, an angel in the religion of the Zoroastrians (which dominated the Persian empire; see *Zoroastrianism*) who had the duty of judging the souls of all who had died. By custom, this grim angel stood before a bridge connecting the world with heaven. He compelled each new dead soul to stand for three days while he weighed carefully the worthiness of the individual to be permitted into heaven. Should they be deemed deserving, they were allowed to cross the bridge with the aid of a beautiful maiden; if found unworthy, they still proceeded ahead, but instead of the waiting arms of a maiden, they found a host of gruesome obstacles, culminating in the shrinking of the bridge to the width of a razor tip. Slicing their feet and hands, the razor caused the sinner to plummet to an awful fate awaiting below, in the Zoroastrian conception of hell.

RAZIEL An angel, called the angel of mysteries, who is the possessor of a staggering amount of information on all matters secret, arcane, and mysterious; his knowledge stems from the fact that he traditionally stands at the very curtains separating God from the rest of Creation and hears and notes everything that is said or done around the throne of the Lord. The angel supposedly wrote down much of this incomparably valuable information in the famous tome called the Book of the Angel Raziel. This grimoire (a type of book said to contain occult and arcane knowledge related to spells and sorcery) was probably actually written during the Middle Ages by one of several Jewish scholars—such as Isaac the Blind or Eleazar of Worms—but this did not keep it from becoming surrounded by a host of legends and tales. The most notable story is the one that has Raziel actually giving the book to Adam.

According to this legend, Raziel felt sorry for Adam and Eve after their expulsion from the Garden of Eden and so gave over his work that Adam might know the true image of God. Other angels, however, took a dim view of this charity. They stole the tome and hurled it into the sea. Instead of punishing Raziel, God commanded Rahab, angel of the sea (whom he apparently would later destroy for excessive pride and disobedience), to fetch it from the watery depths and restore it to Adam. This mighty book thus passed to Enoch, the Old Testament patriarch who acquired such great wisdom that he was eventually taken to heaven and transformed into the angel Metatron.

A part of the Book of the Angel Raziel, from a seventeenth-century edition in the Netherlands.

It was also used by Enoch's descendant Noah and also by King Solomon, who learned from it much of his reputed skill as a sorcerer; after this it disappeared from human history, although a version of it appeared during the Middle Ages. The Book of the Angel Raziel is reputed to contain the 1,500 keys to the mysteries of the universe. Unfortunately these are written in a language so arcane and impossible to decipher (without presumably the aid of Raziel) that not even the greatest angels of heaven are able to figure it out. He is additionally the reputed chief or prince of the order of the erelim, the Hebrew understanding of what was later called the order of thrones. For his compassion and concern for Adam, Raziel is ranked as the special patron for the first human.

REAPER, GRIM A nickname used for the angel of death, most often identified as Azrael. The angel of death is also called simply the reaper, as in the poem by Henry Wadsworth Longfellow, "The Reaper and the Flowers."

RECORDING ANGELS Those angels who are charged with the important task of writing down every human act, both good and evil; these are then used either at the death of each person to determine his (or her) worthiness to enter heaven or at the end of time, when every moment of history is laid bare before God (or Christ) for the final and terrible judgment. The Babylonians accepted the belief in Nebo, the minor deity or spirit who is considered the precursor of the recording angel; he traditionally was held to keep the book in which was written the destinies of all human beings. The most developed of the recording angels were the moakibat (or hafaza), who were mentioned in the Qur'an (see *Moakibat* for details). Other angels considered candidates for the post have included Vrevoil and Dabriel, although there is a possibility that such names denote one angel only, known under different names. In some aspects of Jewish lore the recording angels are known as scribes; they stand before the throne of God and write down all deeds by every human. These are then read out before the heavenly court at the judgment session of heaven to which all souls are subjected and from which there is no appeal.

REGENTS A group or order of angels who are mentioned in John Milton's lesser-known poetic work *Paradise Regained*. He used a similar name—Regent—for one of his fallen angels in *Paradise Lost*.

REMIEL Another name for the angel Ramiel.

RESURRECTION, ANGEL OF THE The otherwise unnamed angel who appeared at the tomb of Jesus after his Resurrection. As was written in the Gospel of Matthew (28:1–7): "Now after the sabbath, toward the dawn of the first day of the week, Mary Magdalene and the other Mary went to see the sepul-

"Why do you look for him here?" inquires the angel of the Resurrection; by Gustave Doré.

chre. And behold, there was a great earthquake: for an angel of the Lord descended from heaven and came and rolled back the stone, and sat upon it. His appearance was like lightning, and his raiment was white as snow. And for fear of him the guards trembled and became like dead men. But the angel said to the women, 'Do not be afraid; for I know that you seek Jesus who has risen, as he said. Come, see the place where he lay. . . .' " There is a tradition that the angel of the Resurrection was Gabriel.

The Four Horsemen of the Apocalypse from the Book of Revelation; by Albrecht Dürer.

🎭 **REVELATION, BOOK OF** The final book of the New Testament, also called the Apocalypse and written by an author named John, said perhaps to be St. John the Evangelist. One of the best known of all scriptural writings, Revelation was composed on the island of Patmos probably during the reign of Emperor Domitian (r. 81–96). It is divided into two parts, a set of letters to seven cities in Asia Minor and then a series of prophetic visions on the unspeakable suffering endured by the faithful, ending with the descent of the new Jerusalem, generally interpreted as the Last Judgment. Full of powerful, even lurid symbolism, Revelation offers up grim images of the seven seals, the seven trumpets, and the seven terrible plagues. Throughout there are references to angels and angelic beings: the six-winged seraphim; the twenty-four elders; "myriads of myriads and thousands and thousands" of angels "heard around the throne"; the seven angels with the seven trumpets; the pillared angel; the Woman Clothed in the Sun; and Michael and the heavenly host, who defeat the dragon and his angels. (See also *Bible*.)

🎭 **RIDWAN** The angel in Islamic lore who is said to be the guardian of the gates of the earthly Paradise.

🙧 **RIKBIEL YHWH** A great angel who is the princely chief of the galgallim, the "wheels," who are to be equated in later angel lore with the cherubim. Rikbiel is one of the highest ranking of all angels in the heavenly host, said to be superior even to such a grand angel as Metatron. In the lore of the Merkabah as reported in the Third Book of Enoch, Rikbiel has charge over the wheels of the chariot (the Merkabah) upon which the throne of God is situated. There are eight wheels, two for each direction, with rivers of fire pouring out from under them. (See also *Galgallim*.)

🙧 **ROME, COUNCIL OF** A synod probably held on October 25, 745, under Pope St. Zachary (r. 741–752) that was concerned with a number of pressing matters, one of which was the question of angels. Church officials at the time were increasingly alarmed at the growing tendency of many of the faithful to give veneration to the angels to such a degree that it bordered on worship, which was to be limited exclusively to God. The synod thus decided to clarify the Church's teaching on angels and removed from the official lists of recognized angels any members of the heavenly host who were not directly supported by Scripture. The result was that the angels Raphael, Gabriel, and Michael were all affirmed by the faith, while many others were stripped from the angelic rolls. The most notable of these demoted angels was Uriel, who was widely followed and was quite well-known among those who had spent any time studying the lore of the angelic. The others included Tubuas, Inias, Simiel, Raguel, Sabaoc, and Adimus. The measure did much to bring some of the faithful back to earth, so to speak, and prepared the way for subsequent theological speculation on angels, which reached its golden age during the twelfth and thirteenth centuries in the writings of such masters of Scholasticism as St. Thomas Aquinas. (See also *Angelology*.)

🙧 **RUHIEL** The angel who has authority over the wind.

🙧 **RULERS** An alternate name used for the angelic choir or order of the dominations.

🙧 **RUMAN** An angel in Islamic lore who works with the two angels Munkar and Nakir. Ruman serves in the infernal regions, greeting each condemned soul that is sent to him and forcing it to sit down and write out each and every evil deed committed while on the earth. In some cases, of course, the writing takes nearly forever, as Ruman is aware of every wicked act, from the smallest to the largest, and waits, impatiently and cruelly, while the sinner scribbles them down. Once they are finished, the poor souls are handed over to Munkar and Nakir for the inflicting of eternal punishments.

SABAOC Also Sabaoth, one of the angels who were declared by a council in Rome in 745 under Pope Zachary to be no longer eligible for veneration by the faithful. He joined several other angels, including Uriel, Simiel, Tubuas, Adimus, and Raguel. (See *Rome, Council of.*)

SABAOTH A Hebrew word meaning "hosts" that has been used over the years to denote the heavenly hosts. In a more personal sense it means an actual angel or, in the Gnostic understanding of the heavenly hierarchy, one of the archons. Sabaoth is also used as a spelling for the angel Sabaoc, who with other angels was removed from official lists by Church officials in 745 as ineligible for veneration by the faithful.

SABRAEL See *Sidriel.*

SAHAQIEL One of the seven great archangels listed in the Third Book of Enoch. According to that source on angelic lore, Sahaqiel is the guardian of the fourth heaven; like all archangels, he is prince of a heavenly host and is attended by 496,000 myriads of ministering angels.

SAINTS AND ANGELS See box on pages 252–253.

SALATHIEL An angel whose name means "I have asked the Lord" and who is one of the great archangels in some Jewish legends.

SAINTS

❦

Throughout history, angels have visited and encouraged the labors of many men and women who were chosen for special missions or considered to be examples of sanctity. In the Old Testament times, angels appeared to patriarchs such as Abraham, Jacob, and Moses and to the prophets Ezekiel, Elijah, and Daniel. Angels, however, have especially cared for saints and holy figures of many faiths.

Perhaps the most detailed relationship between saints and angels has been enunciated by the Catholic Church. The New Testament mentions St. Peter receiving aid from an angel of the Lord and escaping prison. Similarly there are tales of martyrs who were helped by angels to endure their terrible ordeals. In all, there are hundreds of stories about angels and saints. Among the more unusual are those of St. Teresa of Avila, who was aided by angels in her writing (witnesses swore they saw invisible hands scribbling on pages in response to the dictation of St. Teresa); St. Thomas Aquinas, who was regularly visited in dreams by angels, such as the one who suggested to him the topic for his doctoral dissertation; St. Joan of Arc, who was encouraged to go to war by St. Michael; Zita, who was allowed by angels to care for the sick and poor when the heavenly visitors fulfilled her duties as a servant

Francis of Assisi receives the stigmata; by Albrecht Dürer.

by baking bread and cleaning the kitchen of her employers; and St. Francis of Assisi, who beheld a seraphim at the time he received the stigmata. Other saints deserving mention include Gemma Galgani, Rose of Viterbo, Agnese of Montepulciano, Claire of Montefalco, and Frances of Rome. Angels also were said to have appeared to Padre Pio, the modern-era Capuchin friar and recipient of the stigmata.

SAMAEL Also called Sammael, Samil, and even Satan, an angel whose
name has been interpreted as meaning "angel" *(el)* of "poison" *(sam);*
he is considered in legend both a member of the heavenly host (with
often grim and destructive duties) and a fallen angel, equatable with
Satan and the chief of the evil spirits. One of Samael's greatest roles in
Jewish lore is that of the angel of death. In this capacity he is a fell
angel but nevertheless remains one of the Lord's servants. He was
supposedly sent to the world to gather at last the stubborn soul of
Moses after the Lawgiver's death was proclaimed by the angels. One
story assures that Moses did not go gently into the next world, beating the angel so badly with his staff that Samael went blind; only the
intervention of the Lord compelled Moses to surrender his soul (but
even the Lord brought the moral support of Michael, Gabriel, and
Zagzagel). In other tales he stands at the head of each dying person
with a drawn sword. From the tip of his gently hanging sword falls a
single drop of poison into the open mouth of the passing victim; the
looks of abject horror on the faces of the deceased have been attributed to the fact that Samael becomes visible to them at the last moment. The poison has no antidote, and from the actions of Samael
there can be no appeal. (See also *Death, Angel of.*)

As a good angel, Samael supposedly resides in the seventh
heaven, although he is declared to be the chief angel of the fifth
heaven. He may have been the dark angel who wrestled with Jacob,
although many angels are also listed in this post. Far more prevalent
are his incarnations as a wicked fallen angel. He is named in the Third
Book of Enoch as the prince of accusers, making him one of the fell
spirits who hurled accusations against Israel in the court of heaven; in
the same vein he was called the angel of Rome, one of the guardian
angels of nations who became so enamored of the peoples over
whom they had charge that they fell into sin over their biases. Samael
apparently helped bring about the birth of Rome, thereby ensuring
the future conquest of Israel, the destruction of the Great Temple of
Jerusalem in 70 A.D., and the dispersal of the Jews out of the Holy
Land in the cruel migration called the Diaspora. (See also guardian
angels of nations under *Guardian Angels.*)

Samael has been called the chief of the satans, meaning that he
was master of those evil spirits called satans in early Jewish lore. He is
thus considered interchangeable with Satan himself. As the great
tempter, he crept into the Garden of Eden as the serpent and seduced

Eve. Not content with this, however, he is given the infamous credit in one legend for actually fathering Cain, a descent that would do much to explain Cain's more than flawed personality and his penchant for jealousy and murder. Samael possesses twelve wings and, as Longfellow wrote in *The Golden Legend:*

> *The dogs howl when, with icy breath,*
> *Great Sammael, the Angel of Death,*
> *Takes through the town his flight.*

SAMUIL Also Samoil and Semil, an angel whose name means "heard of God" and who is one of the angelic messengers credited with transporting the famous patriarch Enoch to heaven. Samuil is mentioned in the Second Book of Enoch, along with the angel Raguel. Another angel most often mentioned in legend as being responsible for this translation is Anafiel. (See *Enoch* for other details.)

SANDALPHON The tall angel, twin brother of the angel Metatron, and, according to the poet Longfellow, the angel of glory and the angel of prayer. In Greek Sandalphon means "brother," and it is in this role that he is probably best known, for he is the spiritual sibling and close companion of Metatron. This affinity is based largely in the similarities of the two angels; just as Metatron is reputed to have once been the patriarch Enoch, Sandalphon is declared in legend to be the onetime Old Testament prophet Elijah. After his transport to heaven in a fiery chariot, the mighty prophet was turned into an angel, Sandalphon, in order to continue his valuable service to the Lord. While said in some traditions to be in charge of the fourth, sixth, or even seventh heaven, he was actually seen by Moses during the Lawgiver's visit and tour of the third heaven. Moses described Sandalphon as the tall angel, a reference to his incredible height. The angel is one of the tallest beings in all of heaven, his size challenged only by Metatron and Anafiel. Sandalphon is so tall that it would take a journey of five hundred years just to reach from his toes to the top of his head. On the basis of his name, he is also said to be fond of shoes, specifically sandals, wearing them anytime he stands before God. As the angel of prayer he helps carry the prayers of the faithful into heaven, making of them a beautiful and delicate garland to decorate the head of the Lord. (See also *Singing, Angelic.*)

🕸 **SANTRIEL** An angel mentioned exclusively in the Jewish mystical work the Zohar. The angel has only one known duty, unpleasant as it might be: he is to journey to the world of men and gather the bodies of all the dead who in their earthly lives had neglected to honor the Sabbath. The condemned souls are then taken to Gehenna and held up before all of the other sinners so that they might note how the corpses of such wicked people are the breeding ground for worms.

🕸 **SARAQAEL** Also Sariel and Sarakiel, one of the mighty archangels mentioned in the First Book of Enoch. Saraqael has authority over the spirits (or children) of humankind who have sinned in the spirit. He is joined in his duties as an archangel by Gabriel, Raphael, Raguel, Michael, and Suruel. He is also thought in some sources to be synonymous with the mighty angel Uriel.

🕸 **SARIEL** See *Saraqael.*

🕸 **SARIM** The plural name for the Hebrew word *sar* ("prince" or "celestial"), used for several types of angels. The sarim are considered part of the singing angels who reside in heaven and ceaselessly sing the praises of the Lord; they are under the overall authority of the towering angel Tagas. Sarim are also said to be the seventy angels in charge of the nations. According to custom, all of the guardian angels of the nations—with the obvious exception of St. Michael—fell from grace and are now counted among the fallen angels. They can also be termed the great angel princes of heaven, claiming as members such renowned angelic personages as Michael, Metatron, Raphael, Uriel, Sandalphon, Jehoel, and Camael.

🕸 **SASNIGIEL** An angel mentioned in the Third Book of Enoch and ranked as one of the members of the angelic hierarchy. He, like all of the other angelic princes, wears a magnificent crown, which he removes in the presence of one of the angelic princes ranked higher than he in the celestial hierarchy.

🕸 **SATAN** The leader of the fallen angels and one of the embodiments of every kind of evil; he rules over the demons and devils in hell and plots their chronic struggle against God and heaven. One of the most significant figures in religious history, he has been known by a host of names (Lucifer, the Devil, evil one, father of lies, Mephistopheles, Mr.

Scratch, etc.) and has been subject to exceedingly detailed examination by theologians and writers over the centuries. Satan was not, however, always the source of all evil and an unrepentant fallen angel. Indeed, in the Old Testament there is good reason to deduce that he is not even wicked, serving the Lord as a kind of tempting angel (see also *Accusing Angel, The,* and *Mastema*). The Hebrew word *satan* means "the adversary," and in Scripture it seems to denote the title given to an angel who is appointed to work against someone for some divine reason or to tempt a person so as to provide the Lord with a clear picture of their faith. Thus, in the Book of Numbers (22:22), the angel of the Lord is said to stand in the way of Balaam "as his adversary." This concept is perhaps most clear in the early portion of the Book of Job, when the "adversary" (satan)

Satan, the fallen angel, sits plotting his revenge against God; by Gustave Doré.

suggests to God that he should inflict suffering upon Job to test his fidelity. Similar references are found elsewhere in the Old Testament, such as in the Book of Psalms and the First Book of Chronicles.

A change of considerable proportions takes place in the New Testament. Here, and largely henceforth, the satan (adversary) is transformed into Satan, the evil one, the main enemy of the Lord. When Christ reprimands Peter for suggesting that he not go to Jerusalem, he calls him Satan, and that the devil is Satan seems implied throughout the Gospels, especially during the attempted temptation of Christ during his forty days in the desert (Luke 4:1–13). St. Paul describes Satan as the "prince of the power of the air, the spirit that is now at work in the sons of disobedience" (Ephesians 2:2). He is also described as Beelzebub, the prince of demons (Mark 3:22); the adversary (1 Peter 5:8); and a deceiver able to disguise himself as an angel of light (Corinthians 11:14). The most explicit reference, of course, is found in the Book of Revelation with mention of "that ancient serpent, who is called the Devil and Satan, the deceiver of the whole world."

This eschatological outlook would shape the thinking of Christians ever after, so that the devil and Satan became synonymous. Satan's primary purpose is to tempt humanity into sin (Matthew 4:3 and 1 Thessalonians 3:5), the very sin that he helped to create. Thus, to close the historical loop, so to speak, some medieval theologians presented the argument that it was Satan who tempted Eve, either using the serpent as a servant or assuming the guise of the serpent himself. Throughout the Middle Ages brilliant theologians examined both the nature of evil and its chief representatives. This was a fertile period for demonology, during which many of the traditions related to Satan were first formulated and given heightened development.

According to Christian lore, Satan was once one of the mightiest and most beloved angels in all of heaven. In his *Moralia,* Pope St. Gregory the Great wrote that Satan was so great in glory and knowledge that he wore all of the other angels as a mere garment. He was first in knowledge and beauty; some writers have incorrectly declared that during his glory days with the heavenly host he was called Lucifer ("Bearer of Light"), in recognition of his stunning light and burning intelligence, which glowed in the heavens. Aside from his post as a chief minister to the Lord, he was also head or chief of the angelic choirs of the seraphim and virtues (he may also have been prince over the powers and archangels). He was perhaps a member of the seraphim, which makes sense given his luminosity, but St. Thomas Aquinas in his *Summa Theologica,* held that he was actually of the choir of cherubim. The reason, Thomas wrote, was that Satan excelled in knowledge, not love or charity. The former attribute is the hallmark of the cherubim and the latter of the seraphim. Satan also suffered from a staggering (but perhaps understandable) amount of pride. Such was his hubris that when God created humanity he commanded all the angels to bow down. This Satan would not do. When he still refused to follow the command of the Lord, he crossed over the barrier of obedience and became the first angel to sin. Once this choice was made, Satan's pride again refused to let him repent. Joined by other angels, said to have been as much as one-third of all the hosts of the Lord, he declared war upon God. This ended, to no one's surprise, in abject defeat, and the fallen angels were expelled from heaven. The realm to which they were consigned and from which Satan plots endlessly, was hell, thus fulfilling the famous Satanic declaration that it is "better to reign in hell, than serve in heaven" (*Paradise Lost,* Book I). The devil was able to achieve a modicum of revenge upon Creation by drawing Adam and Eve into temptation, making humanity and the world a kind of perpetual battleground. Interestingly, a number of theologians and saints, including Saints Jerome and Gregory of Nyssa, felt that Satan would eventually come around and seek penance for his now innumerable crimes. When this will take place is anyone's guess.

The image of Satan and his minions is firmly established in the conscious mind, thanks to literature, poetry, film, and especially art. In artistic depictions over the centuries, he has assumed an increasingly grotesque visage, in keeping with the more inculcated sense of the struggle between good and evil in the world. He thus assumed the twisted batlike wings, pointed tail, horns, and burning eyes. In time, his dark or even black scaled skin was replaced by the now well-known glowing red. Some elements of his appearance are so well-known that they are virtually caricatures: the horns, tail, red skin, cloven hoofs, and especially the pitchfork.

Satan has definitely brought out the best in writers over the years, figuring in the works of Goethe (*Faust,* where he incarnates as Mephistopheles) and Dryden *(State of Innocence)* and in the masterpieces of Milton and Dante. In Milton's *Paradise Lost,* Satan is one of the major characters, described as the apostate angel, the infernal serpent, glory obscured, and archangel ruined. In Dante's *Divine Comedy* Satan is termed Lucifer and Dis. In Canto XXXIV Dante finds him sitting up to his chest in ice, a punishment fitting one whose heart is now frozen with spite and unable to warm itself with love or charity. There are also numerous films, short stories, and novels, many of which take a lighthearted or whimsical look at Satan's exploits, ambitions, and hopes.

Satan remains the most profound expression of evil. He is a being devoid of love, kindness, compassion, charity, and every other virtue. He struggles endlessly to ensnare the souls of humankind and to sow chaos and woe in the cosmos. So pervasive is his wickedness and so synonymous is he with the absence of goodness that some prefer to look upon him not as an actual fallen angel, but as the personification of evil. While he is not a real being, he represents the sin and dark inclinations of humankind and the horrors they are perpetually tempted to commit. (See also *Fallen Angels, Lucifer, Mastema, Hell,* and *Semyaza.*)

SATQIEL One of the princes of the seven heavens as noted in the Third Book of Enoch. Satqiel is in charge of the fifth heaven, and, as with the other angelic princes, he is attended by 496,000 myriads of ministering angels.

SCOURGING ANGELS The grim name given to the group of angels (called in the Hebrew *malache habbala*) who were beheld by the patriarch Abraham during his visit to paradise.

SCRIBES See under *Recording Angels.*

SEALS See *Merkabah Angels.*

SEASONS, ANGELS OF THE A group of four angels, with their assistants, who have authority or act as patrons of the seasons of the year. The angels are as follows:

spring	Spugliguel, aided by Amatiel and others
summer	Tubiel, aided by Tariel and others
fall	Torquaret, aided by Guabarel and others
winter	Attarib, aided by Amabael and others

DERIVED FROM BARRETT, *THE MAGUS* (1801), AND DAVIDSON, *A DICTIONARY OF ANGELS* (1967).
(See also *Year, Angels of the.*)

SEATS The translation of the Latin *sedes* that was used by St. Augustine in his renowned work *The City of God* to denote what was apparently his idea of an angelic order. It is thought by scholars that the *sedes* should be equated with the choir of the thrones.

SEFIRA The singular of the important angelic beings the sefiroth. (See *Sefiroth* for details.)

SEFIROTH The plural for the sefira, the divine emanations found in the Jewish mystical system of the Qabalah, through which God, as the en-Sof (the Divine), brought into existence all of Creation. Also known as the sephiroth, they can be considered the ten delegated powers of God, controlling the basic structure of the universe and representing ten attributes of the Divine. There were ten holy sefiroth that emanated from the right hand of the Lord and ten unholy sefiroth that were from the left. The holy sefiroth act as his means of interacting with his Creation, as he himself is so vast and unapproachable and so inconceivable in his totality that he is unknowable. Scholars describe them as similar or analogous to the Gnostic concept of the aeons or Plato's idea of the intelligences. The ten holy sefiroth are normally named as Kether (crown); Chocmah or Chokmah (wisdom); Binah (intelligence or understanding); Hesed or Chesed (love); Geburah (power); Tifereth or Tiphereth (beauty); Netzah or Netzach (endurance or victory); Hod (majesty or splendor); Yesod (foundation); and Malkuth (kingdom). The holy sefiroth were also given personification in several angels as a means of extending their expression and function in the world of humanity. Among the sefiroth angels are Michael, Gabriel, Metatron, Raziel, Zadkiel, Camael, and Haniel. (See also *Qabalah*.)

SEGEF An angel mentioned in the work *Jewish Magic and Superstition* by Joshua Trachtenberg. He is to be ranked among the feared angels of destruction and is traditionally invoked at the end of the Sabbath.

SEMALION Probably a variant spelling for the angel Samael; nevertheless, under this name an angel is declared in the Talmud as having proclaimed to the world that Moses had finally died, shouting out, "The Lawgiver is dead!" (See also *Samael*.)

SEMYAZA According to Jewish mythology the leader of the fallen angels, children of heaven who descended from the celestial kingdom and entered into union with the women of the world. Also called Semyaz, Shamazya, and Semiaza, he brought with him two hundred fellow angels; they not only begot children by the women, they taught humanity a variety of useful talents, such as medicine and plants, and some destructive skills as well, including sword making, astrology, and adultery. Most wicked of all were the children of the angels, giants who stood several miles high and brought much suffering to the people of the earth. In vengeance, the Lord dispatched his most powerful angels, including Michael and Gabriel, and they imprisoned the fallen angels in the valleys of the earth. The giants were later wiped out in the Great Flood of Noah fame.

🐚 **SERAPH** The shortened version of the angelic choir of the seraphim, generally used in the singular when referring to one member of that august angelic body. Milton, for example, in his *Paradise Lost,* refers to the faithful seraph Abdiel. (See *Seraphim* for other details.)

🐚 **SERAPHIC DOCTOR** In the Latin *Doctor Seraphicus,* the honorific title given to St. Bonaventure (d. 1274). It is derived from his contributions to the Franciscan order (he is called the second founder of the order, after St. Francis of Assisi) and to the theology of the Church. The Franciscan order is known as the Seraphic order because St. Francis beheld a seraphim when he received his stigmata. Bonaventure's close friend was St. Thomas Aquinas, known as "the Angelic Doctor."

🐚 **SERAPHIEL** Also Serapiel, the chief or prince of the high angelic order of the seraphim. One of the most resplendent of all angels, he is described as having the face of an angel and the body of an eagle, which is full of eyes so many in number that they cannot be counted, each shining forth like the morning star; some are brighter than others, depending on where on his body they are located. He is as tall as the seven heavens and is adorned with a crown that itself would require a journey of 502 years to climb. The crown contains every kind of light and every form of brilliant emanation. As chief of the seraphim, Seraphiel has the main duty of standing by his angelic charges and teaching them every manner of song, psalm, and chant in eternal praise of God. Other possible chiefs of the seraphim have included Michael, Uriel, Jehoel, Metatron, Nathanael, and, before his Fall, Satan. (See *Seraphim* for other details.)

🐚 **SERAPHIM** (Choir) The highest and most splendid of the nine accepted angelic orders as developed by the sixth-century theologian Dionysius the Areopagite and largely embraced by the Christian Church. Not only are the seraphim the highest of the nine choirs, they are ranked first in the first triad of the Dionysian scheme, with the cherubim and the thrones. Without question they are the closest in all of heaven to the very throne of God, and their primary function is to circle the incomprehensibly beautiful throne in perpetual adoration of the Lord, chanting what is called the trisagion: "Holy, Holy, Holy is the Lord of Hosts, the entire earth is full of His Glory" *(Sanctus Sanctus Sanctus Dominus Deus Sabaoth)*; this is a task that is not

Seraphim stand watch over the dead Christ; from an altar cloth, in San Marco, Venice (COURTESY ART RESOURCE).

nearly as monotonous as it might seem to mortals, given the nature of angels (who have perfect powers of concentration) and the delight that such an honor actually brings to the spirits. Known in some Hebrew writings also as the hayyoth, the seraphim are most often identified with fire—not the burning, painful heat of hell, but the redemptive, healing flame of love, for they literally are living flames. The intensity of their adoration and pure love of God pour out of them as a flawless reflection of the divine love that emanates from the Lord. This was touched upon in the apocryphal but interesting Third Book of Enoch, in which was written that every seraphim has sixteen faces (four for each cardinal direction), like the rising sun; each angel radiates such light that even the other holy beings, the cherubim and the thrones, cannot look upon them.

According to Enoch, each seraphim has six wings. This last detail is corroborated by the Old Testament Book of Isaiah (6:1–3): ". . . I saw the Lord sitting upon a throne, high and lifted up; and his train filled the temple. Above him stood the seraphim; each had six wings: with two he covered his face, and with two he covered his feet, and with two he flew." Another reference might be found in the

Book of Revelation (4:8): "And the four living creatures, each of them with six wings, are full of eyes all around and within, and day and night they never cease to sing 'Holy, holy, holy, is the Lord God Almighty who was and is and is to come!' " It is uncertain how many seraphim there are, despite the assurance of the Third Book of Enoch that there are only four, corresponding to the four winds of the world and perhaps seconded by the foregoing passage from Revelation. This does not seem to be supported by lore, which names many angels as members of the choir, such as Michael, Seraphiel, Gabriel, Metatron (he has 36 wings), and even Satan or Lucifer. It has been argued by some angelologists that the four to whom Enoch refers were actually the four chiefs of the choir. As the seraphim circle the throne of God in a stunning and endless chant that is heard throughout all of Creation, it stands to reason that there are scores of them. Enoch also speaks of their useful task of burning the tablets of Satan. It seems that each day Satan is handed by the two wicked accusing angels (Samael, prince of Rome, and Dubbiel, prince of Persia) tablets on which are written the most scandalous and vicious accusations against Israel. These are then given to the seraphim for presentation to the Almighty. The angels, however, simply carry the tablets to the fire next to the throne and burn them. Satan, apparently, never tires of this daily exercise. As seen, the chiefs of the seraphim are listed variously as Seraphiel, Uriel, Nathanael, Michael, Metatron, Jehoel, and Satan, although this was before his Fall.

It is understandable that few seraphim have been seen by mortal eyes. One of the truly fortunate was St. Francis of Assisi (d. 1226), who beheld a crucified Christ being carried aloft by seraphs on Mt. Alvernia in the Apennines in 1224, receiving at the same time the stigmata. The Franciscan order in honor of this event has been called the Seraphic order, and one of its members, St. Bonaventure (d. 1274), the brilliant theologian, is often termed "the Seraphic Doctor" or "the Seraphic Father." (See also *Choirs, Galgallim, Hayyoth,* and *Many-Eyed Ones.*)

Seven Archangels See *Archangels, Seven.*

Seven Heavens See *Heaven.*

Shaitan In Arabic legend, a fallen angel generally identified with the Islamic devil Iblis or Satan. (See *Fallen Angels.*)

🏵 **SHAMIEL** Also Shamael and Shammiel, one of the leaders in Jewish lore of the angelic choirs in their singing the praises of God. Other angels mentioned in this role have included Tagas, Metatron, Radueriel, Asaph, Heman, and Jeduthun. (See also *Music* and *Singing, Angelic*.)

🏵 **SHAMSIEL** Also Shamshiel, a leading angel in the celestial hierarchy whose name means "light of God." He is the angelic guardian of the fourth heaven (although Sahaqiel is often named in this post as well) and is honored as the guardian of Paradise, a title that makes him the chief protector of the Garden of Eden (see also *Eden, Garden of*). Shamsiel is also named as the angel who had the duty of taking Moses on a guided tour of a part of heaven when the Lawgiver visited there at some time during his life. Curiously, in the First Book of Enoch and under the name Sasomaspeel or Samsapeel, he is ranked as one of the fallen angels who descended to the earth and cohabited with women.

🏵 **SHATQIEL** An angel mentioned in the Third Book of Enoch as belonging to the exalted ranks of the princes of the seven heavens, meaning that he may be termed one of the archangels. He is in charge of the fifth heaven and, like his fellows, is attended by some 496,000 myriads of ministering angels. In other sources he is named as the guardian or prince of the fourth heaven.

🏵 **SHEMHAZA** A variation on the name Semyaza. (See *Semyaza*.)

🏵 **SHEPHERD OF HERMAS, THE** A second-century A.D. work, supposedly written by the largely unknown Hermas, that attempts to advance to the reader important Christian virtues, especially the need for penance and the forgiveness of sin. *The Shepherd of Hermas* claims to have been composed as a result of several visions and is organized into three main sections, five visions, twelve mandates, and ten parables or similitudes. The book is of interest to angelologists because of the presence of the angel of penance, who appears to Hermas in his fifth vision, in the guise of a shepherd (hence the work's title). The identity of this angel remains undisclosed in the work, but tradition and legend declare him to be Phanuel or perhaps even Uriel.

🏵 **SIDRIEL** Also Sabrael, a high-ranking angel mentioned in the Third Book of Enoch. He is one of the princes of the seven heavens and is in charge of the first heaven. Thus honored as being one of the archangels, he, like his fellow princes, is attended by 496,000 myriads of ministering angels. As Sabrael he is also often credited with the post of chief or prince of the angelic order of the tarshishim, the Hebrew equivalent of the virtues.

SIMIEL One of the angels removed from official lists of angels to be venerated by the Church in 745 at a council in Rome under Pope Zachary. While revered as an angel for many years, Simiel fell victim to the desire of Church officials to streamline and clarify the proper veneration of angels; thus he was removed from the lists, along with Uriel, Tubuas, Adimus, Sabaoth, and Raguel. (See also *Rome, Council of.*)

SIMSIEL The angel in charge of the day, according to the Third Book of Enoch.

SINGING, ANGELIC One of the greatest abilities and duties of angels. The heavens are said literally to shake with the endless songs of the angelic choirs as they stand in the light of the Lord and sing his praises. The angels most responsible for this activity are the seraphim, the mightiest of all angels, who circle the throne of God and intone the trisagion: "Holy, holy, holy is the Lord of Hosts, the earth is full of His Glory." The seraphim are, of course, joined by the other orders of angels, when they are not sent out on assorted missions. There are as well, if the Third Book of Enoch can be believed, certain choirs that exist solely to sing the Lord's praises, free of any other duties or obli-gations. This naturally is quite an honor, as there can be no higher aspiration than to stand before the Lord and join in the adulation of all Creation toward its Maker. It is possible that there are also entire choirs or ranks of angels (not necessarily to be confused with the actual choirs, such as the seraphim or powers) brought into existence each morning. They chant the trisagion and are then immediately subsumed into the light of God, to be reborn the following day. The heavenly choirs are apparently led by angelic masters. Chief of them is Tagas, although Sandalphon is also reputed to be the master of song. Under him are Jeduthun, Asaph, and Heman. Jeduthun leads the choirs during the evening; Asaph is leader during the night; and Heman is master during the morning. (See also *Music.*)

🪷 **SONS OF GOD** A term found in the Old Testament Book of Genesis (6:4) that is thought to denote angels. The sons of God supposedly came down from heaven and cohabited with the "daughters of men," by whom the sons of God bore children, the giants, the "mighty men that were of old, the men of renown." On the basis of this understanding, the sons of God are titled the fallen angels, for they fell from heaven and surrendered to their lust. Other sources term them the children of heaven, although they were apparently quite prodigal, for they and their offspring brought much suffering and sadness to the world. Other authorities, however, view the sons of God as the bene Elohim, good and holy angels who belong to the order or choir of thrones and who forever stand and sing the praises of the Lord. This latter interpretation would seem to be supported by the Old Testament Book of Job (38:7), where the Lord speaks of "when the morning stars sang together, and all the sons of God shouted for joy . . ." (See also *Bene Elohim.*)

🪷 **SOPERIEL YHWH** Also Sopheriel and Sofriel, two of the mighty angelic princes of heaven in Jewish lore; they have the task of keeping the large books in which are recorded the names of all those who will have life and the names of all those who will die. The names of the princes are Soperiel YHWH ("who puts to death") and Soperiel YHWH ("who makes alive"). They thus possess two of the most important works in all of Creation, reading the names of all who ever shall be born and the exact times and moments of each living person's demise. They are merely record keepers, however, for all that is written and all that shall ever occur does so at the express will of God, whom they attend upon his incomparable throne.

🪷 **SOPHIA** See *Pistis Sophia.*

🪷 **SOQEDHOZI YHWH** An angelic prince in Jewish lore. He has charge over the incredibly delicate and accurate scale in which the souls of all humans are weighed at the time of their judgment before the throne of God. The scales measure their merits against their faults and sins; those found wanting in the merits department are cast out for eternal punishment. Like the other angels who stand in the court of the Lord, Soqedhozi is utterly without pity in the execution of his duties, although, like all angels, his heart grieves at the wickedness of men and women.

🞕 **SOTERASIEL YHWH** A formidable angelic prince whose name means "he who stirs the fire of God" and who is mentioned in the Third Book of Enoch as having authority over the four great chiefs of the River of Fire (the river flowing from the throne of God). He has the privilege of stirring the fiery waters of the river and is the sole angel who grants permission to other angelic princes to enter or leave the so-called Shekinah, often described as the glory that emanates from the Lord. Soterasiel is said to stand seventy thousand myriads of parasangs high, a height that would make him one of the tallest angels in all of heaven.

🞕 **SOULS, CARRIERS OF** One of the important functions of some angels, namely to fetch the souls of the deceased and transport them to the next world. Angels have served as soul carriers to some very prominent figures of the past, such as Adam, Abraham, and Moses, as well as Muhammad, the Prophet. The latter was taken to heaven by the archangel Gabriel, who rode upon Al-Borak, that amazing creature (see *Gabriel*). In the Christian faith the angel most given this duty is Michael. The idea of angelic or spiritual beings transporting the souls of the deceased into the next life is found all over the world. In parts of Asia, for example, a spirit in the form of a butterfly is the carrier, while among the Norse were the proud Valkyrie, the handmaidens of the god Odin, who flew over battlefields and chose the bravest of the warriors to die and journey to Valhalla for an eternity of drinking and merrymaking. Angels, however, are a more direct link between the mortal soul and its Creator, appearing in Jewish, Islamic, and Christian lore. In some accounts every soul is brought before the Lord for judgment, regardless of its ultimate and sometimes obvious disposition. Thus both the blessed and the damned are first carried to heaven and, once there, the Book of Life, containing the list of those chosen from time immemorial, is read to determine if the deceased's name is in it. There is the possibility that the entire life of an individual is read out by the so-called Recording Angels. Each act, good or bad, is presented and the heavenly court—noted for its dispassion—makes its decision, although the ultimate decision of a person's eternal fate remains with God. Yet another recurring motif is that of the soul carrier bringing the soul of a person before an exacting judge, who weighs it upon a scale of infinite sensitivity. If the charity and goodness of the soul outweigh its sin and evil, then the person is to enjoy eternal bliss; there may be a period of purifying and spiritual cleansing for those souls who just *barely* pass the test, but the pleasure at eventual salvation and relief no doubt make the brief sufferings of the purgatory eminently endurable. (See also *Heaven*.)

SPIRIT OF GOD The translated title of the Latin phrase *spiritus Dei* that is used by the noted Christian apologist Lactantius (d. 323) for angels.

SRAOSHA Also Sirush, an angelic being found in the lore of the Zoroastrians, the ancient religion of Persia. He is ranked as one of the amesha spentas, the holy immortals, and is one of the spirits who figure in the afterlife of all humanity. He carries the souls of the deceased to the next world. He is also in some legends a defender of humanity, journeying down to the world to chase away all evildoers, especially the devils and bringers of sin.

STANDARDS What is most likely a force, order, or choir of angels—in John Milton's *Paradise Lost* described by the archangel Raphael as belonging to the "empyreal host." They joined with the gonfalons, hierarchies, orders, and degrees. (See *Gonfalons*.)

STARS The lights of the night sky and the constellations that figure in the lore of angels. As with the planets, nature, and just about everything else, the stars are said to be directed in their paths and function through the assistance or guardianship of angels. In some Jewish legends the stars are said to be under the charge of the angel Kokbiel, while the constellations are under Rahatiel. The stars have also been considered another name for the angels themselves, as seen in the declaration by the Lord in the Old Testament Book of Job (38:4–7):

> *Where were you when I laid the*
> *foundations of the earth?*
> *Who determined its measurements*
> *—surely you know!*
> *Or who stretched the line upon it?*
> *On what were its bases sunk,*
> *or who laid its cornerstone,*
> *when the morning stars sang*
> *together,*
> *and all the sons of God shouted for joy?*

SUKALLIN A type of angelic being found in the mythology of the Sumerians and Babylonians. The sukallin are considered precursors or a foreshadowing of the later angels. (See also *Babylon* and *Nebo*.)

SUMMA THEOLOGICA See under *Thomas Aquinas, St.*

SUN, ANGELS OF THE A title borne by a number of likely angelic candidates. In the lore of Enoch, Galgalliel is listed as having charge over the orb of the sun, but other angels of the sun include Michael, Raphael, Varcan, and especially Uriel. The last angel, whose very name means "fire of God," is perhaps (after Galgalliel) the angelic potentate most deserving of the title.

SURUEL Also Suriel, a mighty archangel, often and variously identified with Uriel, Metatron, and even Ariel. Suruel appears in a number of Jewish legends, including those surrounding the Lawgiver, Moses. With the angel of the burning bush (Zagzagel), he is supposedly one of the main sources of Moses' great knowledge; in recognition of his contributions to the life of Moses, Suruel was permitted by God to descend to the earth at the appointed time and retrieve the mighty soul of the Lawgiver, whose death had been proclaimed by the angel Semalion. Suruel also appears in the First Book of Enoch as one of the grand archangels, with Raphael, Michael, Gabriel, and Saraqael.

SWEDENBORG, EMANUEL Swedish mystic, visionary, and scientist (1688–1772) whose spiritual writings and preaching included extensive thoughts and contact with the angels. The son of a Swedish bishop, he became one of his country's foremost thinkers, authoring the first book in Swedish on algebra and demonstrating proficiency in astronomy, biology, physics, philosophy, chemistry, geology, and even medicine. In 1745, however, he underwent a profound spiritual experience. He claimed to have received a vision from God to preach the divine call and to announce the Second Coming of the Lord. He declared the need to restructure Christianity along pure, cleansed, and authentic lines. While considered eccentric or even demented—he went into trances for days, during which time he supposedly visited the spirit world and conversed with angels—he persevered, writing various books, including *Heaven and Hell, The Five Senses, The Infinite and the Final Cause of Creation,* and especially *Angelic Wisdom: Concerning Divine Love and Wisdom.*

Angels played a central part in the mystical life of Swedenborg. They spoke and sang to him in their unique fashion (see *Language, Angelic*), transmitting into his mind the visions of heaven and their life in that blessed place. While at variance with mainstream Christianity on a host of points, Swedenborg was in agreement that angels exist entirely as messengers and servants of God, deriving their being and all powers from the Lord. What is more, angels accept and embrace God as the source of all things. He thus wrote in *Angelic Wisdom* that "as far as angels are recipients of that spiritual fire and light [by which God appears to the angels], they are loves and wisdoms, but not loves and wisdoms from themselves, rather from the Lord."

Swedenborg's angels are, like those of St. Thomas Aquinas, entirely spiritual, meaning that they can be seen by mortal eyes only through a fleeting corporeal incarnation or by speaking directly into the mind's eye of the mortal they are addressing. They can both speak and write, but their language is incredibly dissimilar to our own, being one of pure and absolute love. It would thus be of little avail to argue or debate with an angel. Instead, the love transmitted by the angel should be allowed to penetrate both the heart and soul.

Some twelve years after Swedenborg's death, an actual faith was established, Swedenborgianism, on the basis of his writings. It began in England and spread to other countries, such as the United States. Swedenborg's books, however, remain largely unknown today, mainly because of their prodigious size and the peculiar, at times indecipherable, style he used in their composition. Nevertheless, he remains one of the more original thinkers on angels, influencing such other writers as Goethe and William Blake.

TADHIEL An angel who appears in Jewish legend as the angel sent by the Lord at the last minute to prevent Abraham from sacrificing his son, Isaac. This action was ascribed in the Old Testament Book of Genesis to an otherwise unnamed angel of the Lord. (See also *Abraham* and *Isaac*.)

TAGAS An angelic prince mentioned in the Third Book of Enoch. He is revered as the chief director of the angelic choirs that sing in eternal praise of the Lord. Presumably he has under his authority such other angelic directors as Asaph, Heman, and Jeduthun. (See also *Singing, Angelic*.)

TALL ANGEL, THE An angel appearing in Jewish legend. He is called the "tall angel" because of his enormous height, unusual even by the standards of heaven, which boasts some staggeringly tall angels among its blessed residents. In this case the angel was encountered by Moses, who was visiting the third heaven at the time and being shown around by the angel Metatron, himself no puny creature. The actual identity of the angel remains somewhat unclear, but according to some sources he was to be identified with Sandalphon, while others declared him to be Nuriel or Hadraniel.

TARSHISHIM The Hebrew name meaning "brilliant [or shining] ones," given to an order of angels generally said to be the equivalent of the later order of angels known as the virtues. Their chief or ruling prince is most often listed as Tarshish; other candidates for the post include Sabrael and Haniel. (See *Virtues* for other details.)

🙏 **TARTARUS, ANGELS OF** Those special angels who reside in Tartarus, classical antiquity's equivalent of Hades or hell. Mentioned in the apocryphal works of the Apocalypse of Paul and the Vision of Paul, the angels of Tartarus have the grim duty of presiding over the terrible punishments given out to the damned souls placed into their hands. The chief of these angels is usually identified as Tartaruchus, but another leader frequently stated is the ubiquitous archangel Uriel. (See also *Hell*.)

🙏 **TATRASIEL YHWH** An angel counted among the foremost princes of heaven, as noted in the Third Book of Enoch.

🙏 **TEARS, ANGEL OF** The title borne by several angels, referring to their penchant for shedding tears for the sinfulness of humanity. Two candidates are Sandalphon and Cassiel, but perhaps the most suitable angelic recipient of the title is Israfel. According to Islamic lore, Israfel stares six times a day into hell and beholds the wickedness of the condemned. So heartrending is this image that the angel bursts into weeping. His tears are so uncontrollable that the Lord himself must stop the flow or the entire world would be flooded. (See also *Israfel*.)

🙏 **TEMLAKOS** Also Temeluch and Temeluchus, an angel with several responsibilities, as reported in the Apocalypse of Peter, a second-century A.D. work purporting to present a revelation of the very Day of Judgment. Temlakos is the protector of all children who were slain by their parents; he is also thought to be the patron of children at the time of their birth and in their early infancy. As for the murderous parents of the children, they are consigned to Gehenna, and Temlakos has the duty of putting them to eternal torture and torment, for, as the Apocalypse declares, "it is the will of God that this be so."

🙏 **THOMAS AQUINAS, ST.** Saint, mystic, philosopher (d. 1274), and one of the foremost theologians in the history of the Catholic Church. Considered an unquestioned authority on matters of theology, St. Thomas was given the title "Angelic Doctor" in honor of his writings and also in recognition of his immense contributions to the Church's understanding and teachings about angels. The main source for his work in angelology was his masterpiece of theology, the enormous *Summa Theologica* (or *Summa Theologiae*). This vast treatise presented the near sum total of Christian doctrine on every conceivable theological topic. One of the sections was devoted to angels. It used as support and source material Scripture and the speculations of the many saints and theologians of previous years, including St. Augustine (who wielded extremely high influence, even in Thomas's era), Pope St. Gregory I the Great, St. Jerome, St. Ambrose, and, of course, the sixth-century writer Dionysius the Areopagite, whose system of organizing the heavenly host into nine choirs was given heightened structure and detailed explanation by St. Thomas.

Thomas wrote: "The angel is the most excellent of all creatures because among all creatures he bears the greatest resemblance to His Creator." The saint considered the angel to be a pure spirit, declaring that the universe itself would be incomplete without them. Further, in his logical and ordered thinking, the angels existed by necessity in a linear universe of ascending spiritual perfection. Aquinas argues that angels fulfill an essential intermediary position between God and corporeal beings. Further, angels, as spiritual creatures, each possess a profound singularity, meaning that every angel is unique, standing virtually as its own species, separate from the other angels in all of Creation. Nevertheless they are grouped together into choirs by virtue of their tasks in the cosmic order and their degree of spiritual perfection, which becomes greater the closer they are to God (see *Choirs* for other details).

In the *Summa* (in the "Treatise on the Divine Government," part I), Thomas examined the realm of angels, using as his method of exposition eight articles, such as whether all angels belong to one hierarchy (Thomas answers "no"); whether within one order there are many angels ("yes"); whether the differentiations in the hierarchies and orders stem from differences in the natures of the angels ("yes"); and whether the names of the angelic orders are correctly given ("yes"). Contrary to popular belief, Thomas did not examine the question of how many angels could fit on the head of a pin. This was purely an invention of the adherents of the philosophical school of the Enlightenment in the eighteenth century and was intended to poke fun at the pedantic tendencies of the old Scholastic thinkers of the Middle Ages. Had Thomas considered the question, however, he would have reached the conclusion (supported by a mountain of scriptural and theological material) that all the angels could fit on the head of a pin because a) they are beings of spirit who take up no actual physical space, and b) anything is possible with the Lord. Thomas is not particularly well-known by the average person today, including the average Catholic, for that matter, but he did much to settle the matter of angels as objects of belief, certified the Dionysian system of nine choirs, and brought to the study of angels an elevated, analytical, and devout mind.

THREE ANGELS The name given to the three otherwise unnamed visitors to the patriarch Abraham in the Old Testament Book of Genesis. The three strangers appeared suddenly at the door of Abraham's tent at the oaks of Mamre. Abraham "lifted up his eyes and looked, and behold, three men stood in front of him. When he saw them, he ran from the tent door to meet them, and bowed himself to the earth, and said, 'My lord, if I found favor in your sight, do not pass by your servant. Let a little water be brought, and wash your feet, and rest yourselves under the tree, while I fetch a morsel of bread, that you may refresh yourselves, and after that you may pass on—since you have come to your servant' " (18:2–5). Scholars and biblical experts have long offered identifications for the three travelers, but the most common, based on Abraham's use of the term "my lord," is that the Lord himself had paid a call, manifesting himself as the Trinity: God, the Son, and the Holy Spirit. While most logical, this explanation has been joined by other proposed identifications. For example, the three have been proclaimed to be God, Gabriel, and Michael; Raphael, Michael, and Gabriel; Gabriel, Michael, and Israfel; or three angels who have no names. That there were two angels accompanying God is seemingly supported by subsequent events, namely the sending of two angels to destroy Sodom and Gomorrah while the Lord continued to speak with Abraham.

THRONE BEARERS The name given to those angels in Islamic lore who carry the throne of God, called the 'Arsh. By custom there are four such angels representing the four divine attributes of requital, providence, mercy, and beneficence. However, on the Day of Judgment eight angels will carry the throne, as declared in the Qur'an (surah 69). In Jewish lore there are also throne angels, the so-called Merkabah Angels, and the seven angels mentioned in the apocryphal Book of the Angel Raziel, who have the high honor of standing in the very presence of the throne of God. The seven throne angels are

EZEKIEL'S THRONES

❧

As for the appearance of the wheels and their construction: their appearance was like the gleaming of a chrysolite; and the four had the same likeness, their construction being as it were a wheel within a wheel. When they went, they went in any of their four directions without turning as they went.

The four wheels had rims and they had spokes; and their rims were full of eyes round about. And when the living creatures went, the wheels went beside them; and when the living creatures rose from the earth, the wheels rose. Wherever the spirit would go, they went, and the wheels rose along with them; for the spirit of the living creatures was in the wheels. When those went, these went; and when those stood, these stood; and when those rose from the earth, the wheels rose along with them; for the spirit of the living creatures was in the wheels.

(EZEKIEL 1:16–21)

Gabriel, Michael, Raphael, Uriel, Phanuel, Israel, and Uzziel. Other sources say that there are actually fifteen throne angels. (See also *Merkabah Angels*.) In Christian traditions the three highest of the choirs in heaven, namely the first triad comprised of the seraphim, cherubim, and thrones, are all close or next to the throne of the Almighty. (See also *Empyrean* and *Heaven*.)

THRONES (Choir) One of the nine choirs of angels, as accepted in lore and determined by the sixth-century theologian Dionysius the Areopagite. Called the ophanim or galgallim in Hebrew traditions, the thrones are also termed the "wheels" and the "many-eyed ones." They belong to the first and highest triad of the heavenly host, standing just below the seraphim and the cherubim; this position makes them some of the most powerful angels in the service of the Lord. According to St. Thomas Aquinas, the thrones have the task of pondering the disposition of divine judgments, meaning that they carry out or fulfill the divine justice of the Lord. Like their counterparts in the first angelic triad, they come the closest of all angels to spiritual

Two members of the choir of thrones; from the Judges and the Elect, Florence
(COURTESY ART RESOURCE).

ANGELIC TRAVEL

While it is romantic to think of angels winging their way through the heavens, harp in hand, this image does little to express the true means by which an angel is actually able to journey from one place to the next. As a spiritual being entirely dependent upon the will of God, all angels are able to travel through Creation as a result of divine empowerment. Such a granted ability permits the angel to move from point to point without traversing the area in between. Thus, for example, Gabriel would be able to move from the seventh heaven to the earth without covering any of the rather presumably large amount of ground between them (although in spiritual terms there is the same distance between the heavens and the world and the components of the smallest atom). Such a conception begins to make clear the very complicated nature of angelic existence. When assuming the form of mortals, of course, angels will accept assorted physical limitations—traveling on trains, planes, and automobiles—as part of the fulfillment of their task among humanity. But their miraculous activities are still present, regularly being accomplished in a manner so unobtrusive and so subtle that mortals are ignorant of their presence; one of these miraculous events is the sudden appearance of a rescuer seemingly out of nowhere and the disappearance of a savior in the middle of nowhere and before the grateful human can even thank the strange benefactor. (See also *Angelophany.*)

perfection and emanate the light of God with mirrorlike goodness. They are, despite their greatness, intensely humble, an attribute that permits them to dispense justice with perfect objectivity and without fear of pride or ambition. Because they are the living symbols of God's justice and authority, they are called thrones and have as one of their symbols the throne.

In some Jewish lore the thrones function within the heavenly scheme of things as either the chariots upon which the throne of God rests (the Merkabah) or as the wheels of the chariot. This imagery is expressed fully in the Old Testament Book of Ezekiel (1:13–21), where they appeared with the cherubim (see box on page 276). Their chiefs are named variously Jophiel, Zaphkiel, Oriphiel, and Raziel. According to lines in John Milton's *Paradise Lost* (Book VI), some of the angels of this choir joined Satan in his war against God and thus shared in the Fall from heaven and were described as "rebel thrones." Clearly, of course, not all the thrones took part, and the bulk of them stayed with the heavenly host. (See also *Choirs, Galgallim, Many-Eyed Ones, Ofanim,* and *Wheels.*)

TIME, SPIRIT OF See *Zeitgeist.*

TRAVEL, ANGELIC See box on page 278.

TREE OF LIFE A belief found in many of the world's religions that there exists a mighty tree of eternal life, standing in some garden or Paradise. The idea is found in Near and Far Eastern cultures, ancient Greece and Rome, and parts of Europe, such as the Norse, who had Yggdrasil, the enormous evergreen ash tree that connected the three realms of Ansgard, Midgard, and Niflheim (heaven, earth, and hell, respectively). The most developed concepts of the tree of life, however, were found among the Jews. In the teachings of the Qabalah the tree is a profound mystical symbol of the cosmic order, with microcosmic and macrocosmic connotations. The structure of the universe, represented by its branches, can correspond both to God and humanity, while depicting a kind of map or layout of the universe. The points of the tree of life, those forces that represent vital aspects of the order of Creation, are embodied by the sephiroth (sefiroth). Each sefira has its own corresponding archangel to provide a kind of angelic personification. There is also a belief that the tree of life, wherever it stands, is guarded by some powerful spirit or angel. According to the Old Testament Book of Genesis, a cherubim, holding a flaming sword, stands watch over the tree. The angel is sometimes identified as Uriel or Raphael, among others.

🌸 **TRUTH, ANGEL OF THE** The generally unnamed angel in Jewish legend who was a staunch opponent of the creation of humanity, with the angel of peace. Both were against the birth of humankind because they, like the earth itself in other tales, perceived that the mortals would turn against God and bring chaos and misery. The Lord, however, grew angry at their impudence and burned both the angel of truth and the angel of peace to ashes, along with the untold number of ministering angels who accompanied them. In tradition, several angels have been named as possessing the title angel of truth, including Amitiel, Gabriel, and even Michael. As the angel was destroyed, it can be deduced that neither Michael nor Gabriel was the original angel of truth; it is possible that Amitiel was incinerated and the position bestowed upon either Gabriel or Michael. Of the two, Gabriel probably has more claim to the title, given his role in announcing momentous news, such as the coming of John the Baptist and Christ in the Christian tradition and the revealing of the Qur'an to Muhammad in the Islamic tradition.

🌸 **TSADKIEL** See *Zadkiel*.

🌸 **TUBUAS** A member of the group of angels who were removed from the ranks of officially recognized celestial hierarchy in 745 by a council in Rome under Pope Zachary. He was joined by Uriel, Adimus, Sabaoth, Simiel, and Raguel. (See also *Rome, Council of.*)

URIEL An oft-named member of the seven archangels and one of the most important angels in all of the heavenly host, with Michael, Gabriel, and Raphael. Unlike those three archangels, however, the existence and labors of Uriel are not supported in any way by the Scriptures, meaning that he is known entirely through legend, tales, and angelic lore. Nevertheless, Uriel, whose name means "fire of God," is truly a formidable angel, so much so that until the eighth century he was accepted entirely as an archangel to be honored by the Church and its faithful.

Uriel is named as both a cherub and a seraph, holding a wide variety of offices and titles: regent of the sun, prince of the sun, angel of the presence, archangel of salvation, patron of prophecy, angel of music, and master of Tartarus. According to the First Book of Enoch, he is the angel over thunder and terror and was sent to Noah to give him warning of the coming deluge. Two characteristics seem to predominate in the legends surrounding Uriel: his sharpness of mind and eye and his total, objective, and impersonal fulfillment of the divine will.

John Milton in *Paradise Lost* described Uriel as "regent of the sun" and "sharpest sighted spirit in all of heaven." Unfortunately his keenness of eye could not see through the cunning disguise of Satan in Book III when the evil one took the form of a cherub and fooled Uriel into permitting him to descend to the earth. The archangel soon realized his error and journeyed by sunbeam to warn Gabriel that Satan was loose in the world.

Uriel possesses an impersonality of such strength that in some customs he was put to work by God as chief of the angels watching over Tartarus, another name for hell. In early writings, such as the Apocalypse of St. Peter, hell was not yet the exclusive domain of demons and devils but was under the control of certain fearsome punishing angels (angels of destruction, wrath, and vengeance), and Uriel was their much-feared leader. In the Apocalypse of St. Peter is a lurid account about Uriel's pitiless treatment of damned souls. Blasphemers, for example, will be hung by their tongues over an unquenchable flame. Along the same lines was the Sibylline Oracles, which assured the reader that on the Day of Judgment the angel will shatter the bars of adamant upon the brazen gates of Hades and call forth for judgment all who reside there. In another aspect of his righteousness, Uriel is named by some sources as being the cherub placed in the Garden of Eden by the Lord to prevent any from entering, wielding a flaming sword to make his point. Uriel is also a candidate for several other notable historical roles: the dark angel who wrestled with Jacob and the angel who gave the Qabalah to humanity.

Long accepted as one of the seven great archangels in the Christian Church, Uriel's position was first scrutinized only in the eighth century. The Christian Church had grown alarmed at the rampant and excessive zeal with which many of the faithful were revering angels. At a council in Rome in 745 under Pope Zachary, seven angels were removed from the ranks of the Church's recognized angels. One of them was Uriel. Although stripped of his post as an archangel, Uriel was still honored by the Church under the name St. Uriel. As an angel he bore the symbols of the scroll and the book; as St. Uriel he had the symbol of an open hand bearing a flame. (See also *Archangels, Seven.*)

URIM AND THUMMIM The dual symbols meaning (respectively) illumination and perfection, used by Jewish priests as important ceremonial letters in the worship of the Lord. The symbols were worn on a breastplate, as described in the Old Testament Book of Exodus (28:29–30): "So Aaron shall bear the names of the sons of Israel in the breastpiece of judgement upon his heart, when he goes into the holy place, to bring them to continual remembrance before the Lord. And in the breastpiece of judgement you shall put the Urim and Thummim, and they shall be upon Aaron's heart, when he goes in before the Lord; thus Aaron shall bear the judgement of the people of Israel upon his heart before the Lord continually." The breastplate with the Urim and Thummim had a divinatory application, serving to act as a mediator between Jehovah and his people and thus revealing the will of the Lord. In this sense the symbols acted in a manner similar to the angels, in that the angelic messengers were also considered a means of hearing or learning of the will of God. A direct connection of the Urim with the angels was made by the poet Friedrich Klopstock in his epic drama *Der Messias* (1794), in which Urim was named as a cherub.

USIEL See *Uzziel*.

UZZAH An angel whose name means "the Lord is strength" and who is listed in the Third Book of Enoch with Azzah and Azael as ministering angels who were against the transformation of the patriarch Enoch into the angel Metatron. They reminded the Lord that Enoch was descended from those who had perished in the Flood for their wickedness and was thus not deserving of the inestimable honor of being taken to heaven and made one of the blessed hierarchy of angels. God, however, replied that the angels had no right to interrupt him and that he had chosen Enoch over all the angels. Taking the hint, the angels arose, greeted Enoch, and bowed down before him as the angelic prince Metatron. According to the account, though, the angels continued to tweak Metatron, calling him "youth" as a reminder that he was the youngest of the angelic company. It is possible that Uzzah can be identified with the fallen angel Semyaza. In the Bible there is a possibly related tale told in 2 Samuel (6:2–7) of Uzzah, a man who violated the law and touched the Ark of the Covenant, whereupon he was struck dead.

UZZIEL Also Usiel, an angel originally in Jewish lore who was ranked variously as a member of the cherubim and of the virtues. In the apocryphal Book of the Angel Raziel, he is one of the seven exalted angels who have the cherished position of standing before the very throne of God. Uzziel is also at times listed as the patron angel or protector of Egypt, a role normally given to Duma or Rahab. John Milton, in his *Paradise Lost* (Book IV), placed Uzziel among the good angels, sent by the angel Gabriel to search high and low for Satan when he came to the earth.

V **ALIANT ONES** A name used in the Old Testament Book of Isaiah (33:7) that is unclear in its original Hebrew meaning but may denote angels. The prophet declares: "Behold, the valiant ones cry without; the envoys of peace weep bitterly." Given that tradition supports the use of this term in such a context, it is not inappropriate to consider "valiant ones" a euphemism for members of the heavenly host.

VALKYRIE The beautiful, mounted, and armor-clad maidens of Norse mythology, immortalized in the music of Richard Wagner, especially his famous piece "Ride of the Valkyrie." The Valkyrie were said to be the handmaidens of Odin, numbering seven, nine, or twelve, and characterized by their flying steeds, drawn swords or brandished spears, and gleaming armor. They were sent down by the god to fly over battlefields to fetch from among those engaged in bloody conflict all whom they had chosen to meet their glorious end in combat. They also picked from among the fallen the most heroic and deserving warriors, who were then carried by the Valkyries to Valhalla, where they took up their places among the honored dead; they were waited upon by the Valkyrie and served both mead and ale, which they drank from the skulls of those they had defeated. The Valkyrie are often looked upon as primitive or pagan precursors of the angels, fulfilling a mission similar to that of the angels in that they gathered the souls of the dead and brought them to their eternal reward. (See also *Souls, Carriers of.*)

VARCAN An angel mentioned in Thomas Heywood's 1623 work *The Hierarchy of the Blessed Angels,* said to possess authority over the sun. This, of course, makes him one of several angels with this supposed power, including Uriel, Galgalliel, and Michael. (See also *Sun, Angels of the.*)

VENGEANCE, ANGEL OF The title used for a group of angels who exact some form of vengeance or retribution upon sinners; they are, like all angels, entirely at the service of the Lord, fulfilling their often grim duties only at the express command of God and never through some personal whim or desire. Perhaps equatable with the angels of destruction and even the angels of wrath, the angels of vengeance are said in Jewish lore to number twelve (as one angel wiped out an entire Assyrian army of 185,000 in one night and two others destroyed Sodom and Gomorrah, it may be assumed that the Lord does not need more than twelve); among those mentioned by name are some of the usual and most powerful personages of the heavenly host—Michael, Raphael, Gabriel, Metatron, and Uriel—along with some lesser-known angels, such as Nathaniel, Jehoel, and Zagzagel.

VICTOR The angel who, in Irish lore, appeared to St. Patrick (d. 461) in the hopes of convincing the saint to return to Ireland and bring with him the light of the Christian faith. While a youth in Roman Britain during the early fifth century, Patrick had been kidnapped by Irish raiders and sold into slavery in Ireland. After years of servitude he underwent a personal conversion and, through the intercession of a voice, managed to escape back to his homeland. Some legends declare the voice to have been the angel Victor. The angel came to Patrick several years later, imploring him to go back to the Irish, not as a slave but as a missionary. Patrick apparently heeded the words of Victor and so became one of the world's most famous and beloved saints.

VICTOR ANGELS The vivid description used by John Milton in *Paradise Lost* (Book VI) for the triumphant angels of heaven, who waged war upon their fallen brethren:

> *Now when fair morn orient in heaven appeared*
> *Up rose the victor angels, and to arms*

The matin trumpet sung: in arms they stood
Of golden panoply, refulgent host
Soon banded . . .

🕮 **VIRGIN MARY** See under *Mary, Virgin;* see also *Queen of the Angels.*

🕮 **VIRTUES** (Choir) One of the nine choirs of angels as listed by the sixth-century theologian Dionysius the Areopagite. The virtues are ranked fifth in the heavenly host and belong to the second triad of angelic orders, with dominations and powers; as members of the second triad, they take part in the duties given to the three choirs, namely the ordering of the universe. The virtues specifically preside over the elements of the world and the process of celestial life. Thus all heavenly bodies—from the stars and planets to the galaxies themselves—are kept in their divinely appointed routes and progress. On earth the angels maintain a watch over nature, marking and guiding every facet of natural life: rain, wind, snow, etc. St. Thomas Aquinas, in his *Summa Theologica,* noted that virtues also fulfill the divine effects that interrupt the ordinary functioning of nature. In Aquinas' convoluted language he means the virtues are in charge of miracles. As if these duties were not enough, the angels also assist humanity by bestowing grace and valor within the mortal heart. They give encouragement to the human to turn always to the good and help bolster the person's will to endure hardship and suffering and to have the personal strength to turn ever toward God. As the angels in charge of miracles, they receive their orders from the powers, but they also are connected closely to the saints.

In legend, two angels from this choir served as the angels of the Ascension, appearing at the moment of the Ascension of Christ (see *Ascension, Angels of*). The virtues are called in the Hebrew the malakim and the tarshishim. Their chiefs are listed variously as Gabriel, Michael, Tarshish, Peliel, Barbiel, and Uzziel. (See also *Choirs.*)

🕮 **VOHU MANAH** A member of the amesha spentas, the holy immortals of Zoroastrian thought, who stands as the "good mind" or "good thought" and is credited with revealing to the prophet Zoroaster in the late seventh century the secrets of what later became Zoroastrian belief. Vohu Manah was revered as the first and foremost of the amesha spentas, the early equivalent of the archangels. (See also *Zoroastrianism.*)

🏵 **VRETIEL** Another spelling for the angel Vrevoil.

🏵 **VREVOIL** Also Vretiel, Vretil, and Pravuil, an important archangel in the celestial hierarchy who keeps the sacred record of all of the knowledge and the deeds of the Lord. Perhaps to be identified with the archangel Uriel and similar in function to the ancient Egyptian god Thoth or the later Hermes Trismegistos, Vrevoil is described in the Second (Slavonic) Book of Enoch as being the swiftest in wisdom of all the archangels. It was Vrevoil who was supposedly commanded by the Lord to bring forth the books from the heavenly treasury and to dictate to Enoch unceasingly for thirty days and thirty nights; in the end, Enoch, using pen and ink provided by the angel, would write 366 books concerning virtually every form and kind of knowledge. (See also *Recording Angels*.)

WAR IN HEAVEN The name given to the bitter struggle that erupted in heaven between the forces of Satan and his fellow fallen angels and the heavenly host under St. Michael the Archangel. The cause of the war was the rejection of God by Satan and his cohorts. The most commonly given reason for the rejection was the unbearable pride of Satan, who refused to bow down before mankind as the Lord had demanded. Precisely how many angels joined Satan is unclear, but some sources declare that at least one-third of the entire heavenly host fell into sin, a number placed during the Middle Ages at 133,306,668; in sharp contrast with this group was the minor rebellion of the two hundred angels listed in the First Book of Enoch.

Regardless of the causes of the fall, the war in heaven could end in only one way: the corrupt and sinful angels were unable to resist for long against the hosts of the Lord, as was made clear in the Book of Revelation (12:7–9):

> *Now war arose in heaven, Michael and his angels fighting*
> *against the dragon; and the dragon and his angels fought, but*
> *they were defeated and there was no longer any place for them in*
> *heaven. And the great dragon was thrown down, that ancient*
> *serpent, who is called the devil and Satan, the deceiver of the*
> *whole world—he was thrown down to the earth, and his angels*
> *were thrown down with him.*

While unable to defeat God—a rather absurd notion—the fallen angels were able to survive the war, arriving in the dreadful realm of hell. In this place of torment where the devils and demons live with the perpetual misery of having rejected their Creator, the legions of darkness scheme to overthrow the very pillars of heaven, even though they know within their twisted hearts that such an achievement is utterly impossible. These schemes will produce one last effort to overcome the heavenly host, a campaign that will come at the end of time, during which the chosen souls on the earth will be tormented and the world will be virtually destroyed. The final conflict will then be fought, and

The angels engaged in the great struggle in *Paradise Lost;* by Gustave Doré.

once again the fallen angels will be defeated. But this time their loss will be total. The legions, with their king, will be bound into imprisonment, an event Satan is able to see every moment and which he will not and cannot do anything to prevent. (See box on page 290; see also *Fallen Angels.*)

WARRIORS The name used for certain angels by Satan in John Milton's *Paradise Lost* (Book I). The name is probably a reference to angels in general or perhaps to some rank of the celestial hierarchy, for Satan, soon after arriving in hell, summons his fallen legions:

> *He called so loud, that all the hollow deep*
> *Of hell resounded. "Princes, potentates,*
> *Warriors, the flower of heaven, once yours, now lost,*
> *If such astonishment as this can seize*
> *Eternal spirits . . ."*

WAR IN HEAVEN

And clamor such as heard in heaven till now
Was never, arms on armor clashing brayed
Horrible discord, and the madding wheels
Of brazen chariots raged; dire was the noise
Of conflict; overhead the dismal hiss
Of fiery darts in flaming volleys flew,
And flying vaulted either host with fire.
An inextinguishable rage; all heaven
Resounded, and had earth been then, all earth
Had to her center shook. What wonder? When
Millions of fierce encountering angels fought
On either side, the least of whom could wield
These elements, and arm him with the force
Of all their regions: how much more of power
Army against army numberless to raise
Dreadful combustion warring, and disturb,
Though not destroy, their happy native seat;
Had not the eternal king omnipotent
From his stronghold of heaven high overruled
And limited their might. . . .

(PARADISE LOST, BOOK VI)

WATCHERS Also termed the grigori, a group of angels who figure in Jewish legend; they are reputed to have members who fell into sin and others who stayed devoted to the cause of the Lord. Originally the watchers were apparently some of the most august angels in all of heaven. They never slept, kept eternal vigilance over heaven, and were some of the tallest beings in all creation. According to the Book of Jubilees (supported to some degree by the First Book of Enoch), they were sent to earth to give instruction to mortals on nature and other knowledge considered useful for them to have by the Lord. Unfortunately several watchers became enamored with human women and so cohabited with them. Their offspring were the nephilim, the giants who were mentioned in the Book of Genesis and who supposedly troubled the world with their cruelty and predilection for evil; the nephilim were all but exterminated in the Flood. The fallen watchers, meanwhile, were imprisoned in some unpleasant part of heaven (a bit of an oxymoron), where they languish in disgrace. The ranks of the evil watchers include Semyaza, Azazel, Sariel, and Satan-el, while the holy watchers claim such notables as Raphael, Uriel, and Michael.

There is also another group of mighty angels called the watchers. Known in the Hebrew as the *irin* or *irin qaddisin,* these angels are said in the Third Book of Enoch to number only two and are the close companions of the holy ones (*qaddisin*). They are, like the holy ones, greater than all the other angels combined, matched by no other creatures in the entire heavenly host. They reside directly next to the very throne of God and, with the holy ones, act as the court officials of heaven, debating every case that comes before the blessed throne. The watchers and the holy ones were mentioned in the Book of Daniel (4:17), and their pronouncements are heard throughout all of the heavens: "The sentence is by decree of the watchers, the decision by the word of the holy ones, to the end that the living may know that the Most High rules the kingdom of men, and gives it to whom he will, and sets over it the lowliest of men." (For other details, see *Qaddisin.*)

WEEK, ANGELS OF THE The angels who have authority over the seven days of the week—in much the same fashion as there are angels presiding over the planets, hours of the day, and months of the year. The angels give their particular day their special attention and in legend can be invoked to assist a person in some endeavor or need. The

Sunday	Monday	Tuesday	Wednesday	Thursday	Friday	Saturday
Michaël	Gabriel	Camael	Raphaël	Sachiel	Anaël	Cassiel
name of the 4.th Heaven	name of the 1.st Heaven	name of the 5.th Heaven	name of the 2.d Heaven	name of the 6.th Heaven	name of the 3.d Heaven	No Angels ruling above the 6.th Heaven
Machen.	Shamain.	Machon.	Raquie.	Zebul.	Sagun.	

The symbols of the angels of the week; from Barrett's *The Magus*.

angels and their days are as reported in *The Magus* (1801) by Francis Barrett:

Sunday: Michael
Monday: Gabriel
Tuesday: Camael
Wednesday: Raphael
Thursday: Sachiel
Friday: Anael
Saturday: Cassiel

WHEELS The nickname given to the angelic members of the choir or order of thrones. The name is derived from the Hebrew word *ophanim* (later galgallim, "wheels" or "spheres"), itself based on the vivid description of these angels found in the Old Testament Book of Ezekiel (1:13–19). The angels are also called the "many-eyed ones." (See *Thrones* for details.)

WIND, ANGELS OF THE Angels who possess special authority over the winds of the earth. There are generally reputed to be four such angels, one for each of the cardinal points of direction, south, north, east, and west, although in the ever-useful Third Book of Enoch Ruhiel is named as being in charge of the wind, with Zaamiel in control of whirlwinds. Other chiefs of the wind mentioned in various sources are Rujiel, Ben Nez, and Moriel. The Book of Revelation (7:1) declares: "I saw four angels standing at the four corners of the earth, holding back the four winds of the earth, that no wind might blow on earth or sea or against any tree." There are also scriptural references that indicate that angels may actually assume the very incarnation of the wind. In the Book of Psalms (18:10), for example, it is written: "He rode on a cherub, and flew; he came swiftly upon the wings of the wind." And in Hebrews (1:7): "Of the angels he says, 'Who makes his angels winds, and his servants flames of fire.' "

WINGS OF ANGELS Probably the most recognized attribute of every angel. The wings of the angel are its most significant identifying feature, more so than even the harp or halo; likewise, demons, devils, and the other fallen angels are readily distinguished by their own wings, once as beautiful as their angelic brethren's, but now hideous, barbed, batlike appendages. Many writers on angels point out—many in jest or humorous speculation—that angel wings, especially as they have been depicted by medieval and Renaissance artists, could not possibly support the weight of an angel sufficiently to get the angel off the ground, let alone fly it around the universe. Malcolm Godwin, in his charming work *Angels* (1990), for example, includes useful diagrams and points out that a tall angel would need a wingspan of between 36 and 120 feet!

Such speculation naturally applies common sense and physics to a particular subject for which neither is well suited. Angels are depicted with wings for a number of reasons, none of which have much to do with flying in a terrestrial sense. The possession of wings by a spiritual being helps to stress several important aspects. First, wings imply spiritual power, the symbol of granted authority to achieve some purpose or complete some task. In the case of angels, it connotes that the angel has received a mission from God. This understanding is similar to the ancient customs of supernatural entities, such as spirits or souls, having wings. In *Phaedrus,* Plato has Socrates declaring of a spirit: "Thus when it is without flaw and winged, it travels on high and controls the entire world." Wings additionally symbolize spiritual flight and travel. The god Hermes, for example, had wings on his feet. To angels, wings are merely a means of giving expression to their innate capacity to journey anywhere in the Creation at a moment's notice.

The link between angels and wings is a venerable one. Its roots can be traced to the statues found in Babylon and Persia, the Greek ideas (as expressed by the aforementioned Plato), and the Roman conceptions of the genii and Victory; the latter was particularly significant, as the Winged Victory, a revered statue, personified pagan ideals and stood in the Senate chamber of Rome, the Curia. During their many enforced years in Babylon, the Jews adopted crucial ideas about angels and angel-like beings, including those of wings and angelic flight. (See also *Babylon*.) In the Old Testament the seraphim and cherubim are both described as possessing wings. The seraphim had six wings, while the cherubim had four wings. In the Qur'an it is written: "Praise to Allah, the Originator of the heavens and the earth, the Maker of the angels, messengers flying on wings, two, and three, and four" (surah 35:1).

Several examples of wings; from *Angel Carrying a Column,* by Melozzo da Forlì, Loreto (COURTESY ART RESOURCE).

Flight is implied in the Old Testament with such passages as that in the Book of Daniel in which an angel of the Lord descends from heaven. It is even more explicit in the New Testament. Angels are flying in Luke's account of the Nativity and in the Book of Revelation.

In art, angel wings make manifest the special place of the angels in the service of God, acting as mediators between the divine and human, with the ability to fly between both spheres of existence. Curiously, despite the scriptural references, early Christian artists did not paint angels with wings until after the formal emancipation of the Christian Church from Roman persecution in the early fourth century. The reasons for this most likely are found in the pagan winged genii (see *Genius*) and the Victory; every effort was made to differentiate between idolatrous practices and authentic Christian teaching, and this extended to art. Once established as the faith of the Roman world, wings were added and would become a staple of artistic renderings, reaching glorious heights during the Renaissance. It is a matter of speculation whether angels must earn their wings, as was declared by Clarence, the hopeless angel of *It's a Wonderful Life* (1946). He is an angel second class who has not yet earned his wings; of course, he wins them by the end of the film—an achievement confirmed by the ringing of a little bell (in keeping with an old tale that every time a bell rings, an angel receives his wings). (See also *Art, Angels in,* and *Travel, Angelic.*)

WISDOM See *Pistis Sophia.*

WOMAN CLOTHED WITH THE SUN A profound vision described in the Book of Revelation, commonly interpreted as a symbolic representation of the Virgin Mary: "And a great portent appeared in heaven, a woman clothed with the sun, with the moon under her feet, and on her head a crown of twelve stars; she was with child and she cried out in her pangs of birth, in anguish for delivery." The Woman Clothed with the Sun is menaced by a great red dragon, with seven heads and ten horns, with seven diadems upon his heads, eager to eat the child when he is born. But the child is rescued from the dragon's clutches and hidden, all part of the exceedingly enigmatic text of Revelation. (See *Revelation, Book of.*)

WORMWOOD A mysterious being, commonly named an angel, who is mentioned in the Book of Revelation (8:10–11): "The third angel blew his trumpet, and a great star fell from heaven, blazing like a torch, and it fell on a third of the rivers and on the fountains of water. The name of the star is Wormwood. A third of the waters became wormwood, and many men died of the water, because it was made bitter." This grim episode is clearly based on the Old Testament Book of Jeremiah, in which is written: "Behold, I will feed this people with wormwood, and give them poisonous water to drink." In botany, wormwood is recognized as one of several bitter plants used in the making of absinthe, but many scholars have interpreted the Wormwood of Revelation to be a dread angelic spirit, perhaps a prince of the air, who shall chastise the wicked and bring death to many. Wormwood has figured in several fictional tales, most notably *The*

Screwtape Letters by C. S. Lewis, in which the junior devil Wormwood receives a series of letters from his uncle, Screwtape, a high-ranking member of the netherworld.

WRATH, ANGELS OF The name of several fearsome angels, also termed the angels of anger. They were supposedly encountered by Moses during his visit to heaven, as recounted in the apocryphal Revelation of Moses. According to that lively work, Moses met them in the seventh heaven. Among those identified as angels of wrath have been Af, Hemah, and Kezef. The Book of Revelation also notes seven angels of wrath who will appear at the time of the Last Judgment.

APHON Also Zephon, an angel who appears in John Milton's *Paradise Lost*. Probably a member of the cherubim, he flies to earth with his fellow angel Ithuriel to hunt for Satan, who is loose in the world. (For details, see under Zephon.)

XATHANAEL See *Nathaniel*.

YAASRIEL A kind of recording angel in Jewish legend, although he does not write down the deeds of all human beings like other similar angels; in some ways Yaasriel has a far more important job. He has authority over seventy holy pencils (presumably never in need of sharpening) with which he perpetually inscribes on celestial shards the ineffable names of God.

YAHOEL Also termed Jehoel in some accounts, an angel who is often thought to be synonymous with the great angel Metatron. According to Jewish lore, Yahoel was one of the angels connected to Abraham, supposedly serving as his tour guide in heaven when the patriarch paid a visit to paradise, as recorded in the apocryphal work called the Testament of Abraham. He also was said to have taught Abraham the Torah and the Pentateuch (the first five books of the Hebrew Old Testament: Genesis, Exodus, Leviticus, Numbers, and Deuteronomy).

YAHRIEL An angel in Jewish lore who is credited with authority over the moon. He is only one of several angels who have received this title. (See *Moon, Angel of the.*)

YAZATAS A type of angelic being found in the ancient religion of Zoroastrianism. The yazatas were considered minor angels in the service of the powerful archangel-like spirits of the amesha spentas (the holy immortals). The yazatas concerned themselves with virtually every aspect of human affairs, safeguarding and watching over such

minute details of existence as the hours of the day and the minutes of
the hour. Their chief or prince was Mithra (or Mihr), who eventually
became a god in the lands of the Roman Empire under the name of
Mithras, one of the empire's many eastern deities who found appeal
among the often jaded population. As the head of the yazatas, Mithra
was considered the embodiment of truth and light, assisting the powerful deity Ahura Mazda. (See also *Zoroastrianism*.)

YEAR, ANGELS OF THE Those angels who have rulership or gover-
norship over each of the months of the year, just as there are angels
for each day of the week, each hour of the day, and even the signs of
the zodiac. As recorded in the occult work *Dictionnaire Infernal*
(1825–1826) by Collin De Plancy, the designated angels are as follows:

January:	Gabriel	July:	Verchiel
February:	Barchiel	August:	Hamaliel
March:	Machidiel	September:	Uriel
April:	Asmodel	October:	Barbiel
May:	Ambriel	November:	Adnachiel
June:	Muriel	December:	Hanael

YEFEFIAH Also Yofiel, an angel credited with teaching Moses the secrets of the mystical lore of the Qabalah. He is also often identified
with the angel Iofiel and hence can be considered synonymous with
Jophiel.

YOFIEL See *Yefefiah*.

ZA'AFIEL An angel who has control over all hurricanes, as recorded in the Third Book of Enoch; his control does not extend to every kind of storm, however, for those are of concern to Za'amiel. Za'afiel is ranked as one of the angelic princes with rulership over the elements of the world.

ZA'AMIEL An angel reported in the Third Book of Enoch as being in charge of all great winds and storms, save for hurricanes, which are the province of his fellow angel Za'apiel. He is one of the angelic princes who guide the natural elements of the world.

ZA'APIEL See *Za'afiel.*

ZABKIEL An angel, not to be confused with Zadkiel, who is the reputed chief or prince of the angelic choir of the thrones. Other angels ranked as chief include Orifiel, Jophiel, and Raziel.

ZADKIEL A notable angelic personage with quite a varied portfolio. Also called Tzadkiel, Satqiel, and Zachiel, he is considered one of the seven archangels, with such eminent angels as Gabriel and Michael, in the traditions of the Third Book of Enoch, which means that he is the chief of one of the seven heavens (the fifth) and is attended by 496,000 myriads of ministering angels. In Jewish lore Zadkiel is said to be the angel who appeared to Abraham on Mount Moriah and prevented the patriarch from sacrificing his son, Isaac; in honor of this event, Zadkiel's traditional symbol is a dagger, the weapon Abraham was prepared to use—obedient to God's command—in sacrificing his beloved son. Zadkiel is reputed to be one of the companions, with the angel Zophiel, of Michael the Archangel anytime that captain of the hosts of the Lord goes into battle with his mighty standard unfurled. He is also honored as the chief or prince of the choir or order of dominations, an angel of mercy and excellent memory, and the angel with rulership over the planet Jupiter. Other possible chiefs of the dominations are Muriel and especially Hashmal. Zadkiel was the name adopted by Richard James Morrison (1795–1874), author of *Herald of Astrology* (1831), which was known subsequently as *Zadkiel's Almanack.*

ZAGZAGEL An angel associated with the many legends surrounding the Lawgiver, Moses. He is revered as the so-called Angel of the Burning Bush (see *Burning Bush, Angel of the,* for details) and supposedly taught Moses the profound knowledge of the ineffable names of God, the power that Moses used during his journey to heaven to bring several arrogant angels to their knees. Zagzagel is also said to have joined the Lord, Michael, and Gabriel in the much-grieved expedition from heaven to the earth to fetch the soul of Moses after the Lawgiver's death and its announcement by the angel Semalion. With Gabriel and Michael, Zagzagel supposedly prepared the grave of Moses and lovingly placed the Lawgiver into the earth. By custom he resides in the seventh heaven with the Lord, even though one of his areas of concern is safeguarding the fourth heaven. He also speaks seventy languages and is a renowned tutor, lecturing even to his fellow angels.

ZAKZAKIEL YHWH One of the foremost princes in the celestial hierarchy who has the task, according to Jewish legend, of recording the merits of Israel upon the very throne of the Lord. He is superior to the prince Gallisur YHWH but is inferior in rank to the prince Anapiel YHWH, keeper of the keys of the heavenly palace.

ZAKUM An angel who, as reported in Jewish legend, conspired with the angel Lahash to prevent an important prayer of Moses from reaching the ears of the Lord. This crime was so terrible that Lahash repented and was subsequently punished rather severely; Zakum, however, did not apparently have a guilty conscience, but his fate remains unknown. It is possible that he was destroyed, like Af and several other angels in lore who committed the transgression of getting in the way of the Lord and the mighty Lawgiver.

ZAPHIEL See *Zophiel*.

ZAPHKIEL See *Zophiel*.

ZARALL With Jael, one of the two cherubim who were placed upon the mercy seat of the Ark of the Covenant. (For details, see *Ark of the Covenant*.)

ZAZRIEL YHWH One of the great angelic princes of the celestial hierarchy, as reported in the Third Book of Enoch. He is superior in rank to Sasnigiel YHWH but is beneath Geburatiel YHWH, being compelled anytime he comes into his presence to fall prostrate and remove his glorious crown. There is, apparently, a considerable set of protocols among the angels.

ZEHANPURYU YHWH A truly formidable angelic prince who is revered in Jewish lore as the prince of the Divine Presence, one of the gatekeepers of the grand palace of the Lord in the seventh heaven, and an angel said to be ranked higher even than Metatron. According to the Third Book of Enoch, he is "glorified and dreaded" by the entire heavenly household, but even Zehanpuryu removes his crown and falls prostrate when he meets the angelic prince Azbogah YHWH.

ZEITGEIST Known in English as "the spirit of time," the name adopted by the esoteric philosopher and founder of anthroposophy Rudolf Steiner (1861–1925) for the archangel Michael in the sense of the angel's efforts to give assistance to humanity in its struggle against the evil beings of the era, specifically Ahriman and what he saw as the impending Antichrist (namely Adolf Hitler, whose rise Steiner foretold). The activities of Michael were detailed in Steiner's *The Mission of the Archangel Michael*. The term Zeitgeist is also used to express the moral and social attitudes and tendencies of a given period.

ZEPHON An angel best known through his appearance in John Milton's *Paradise Lost*. Said in Jewish lore to be a cherubim and one of the protectors of paradise, in *Paradise Lost* (Book IV) he and Ithuriel, a fellow cherub, are sent by Gabriel to hunt for Satan, who has come to earth. They find the prince of evil squatting next to the ear of the sleeping Eve, whispering temptations. Touching Satan, the angels are alarmed by his sudden transformation into "the grisly king," but Zephon scornfully declares to him:

> *Think not, revolted spirit, thy shape the same,*
> *Or undiminished brightness, to be known*
> *As when thou stoodest in heaven upright and pure;*
> *That glory then, when thou no more wast good,*
> *Departed from thee, and thou resemblest now*
> *Thy sin and place of doom obscure and foul.*
> *But come, for thou, be sure, shalt give account*
> *To him who sent us, whose charge is to keep*
> *This place inviolable, and these from harm.*

ZI'I'EL An angel mentioned in the Third Book of Enoch and listed as being in charge of tremors. He is apparently joined by the angel Ra'asiel, who is the chief of earthquakes.

ZIQIEL An angel listed in the Third Book of Enoch as being in charge of comets. He is also probably the ruling prince of meteors as well.

ZODIAC, ANGELS OF THE The tradition that there are ruling angels who watch over or govern the twelve signs of the zodiac. They are often to be considered synonymous with the various angels of the months of the year. Specifically, the angels of the zodiac are as follows:

Capricorn:	Hanael	Cancer:	Muriel
Aquarius:	Gabriel	Leo:	Verchiel
Pisces:	Barchiel	Virgo:	Hamaliel
Aries:	Machidiel	Libra:	Uriel
Taurus:	Asmodel	Scorpio:	Barbiel
Gemini:	Ambriel	Sagittarius:	Adnachiel

(FROM LENORMANT, *CHALDEAN MAGIC*; AND DAVIDSON, *A DICTIONARY OF ANGELS*)

❧ **ZOPHIEL** Also Zaphiel and Zaphkiel, an angelic prince named as one the chiefs of the angelic choir of cherubim (with such other princes as Gabriel, Raphael, Uriel, Ophaniel, and, before his fall, Satan). He is also sometimes said to be chief of the thrones; the ruling angel of the planet Saturn; and the special patron of Noah, guiding him in the building of the ark and helping to ensure the survival of his family. In *Paradise Lost* by John Milton (Book VI), Zophiel was described as "of cherubim, the swiftest wing," using his speed to help muster the heavenly host against the fallen angels. However, in the work of Friedrich Klopstock, *Der Messias,* Zophiel was the standard-bearer of the infernal armies. It is possible that he can be equated with the angel Zaphkiel—listed as an archangel and head of the choir of thrones—but some scholars dispute this.

❧ **ZOROASTRIANISM** Also called Mazdaism, the chief religion of ancient Persia (the region of modern Iran) that was preached by the prophet Zoroaster in the sixth century B.C. Considered a dualistic faith, it taught that the earth was a bitter battleground between good and evil, a conflict in which God would inevitably triumph. The highest and central deity of Zoroastrianism was Ahura Mazda, creator of heaven and earth. This god was supported by the so-called Holy Immortals, the amesha spentas, six or seven beings considered the equivalent of the archangels. The enemy of Ahura Mazda was Ahriman, the prime source of evil, who was supported by a host of wicked spirits, the opposite beings of the amesha spentas. In later forms of Zoroastrianism, Ahura Mazda (in the shape of Ormazhd) was placed on nearly an equal level with Ahriman. The two struggle for supremacy, with humanity between them; each human must choose to pursue a life of ethical and moral rectitude or one of sin. This system thus made the adherents of Zoroastrianism exceedingly moral individuals, and the faith itself is quite optimistic. Its members have the confidence that in the end Good will triumph. This final victory will come at the close of the fourth age (there are four ages, each around three thousand years), when there will occur the frashkart, the cleansing of the universe of all sin and wickedness. (See also *Ahura Mazda, Amesha Spentas, Fravashi,* and *Rash.*)

❧ **ZUTU'EL** An angel who appears in the First Book of Enoch. He resides past the Erythrean Sea and was visited by the patriarch Enoch during his journeys.

SUGGESTED READING LIST

Adler, Mortimer. *The Angels and Us.* N.Y.: Macmillan, 1982.

Alter, R. *The Art of Biblical Narrative.* N.Y.: Basic Books, 1981.

Anderson, Joan. *Where Angels Walk.* N.Y.: Ballantine Books, 1992.

Apocrypha, The. Hyde Park, N.Y.: University Books, 1962.

Apocrypha, The Oxford Annotated. N.Y.: Oxford University Press, 1965.

Apocrypha and Pseudepigrapha of the Old Testament. London: Oxford University Press, 1913.

Apocryphal New Testament, The. N.Y.: Peter Eckler, publ., 1927.

Aquinas, Thomas. *Summa Theologiae,* 5 vols. Westminster, Md.: Christian Classics, 1981.

Bamberger, Bernard J. *Fallen Angels.* Philadelphia, Penn.: The Jewish Publication Society of America, 1952.

Barnstone, Willis, ed. *The Other Bible.* San Francisco: Harper & Row, 1984.

Baron, Salo W. *A Social and Religious History of the Jews,* 18 vols. Philadelphia: Jewish Publication Society, 1952–1983.

Barrett, Francis. *The Magus.* London: Lackington, Allen & Co., 1801.

Bennett, William J. *The Book of Virtues.* N.Y.: Simon & Schuster, 1993.

Ben-Sasson, H. H., ed. *A History of the Jewish People.* Cambridge: Harvard University Press, 1976.

Berefelt, Gunnar. *A Study on the Winged Angel.* Stockholm, Sweden: Almquist and Wiksell, 1968.

Blackmore, Rev. Simon. *The Angel World.* Cleveland: John Winterich, 1977.

Boros, Ladislaus. *Angels and Men.* N.Y.: Seabury Press, 1976.

Brewer, Rev. Cobham. *A Dictionary of Miracles.* Detroit: Gale Research Co., 1966.

Budge, E. A. Wallis. *Amulets and Talismans.* New Hyde Park, N.Y.: University Books, 1961.

Bunson, Matthew. *The Angelic Doctor: The Life and World of St. Thomas Aquinas.* Huntington, Ind.: OSV, 1995.

———. *Encyclopedia of the Middle Ages.* N.Y.: Facts on File, 1995.

Burnham, Sophy. *A Book of Angels.* N.Y.: Ballantine Books, 1991.

_____. *Angel Letters.* N.Y.: Ballantine Books, 1991.

Cameron, Ann. *The Angel Book.* N.Y.: Ballantine Books, 1977

Charles R. H. *The Book of Enoch.* Oxford: Clarendon Press, 1912.

_____. *The Book of Jubilees or The Little Genesis.* London: Society for Promoting Christian Knowledge, 1917.

_____. *The Apocrypha and Pseudepigrapha of the Old Testament,* 2 vols. Oxford: Clarendon, 1913.

Charlesworth, James H. *The Old Testament Pseudepigrapha,* 2 vols. N.Y.: Double-day, 1983.

Chearney, Lee Ann, ed. *The Quotable Angel.* N.Y.: Wiley and Sons, 1995.

Christian, Paul, ed. *The History and Practice of Magic,* 2 vols. N.Y.: Citadel, 1963.

Church, F. Forrester. *Entertaining Angels.* San Francisco: Harper & Row, 1987.

Clayton, George. *Angelology.* N.Y.: H. Kermot, 1851.

Collins, James D. *The Thomistic Philosophy of the Angels.* Washington, D.C.: Catholic University of America Press, 1947.

Connell, Janice T. *Angel Power.* N.Y.: Ballantine, 1995.

Daniel, Alma; Wyllie, Timothy; and Ramer, Andrew. *Ask Your Angels.* N.Y.: Ballantine, 1992.

Danielou, Jean. *The Angels and Their Mission.* Westminster, Maryland: The Newman Press, 1957.

Davidson, Gustav. *A Dictionary of Angels.* N.Y.: The Free Press, 1971.

De Plancy, Collin. *Dictionnaire Infernal,* 4 vols. Librairie Universelle, 1825–1826.

Dickason, C. Fred. *Angels, Elect and Evil.* Chicago: Moody Press, 1975.

Drakos, Mary. *Angels of God, Our Guardians Dear: Today's Catholics Re-discover Angels.* Ann Arbor, Mich.: Charis Books, 1995.

Field, M. J. *Angels and Ministers of Grace.* N.Y.: Hill and Wang, 1971.

Frazer, Sir James George. *The Golden Bough.* N.Y.: Macmillan, 1951.

Freeman, Hobart. *Angels of Light.* Plainfield, N.J.: Logos International, 1969.

Freeman, Eileen. *Touched by Angels.* N.Y.: Warner Books, 1993.

Fuller, J.F.C. *The Secret Wisdom of the Qabalah.* London: The Occult Book Society, n.d.

Gaebelin, A. C. *The Angels of God.* Grand Rapids, Mich.: Baker Book House, 1924.

Garfield, Laeh Maggie and Grant, Jack. *Angels and Companions in Spirit.* Berkeley, Calif.: Celestial Arts, 1995.

Gaster, Theodore. *The Dead Sea Scriptures in English Translation.* N.Y.: Doubleday, 1956.

Gilligan, W. Doyle, ed. *Devotion to the Holy Angels.* Houston: Lumen Christi Press, 1990.

Gilmore, Don. *Angels, Angels Everywhere.* N.Y.: Pilgrim, 1981.

Ginzberg, Louis. *The Legends of the Jews,* 7 vols. Philadelphia: The Jewish Publication Society of America, 1954.

Giovetti, Paola. *Angels: The Role of Celestial Guardians and Beings of Light.* York Beach, Maine: Samuel Weiser, 1993.

Godwin, Malcolm. *Angels: An Endangered Species.* N.Y.: Simon & Schuster, 1990.

Goldman, Karen. *The Angel Book.* N.Y.: Simon & Schuster, 1992.

Graham, Billy. *Angels: God's Secret Agents.* N.Y.: Pocket Books, 1975.

Hahn, Emily. *Breaths of God.* N.Y.: Doubleday, 1971.

Hall, Manley P. *The Blessed Angels.* Los Angeles: The Philosophical Research Society, 1980.

Hanson, Jeanne, ed. *The Poetry of Angels.* N.Y.: Crown, 1995.

Hart, Rob van der. *Theology of Angels and Devils.* Cork, Ireland: The Mercier Press, 1973.

Harvey, Gail. *On the Wings of Angels.* N.Y.: Gramercy Books, 1993.

Heywood, Thomas. *The Hierarchy of the Blessed Angels.* London: Adam Islip, 1635.

Hodson, Geoffrey. *Brotherhood of Angels and of Men.* London: Theosophical Publishing House, 1973.

Holden, Ursula. *Fallen Angels.* N.Y.: Methuen, 1979.

Howard, Jane. *Commune with the Angels.* Virginia Beach, Va.: A.R.E. Press, 1992.

Hubbs, Juliet and Monaco, Nora. *Celestial Wisdom Cards.* N.Y.: Crown, 1995.

Huber, Georges. *My Angel Will Go Before You.* Westminster, Md.: Christian Classics, 1983.

Humann, Harvey. *The Many Faces of Angels.* Marina del Rey, Calif.: DeVorss & Co., 1986.

Joppie, A. S. *The Ministry of Angels.* Grand Rapids, Mich.: Baker Book House, 1953.

Jovanovic, Pierre. *An Inquiry into the Existence of Guardian Angels.* N.Y.: M. Evans, 1995.

Jung, Leo. *Fallen Angels in Jewish and Christian and Mohammedan Literature.* N.Y.: Ktav Publishing House, 1926.

Langton, Edward. *Essentials of Demonology.* London: The Epworth Press, 1949.

_____. *Good and Evil Spirits.* London: Society for Promoting Christian Knowledge, 1942.

Latham, Henry. *A Service of Angels.* Cambridge: Deighton, Bell, & Co, 1896.

Leavell, Landrum. *Angels, Angels, Angels.* Nashville, Tenn.: Broadman Press, 1973.

Lewis, C. S. *The Screwtape Letters.* N.Y.: Macmillan, 1943.

Lloyd, Marjorie Lewis. *It Must Have Been an Angel.* Mountain View, Calif.: Pacific Press, 1980.

Lockyer, Herbert. *The Mystery and Ministry of Angels.* Grand Rapids, Mich.: Eeerdmans Publishing, 1958.

Lord, Bob and Penny. *Heavenly Army of Angels.* Birmingham, Ala.: Journeys of Faith Publications, 1991.

MacDonald, Hope. *When Angels Appear.* Grand Rapids, Mich.: Zondervan Publishing House, 1982.

MacGregor, Geddes. *Angels: Ministers of Grace.* N.Y.: Paragon House, 1988.

Maclean, Dorothy. *To Hear the Angels Sing.* Hudson, N.Y.: Lindisfarne Press, 1980.

Malz, Betty. *Angels Watching over Me.* Old Tappan, N.J.: Revell, 1986.

Mandino, Og. *The Twelfth Angel.* N.Y.: Ballantine Books, 1993.

Margolies, Morris. *A Gathering of Angels.* N.Y.: Ballantine Books, 1994.

Mark, Barbara and Griswold, Trudy. *Angelspeake: A Guide. How to Talk with Your Angels.* N.Y.: Simon and Schuster, 1995.

Mathers, S. L. MacGregor, ed. *The Greater Key of Solomon.* Chicago: de Laurence, 1914.

_____. *The Kabbalah Unveiled.* London: George Redway, 1887.

Miller, Leslie Miller. *All about Angels.* Glendale, Calif.: 1976.

Moolenburgh, Hans. *A Handbook of Angels.* Saffron Walden, England: C.W. Daniel Co., 1984.

_____. *Meetings with Angels.* Saffron Walden, England: C.W. Daniel, 1992.

Morse, Melvin, M.D. *Transformed by the Light.* N.Y.: HarperCollins, 1992.

Mould, Daphne. *Angels of God.* N.Y.: Devin Adair, 1963.

Newhouse, Flower A. *Rediscovering the Angels.* Wheaton, Ill: Theosophical Publishing House, 1986.

Odeberg, Hugo, ed. and trans. *3 Enoch or the Hebrew Book of Enoch.* N.Y.: Cambridge University Press, 1928.

O'Sullivan, Paul. *All about the Angels.* Rockford, Ill.: Tan Publishers, 1990.

Paine, Randall. *The Angels Are Waiting.* St. Paul, Minn.: The Leaflet Missal, 1988.

Palmer, Tobias. *An Angel in My House.* Notre Dame, Ind.: Ave Maria Press, 1975.

Parente, Alessio. *Send Me Your Guardian Angel.* Amsterdam, N.Y.: Noteworthy, 1983.

Patterson, Robert M. *The Angels and Their Ministrations.* Philadelphia: Westminster Press, 1900.

Peterson, Erik. *The Angels and the Liturgy.* N.Y.: Herder & Herder, 1964.

Pruitt, James. *Angels Beside You.* N.Y.: Avon, 1994.

Ramer, Andrew. *Angel Answers.* N.Y.: Pocket Books, 1995.

Regamey, Reginald. *What Is an Angel?* N.Y.: Hawthorn Books, 1960.

Reynolds, Dana. *Be an Angel.* N.Y.: Simon and Schuster, 1994.

Ronner, John. *Do You Have a Guardian Angel?* Murfreesboro, Tenn.: Mamre Press, 1985.

_____. *Know Your Angels.* Murfreesboro, Tenn.: Mamre Press, 1993.

Saint Michael and the Angels. Rockford, Ill.: Tan Books, 1983.

Schlink, Basilea. *The Unseen World of Angels and Demons.* Old Tappan, N.J.: Chosen Books, 1986.

Schneweis, Emil. *Angels and Demons According to Lactantius.* Washington, D.C.: Catholic University Press, 1944.

Scholem, Gershom. *Major Trends in Jewish Mysticism.* N.Y.: Schocken Books, 1941.

Schouppe, F. X., S. J. *The Dogma of Hell.* Rockford, Ill.: Tan Books, 1989.

Snell, Joy. *The Ministry of Angels, Here and Beyond.* N.Y.: Citadel, 1959.

Steiger, Brad. *Guardian Angels and Spirit Guides.* N.Y.: Plume, 1995.

Steiner, Rudolf. *The Mission of the Archangel Michael,* trans. Lisa de Monges. N.Y.: Anthroposophic Press, 1961.

_____. *The Work of the Angels in Man's Astral Body.* London: Anthroposophical Publishing Co., 1960.

Steinsaltz, A. *The Essential Talmud.* N.Y.: Basic Books, 1976.

Sumrall, Lester F. *The Reality of Angels.* Nashville, Tenn.: T. Nelson, 1982.

Swedenborg, Emanuel. *Heaven and Its Wonders and Hell.* N.Y.: Swedenborg Foundation, 1956.

Taylor, Terry Lynn. *Answers from the Angels.* Tiburon, Calif.: H. J. Kramer, 1993.

_____. *Guardians of Hope.* Tiburon, Calif.: H. J. Kramer, 1992.

_____. *Messengers of Light.* Tiburon, Calif.: H. J. Kramer, 1990.

Trachtenberg, Joshua. *The Devil and the Jews.* Philadelphia: Jewish Publications Society, 1961.

_____. *Jewish Magic and Superstition.* N.Y.: Behrman's Jewish Book House, 1939.

Underhill, James. *Angels.* Shaftesbury, Dorset: Element, 1994.

Waite, Arthur Edward. *The Book of Black Magic and of Pacts.* Chicago: de Laurence Co., 1940.

_____. *The Book of Ceremonial Magic.* New Hyde Park, N.Y.: University Books, 1961.

_____. *The Holy Kabbalah.* New Hyde Park, N.Y.: University Books, n.d.

_____. *The Lemegeton, or The Lesser Key of Solomon,* N.Y.: Wehman Bros., 1916.

Walsh, Michael, ed. *Butler's Lives of the Saints.* San Francisco: Harper & Row, 1984.

Ward, Theodore. *Men and Angels.* N.Y.: Viking Press, 1969.

Waters, Clara Clement. *Angels in Art.* Boston: L. C. Page & Co., 1898.

Webber, Marilynn and William. *A Rustle of Angels.* Grand Rapids, Mich.: Zondervan Publishing House, 1994.

West, R. H. *Milton and Angels.* N.Y.: Viking Press, 1969.

Wilson, Peter Lamborn. *Angels.* N.Y.: Pantheon Books, 1980.

Wulfing, Sulamith. *Angels.* Werkerke, Holland, 1980.

Zohar, the, trans. Harry Sperling and Maurice Simon, 5 vols. London: The Soncino Press, 1956.